AS NORMAL
AS POSSIBLE

T0345343

Queer Asia

The Queer Asia book series opens a space for monographs and anthologies in all disciplines focused on non-normative sexuality and gender cultures, identities and practices in Asia. Queer Studies and Queer Theory originated in and remain dominated by North American and European academic circles, and existing publishing has followed these tendencies. However, growing numbers of scholars inside and beyond Asia are producing work that challenges and corrects this imbalance. The Queer Asia book series — first of its kind in publishing — provides a valuable opportunity for developing and sustaining these initiatives.

Other Titles in the Queer Asia Series

Undercurrents: Queer Culture and Postcolonial Hong Kong
Helen Hok-Sze Leung

Obsession: Male Same-Sex Relations in China, 1900–1950
Wenqing Kang

Philippine Gay Culture: Binabae to Bakla, Silahis to MSM
J. Neil C. Garcia

Editorial Collective

Chris Berry (Goldsmiths, University of London)
John Nguyet Erni (Lingnan University)
Peter Jackson (Australian National University)
Helen Hok-Sze Leung (Simon Fraser University)

International Editorial Board

Dennis Altman (La Trobe University, Australia)
Evelyn Blackwood (Purdue University)
Tom Boellstorff (University of California, Irvine, USA)
Pimpawan Boonmongkon (Mahidol University)
Judith Butler (University of California, Berkeley, USA)
Ding Naifei (National Central University, Taiwan)
David Eng (University of Pennsylvania, USA)
Neil Garcia (University of the Philippines, Diliman)
David Halperin (University of Michigan, Ann Arbor, USA)
Josephine Chuen-juei Ho (National Central University, Taiwan)
Annamarie Jagose (University of Auckland, New Zealand)
Song Hwee Lim (University of Exeter)
Kam Louie (University of Hong Kong)
Lenore Manderson (Monash University, Australia)
Fran Martin (University of Melbourne, Australia)
Mark McLelland (University of Wollongong)
Meaghan Morris (Lingnan University, Hong Kong)
Dédé Oetomo (University of Surabaya, Indonesia)
Cindy Patton (Simon Fraser University, Canada)
Ken Plummer (University of Essex)
Elspeth Probyn (University of Sydney, Australia)
Lisa Rofel (University of California, Santa Cruz)
Megan Sinnott (Georgia State University)
John Treat (Yale University, USA)
Carol Vance (Columbia University, USA)
Audrey Yue (University of Melbourne)

AS NORMAL AS POSSIBLE

Negotiating Sexuality and Gender in Mainland China and Hong Kong

Edited by
YAU CHING

香港大學出版社
HONG KONG UNIVERSITY PRESS

Hong Kong University Press
14/F Hing Wai Centre
7 Tin Wan Praya Road
Aberdeen
Hong Kong
www.hkupress.org

© Hong Kong University Press 2010
First paperback printing 2010
Reprinted 2011

ISBN 978-962-209-987-6

British Library Cataloguing-in-Publication Data
A catalogue copy for this book is available from the British Library

Printed and bound by Condor Production Co. Ltd., Hong Kong, China

Contents

List of Illustrations   vii

List of Contributors   ix

Dreaming of Normal While Sleeping with Impossible: Introduction   1
    Yau Ching

I   Travelling Bodies

1.   Outcast Bodies: Money, Sex and Desire of Money Boys   15
    in Mainland China
    Travis S. K. Kong

2.   Lesbianism among Indonesian Women Migrants in Hong Kong   37
    Amy Sim

3.   Tung Lo Wan: A Lesbian Haven or Everyday Life?   51
    Denise Tse Shang Tang

II   Communities

4.   GID in Hong Kong: A Critical Overview of Medical Treatments   75
    for Transsexual Patients
    Eleanor Cheung

5.   Opening Up Marriage: Married Lalas in Shanghai   87
    Kam Yip Lo Lucetta

6.   My Unconventional Marriage or *ménage à trois* in Beijing   103
    Xiaopei He

III **Representations**

7. Porn Power: Sexual and Gender Politics in Li Han-hsiang's   111
   Fengyue Films
   Yau Ching

8. Queering Body and Sexuality: Leslie Cheung's Gender   133
   Representation in Hong Kong Popular Culture
   Natalia Sui-hung Chan

9. Performing Gender, Performing Documentary in   151
   Post-socialist China
   Shi-Yan Chao

Notes   177

Glossary   189

Worked Cited   195

Index   215

Illustrations

Figures

6.1	Xiaopei He's wedding gown	106
6.2	Xiaopei He dressing up as a bride or drag	106
6.3	Xiaopei He with her wedding accessories	107
6.4	Xiaopei He with her "father"	107
6.5	Doudou and Xiaopei He's "father"	108
6.6	Guests at Xiaopei He's wedding	108
6.7	Question-and-answer session at Xiaopei He's wedding	109
6.8	Proud father holding the certificate at Xiaopei He's wedding	109
7.1	Freeze frame at the ending of *That's Adultery!*	131
8.1	Leslie Cheung's drag on stage, 1997	137
8.2	Leslie Cheung's dandy look in the 1980s	141
8.3	Leslie Cheung: "White Angel"	145
8.4	Leslie Cheung: "Pretty Boy"	145
8.5	Leslie Cheung: "Man in Skirt"	145
8.6	Leslie Cheung: "Latin Lover"	145
8.7	Leslie Cheung in "Opera Coat"	145
9.1	Still from *Tang Tang*	153
9.2	Still from *Tang Tang*	154
9.3	Still from *Tang Tang*	155
9.4	Still from *Mei Mei*	164
9.5	Still from *Mei Mei*	168

Contributors

Natalia Sui-hung CHAN is an assistant professor in the Department of Cultural and Religious Studies at the Chinese University of Hong Kong. She is on the editorial board of *Envisage: A Journal Book of Chinese Media Studies in Taiwan*, and her recent publications in Chinese include *Decadent City: Hong Kong Popular Culture* (Hong Kong: Oxford University Press, 1996), *City on the Edge of Time: Gender, Special Effects and the 1997 Politics of Hong Kong Cinema* (Hong Kong: Oxford University Press, 2002), *Female Heteroglossia: Media and Cultural Readings* (Hong Kong: Youth Literary, 2002) and *Butterfly of Forbidden Colors: The Artistic Image of Leslie Cheung* (Hong Kong: Joint Publishing, 2008).

Shi-Yan CHAO is a Ph.D. candidate in Cinema Studies at New York University. Having published various articles in Chinese, he is currently working on a dissertation on Chinese *tongzhi*/queer media.

Eleanor CHEUNG is currently conducting research on transgender subjectivities in the Faculty of Education at the University of Hong Kong. She is an active member in the LGBTIQ community in Hong Kong, including being one of the founding members of HKqUeer Campus, a network for sexual and gender minorities at the University of Hong Kong.

Xiaopei HE is a long-term activist from Beijing involved with women and *tongzhi* organizing since the 1990s. She holds Ph.D. and masters' degrees in gender, sexuality and cultural studies, and is now the executive director of Pink Space Culture and Development Centre, a Beijing-based NGO working on sexuality which conducts research and advocacy.

KAM Yip Lo Lucetta received her Ph.D. from the gender studies programme of the Chinese University of Hong Kong and is currently an assistant professor in the Department of Journalism and Communication, Chu Hai College, Hong

Kong. Her publications include "TB zhe xingbie" (Gender: TB), in *E-Journal on Hong Kong Cultural and Social Studies* 2 (September 2002); "Noras on the Road: Family and Marriage of Lesbian Women in Shanghai", in *Journal of Lesbian Studies* 10.3/4 (July 2006); "Recognition through Mis-recognition: Masculine Women in Hong Kong", in *AsiaPacifiQueer: Rethinking Gender and Sexuality in the Asia-Pacific* (edited by Fran Martin and Peter Jackson et al., University of Illinois Press, forthcoming); "Queer Guise for the Straight Guy: The Construction of Metrosexuals in Hong Kong", in *Mainstreaming Gender* (edited by Fanny Cheung et al., forthcoming). Kam and James Welker are editors of "Of Queer Import(s): Sexualities, Genders, and Rights in Asia", a special issue for *Intersections: Gender, History and Culture in the Asian Context* (issue 14, Autumn 2006). She also edited *Yueliang de shaodong — tata de chulian gushi: women de zhishu* (Lunar desires: Her first same-sex love in her own words) (Hong Kong: Cultural Act Up, 2001), the first anthology of lesbian writing from Hong Kong and Macau.

Travis S. K. KONG is an assistant professor in the Department of Sociology at the University of Hong Kong. His research expertise is on gay men and lesbians, sex workers, and people with HIV/AIDS in Chinese communities. His recent projects are researching Chinese masculinity (gay men and male sex workers) and examining queer politics in Chinese communities. His articles have appeared in books, encyclopedias, and journals such as *Body & Society, Sexualities,* and *Gender, Work and Organization.* Kong is also a cultural activist who works for many non-governmental organizations.

Amy SIM is currently teaching in the Department of Sociology at the University of Hong Kong. Prior to her graduate studies in cultural anthropology at the Department of Sociology, the University of Hong Kong, Sim has worked in a regional NGO in Asia for five years on issues of sustainable development. Her research interests are in migration, NGOs, social movements, labor activism, gender and sexuality in East and Southeast Asia.

Denise Tse Shang TANG is currently an assistant professor in the Graduate Institute for Gender Studies at Shih Hsin University, Taipei. Born in Hong Kong, she received her M.A. in educational studies from the University of British Columbia, Canada, and her Ph.D. from the Department of Applied Social Sciences at the Hong Kong Polytechnic University. Her research interests include queer pedagogy, lesbian spaces in Hong Kong, gender and sexualities, new media and visual culture. Since 1994, she has worked with marginalized populations in community-based organizations (Vancouver BC, Seattle and San Francisco) in the fields of violence against women, juvenile justice, queer youth, aboriginals, mental health, substance use and HIV / AIDS. Taking a break from social services, she returned to Hong Kong in 2003 and became the festival director of the Hong Kong Lesbian and Gay Film Festival in 2004 and 2005.

YAU Ching is an associate professor in the Department of Cultural Studies at Lingnan University, Hong Kong. She received her Ph.D. in media arts from Royal Holloway College, University of London and has also received a Rockefeller Post-doctoral Humanities Fellowship, New York Foundation for the Arts Fellowship, Asian Cultural Council Arts Fellowship, Japan Foundation artist-in-residence and several Hong Kong Arts Development Council grants. Known locally as a writer, filmmaker and cultural activist, she is a founding member of Nutong Xueshe, an LBGTQ-based organization for cultural advocacy and public education, and serves as executive board member for Midnight Blue, a male sex workers' support network in China and Hong Kong. She has authored five books in Chinese, including *Sexing Shadows: A Study of Representation of Gender and Sexuality in Hong Kong Cinema* (Hong Kong Film Critics' Society, 2005), *The Impossible Home* (Hong Kong: Youth Literary, 2000), a book in English, *Filming Margins: Tang Shu Shuen, a Forgotten Hong Kong Woman Director* (Hong Kong: Hong Kong University Press, 2004) and has edited *Sexual Politics* (Hong Kong: Cosmos, 2006). Her most recent English publication is "Performing Contradictions, Performing Bad-Girlness in Japan", a chapter in Kathy E. Ferguson and Monique Mironesco (eds.), *Gender and Globalization in Asia and the Pacific: Method, Practice and Theory* (Honolulu: University of Hawai'i Press, 2008). Her first feature film *Ho Yuk (Let's Love Hong Kong)* won the Critics' Grand Prize for Fiction at Figueira da Foz International Film Festival, Portugal in 2002.

Dreaming of Normal While Sleeping with Impossible: Introduction

Yau Ching

Issues related to sexuality have emerged in China and Hong Kong[1] in unprecedented ways in the past several years. The growth of religious fundamentalisms and global gay discourses, heightened media attention linking the rising AIDS figures primarily to the gay community, *tongzhi*[2] activist movements, struggles and public demands of sex workers, have all contributed to this new visibility. In Hong Kong, tensions are rapidly rising within the growing impact of the religious neo-liberal front fueled with reclaimed (reimagined) post-1997 Chinese moralism *vis-à-vis* glocalized movements of sexual rights. Normative institutions for the regulation of sexuality including faith-based organizations and megachurches in Hong Kong and to a less successful degree in China, and government bureaucracies across the region, have adopted activist strategies to act in unprecedented unison, and with great speed, triggering waves of moral panic[3] in their campaigns against sexual minorities and representations including but not limited to LBGTIQ and sex workers' movements, pornography and queer mainstreaming, in order to restabilize their stronghold and perpetuate their privileges. As a result, non-normative sexual subjects and communities have been brought centre stage and often stigmatized *together* due to their "abnormal/shameful" gender identities, object choices and/or sexual practices, while *tongzhi* activists—often in alliance with other pro-sexual rights groups—are striving to fight back. There is a very urgent need for intellectual work to more acutely articulate, understand and analyze the complexity of the issues raised, the subject formations concerned, and the ways in which different norms line up and become synonymous with one another. This work will contribute to building situated knowledges that will strengthen the discursive power of non-normative sexual-subjects-in-alliance, enabling them to fight against the stigmatization and facilitate more visibility of variance and differences.[4]

This book showcases the work of emerging and established scholars — working mostly outside Euro-America—on contemporary *tongzhi* studies. As one of the first sustained collections of writings on non-normative sexual subjectivities and sexual politics in Hong Kong and China post-1997 published in English, many of the writers included here are uniquely first-generation. Unlike the Euro-American academia where gender (umbrella word including sexuality) and queer studies have been rapidly proliferating at the risk of becoming normalized, these fields are still marked in Mainland China and Hong Kong as territories for the impossible and unthinkable, inhabited by stigma, silence, risk and frustration. In most universities in China and almost all universities in Hong Kong, postgraduate students are guided away from working on topics concerning queer studies *and/or* sexuality; scholars are discouraged from pursuing or publishing research in these fields. As a result, queer studies scholars have produced relatively little scholarship outside the contexts of Europe, North America and Australia. Scholars based in Asia have had remarkably little opportunity and freedom to access the resources needed to conduct and publish studies regarding LBGTIQ communities and non-normative sexual practices, in our own languages even, not to mention in English. Both of these histories have contributed to a systemic suppression of sexuality and a perpetuation of varieties of hybrid heteronormativities (that also need study) in the formulation and institutionalization of knowledge. In this light, most of the research presented here is *primary* research, literally—most of the topics and/ or communities studied here have not been studied before. All the authors here conducted their research primarily in a language other than English. Subjects previously unthinkable in the societies they live in *and* in English are be(com) ing named, spoken, articulated, and communicated through this project. This book could therefore be seen, by its writers as well as its readers, as an act of disclosure. Like most acts of disclosure, a certain strategic essentialism would be considered historically necessary by writers in this book while the collection as a whole resists the normalizing logic of the modernized privileged queer agent.[5] As a project of "continuous deconstruction of the tenets of positivism at the heart of identity politics", the Euro-American critique of queer studies "disallows any positing of a proper subject of or object for the field by insisting that queer has no fixed political referent" (Eng, Halberstam and Muñoz 3). However, in many parts of the rest of the world today, identity politics have not made their way into a core part ("heart") of our culture as most subjects could not afford to politicize one's identity. The Chinese translation of "queer" has also been largely unable to go beyond academic circles in China and Hong Kong.[6] With *Queer Eye for the Straight Guy* widely consumed on Hong Kong mainstream television (entitled in Chinese as *Fenhong jiu bing*, literally meaning *The Pink Rescue Team*, thus avoiding the untranslatability of "queer" and the potential confrontation in the suggested opposition/separation between queer and straight) and on YouTube, queer consumerism has popularized itself as one of the coolest parts of Western globalization. By rechanneling expressions of seemingly non-normative desires *only* into commodity culture this form of queerness helps to serve rather than challenge the hegemonic hierarchies of sexualities.

Resistance to the (queer) normativity seemingly offered by the American-centric (subjectless) agent, as summarized by Eng, Halberstam and Muñoz, also needs to be problematized. In this age of globalized "queer liberalism", not only does that normativity need to be foregrounded and interrogated as "variegated, striated, contradictory" (Villarejo), it is also important to remember that normativity as a relative ideal might not be accessible for many people in most parts of the world. As a performative façade fraught with fission, consumed and upheld with ongoing-but-never-to-be-exposed sacrifices and sweat, it is practically impossible and thus always desirable. I began to learn this from the following experience. Undergraduates in Cultural Studies at the school where I teach are required to work on an article-length thesis under supervision in their final year. Last year one of my students, K., wanted his thesis to be on "Straight-boy Complexes of Hong Kong Gays". Mainly based on his self-inquiry, his personal observations of friends around him, interviews and focus group discussions with friends and acquaintances, his project tried to understand how and why Hong Kong gay boys—especially "sissies" like himself—seemed to have an unyielding fixation on straight-looking guys in spite of repeated hurt, rejection and shaming. In the second tutorial, in my most gentle and understanding voice, I asked him if he had considered these "complexes" as constituted at least partly by self-loathing homophobia. Much to my surprise, with a big nodding smile he responded he had certainly asked himself *this*. He didn't tell me what his answer was. Later in his paper, he concluded by suggesting that these fantasies to date or *have* straight boys might be closely akin to a naturalized/socialized desire to access normativity—to be as close to being normal as possible because it is through sleeping with straight boys that one can imagine *being close to* getting married, having children and building families. Thus the moment of being closest to normativity is also the moment of confirming the impossibility of one's desire is also the moment of knowing one's queerness. It is only upon acknowledgement of one's not being straight that one needs to put one's finger on straightness in other ways, including in ways apparently impossible. In other words, my simplistic and presumptuous question had failed to register the complex processes of construction of and negotiation with normativity *within* subjects who are deprived of the right or the option or resist to be normal to start with. With "As Normal As Possible"—

the title of this collection—the emphasis is on the two "as"es; how its meanings change *aaaasssss* it moves along the conditions that define it. In what ways does normativity produce (im)possibilities for our sexualities; how do we stretch and resist the hegemony of normativity *and* survive to redefine, make productive and/or transform its violence and tensions in our be(come)ings? When it is given that certain forms of sexuality could not be "normal" period, the challenges for the continual and thriving existence of non-normative sexual subjects reside between the operations of at least these two levels (among others) *simultaneously*: accessing "normal" as a possibility *and* transforming "normal" into "possible".

Different Normativities

As what is considered "queer" might vary from context to context, what is constructed, desired and/or resisted as normative also varies across different bodies and communities. This collection seeks to highlight the context-specificity of normativity and the ways in which different individuals'/communities' love-and-hate relationships with normativity are also manifested and negotiated differently at different historical moments, fine-tuned according to the different power structures of each context and making different meanings. For male sex workers who serve primarily men (in local parlance "money boys") in contemporary Mainland China, the neo-liberal ideology of achieving upward class mobility and adopting a cosmopolitan lifestyle signifies more normativity than concerns regarding sexual identity or health. For Indonesian domestic helpers in Hong Kong, the prescribed feminine role of getting married, serving one's husband and having kids at home exerts tremendous pressure on the migrant workers' lives, thus informing and configuring their choices of migrancy, transgenderism and exploration of same-sex desires and practices. Compared to female migrant workers in Hong Kong and lesbians in Shanghai, Hong Kong lesbians are less confronted with the pressure to get married, but they suffer nonetheless from the expectations of their being straight-behaving, income-aspiring or income-earning hard-working girls at school, at work and at home. Their need for lesbian-only spaces expresses a desire for a buffer and comfort zone to work out and manage the stress that comes with their non-normative identities and to gain more bargaining power within a highly condensed capitalist normativity. In desiring to access this normativity, the women in Tang's study identify—not without contradictions—with a visible queer consumerism, and an affirmative discourse on lesbian sexuality as (close-to-)normal possibilities. In Shanghai *lalas'* (a Chinese term for women with same-sex desires) experimentation with "fake marriage" in order to act "normal", they have created new forms of intimacy and familial relations in the interstices between heterosexual and same-sex relationships. A reading of some pornographic period dramas made in 1970s–1990s Hong Kong suggests that the assumed normative ideal of monogamous marriage based on romantic equalitarian love between opposite genders is a very recent invention and might not be quite universalized or even desirable in contemporary Chinese imaginaries that retain memories of our literary past. Yet, for an openly queer icon Leslie Cheung Kwok-wing (who starred in films including *Rouge*, *Farewell My Concubine* and *Happy Together*, among others) operating in an increasingly or more overtly homophobic post-1997 Hong Kong, he found himself exhausting all his energies and creativity in negotiating with the limits of masculine- and hetero-normativity. In films representing transgender subjects in China today, realism, essentialized genders and assumed mutual exclusivity of homosexuality and heterosexuality are explored and critiqued as sites of normativity, whereas for transsexuals who are inevitably subject to the violence of Hong Kong's medical system, a stable and changed gender offers simultaneously the promise for normativity as well as the means for self-invention.

Different Chinese

In providing grounded and original fieldwork, as well as critical applications from the wider fields of sociological studies, public health, cultural and film studies, this interdisciplinary collection taps on the one hand, the denaturalizing of disciplinary boundaries and assumptions in Euro-American queer studies, and on the other, demonstrates the study of Chinese sexuality as an emergent field currently emanating from multiple disciplines. This book will hopefully help to just begin queering and re-sexualizing established academic disciplines, anthropology, sociology and cinema studies, to name a few, in putting together a long overdue initial knowledge base on sexuality and queer politics in China, including Hong Kong. Using a variety of methodologies ranging from ethnographic studies, documentation of activist happenings, to institution and textual analysis, it builds on existing scholarship to further diversify the study of sexuality as well as produce differences within the study of "Chinese" sexualities. As it is impossible to study sexuality in Hong Kong as a subject in isolation without studying its embeddedness in other domains such as class, educational backgrounds, religion, gender, ethnicity, and various relationships to westernization-cum-modernization, nationalism and colonialism, I envision this collection as potentially posing new and exciting challenges to queer studies pioneered but also now still somewhat shadowed by the Euro-North American axis.

Recent studies of male and female same-sex desires in early modern, modern and contemporary Chinese studies tend to privilege the site of China, at times with a comparative reference to Taiwan, but have understudied other Chinese-speaking cultures, most notably that of Hong Kong. While studies on Japan and Thailand have contended that local gender and sexual identities are shaped as much by traditional cultural trajectories as by the reworkings of globalization through the negotiative frameworks of the nation-states, this anthology seeks to examine the processes of (re)genderization and sexualization of Chinese cultures today via cities including Hong Kong, Shanghai and Beijing. The changing configurations of sexualities are studied in light of the destabilizing, internally differentiated and contested notions of the Chinese nation-state through its conflicted relations with regional and local territories such as Hong Kong, whose cultural and geographical boundaries also need to be problematized by the presence of its large population of immigrants and migrant workers, with Indonesians as a prominent case in hand.

Structure and Chapters

This collection chooses as its starting point considerations of late-twentieth-century global and local movement of labour that have reconfigured class, urban-rural, ethnic and gender hierarchies and their mutual embeddedness with sexual identifications and practices. For many in China, sex work is an attractive occupation which can provide more economic reward than that of an average (manual or even white collar) worker. As Warner notes, sex workers are the most visible examples whose gender identity and object choice could pass as normal yet they nonetheless "find themselves despised as queer because of their sexual practice" (37). Constructed by the rapidly compressed economic development of China today, sex work is a possible means to make one more "normal", while simultaneously making the subject an "abject disgrace" as well as an agent who enables new possibilities for oneself and for others. China's joining the World Trade Organization not only intensifies the already severe urban-rural inequality but further accelerates the growth of a migrant labor underclass, many of whom become sex workers in cities. The majority of clients for sex workers in Southern China are tourists from Hong Kong; the majority of sex workers in Hong Kong today are from the Mainland. While sex work is a popular profession in China and Hong Kong, the Chinese sex trade remains under-studied and most scholarly work done on the subject is available only in Chinese. Part one of this book re-frames sexualities closely related to Chinese cultural trajectories as well as drastic socio-economic changes around work and around spatial and bodily shifts. It begins with focusing on an area which is often overlooked in existing scholarship: male sex workers.[7] Based on forty-five in-depth interviews of money boys mainly coming from rural or semi-rural areas to big cities in China, Kong's study facilitates understanding of these triply-stigmatized (rural-urban migrants, sex workers *and* engaged in homosexual behaviours) subjects' own perception of risk, intimacy and mobility in relation to their structural constraints and work experiences, analyzing the relationship between poverty, homelessness and sex work in light of the political economy of sexuality, and the "circuit of desire" that links up sexuality with tourism, work and love under the thesis of transnationalization of bodies. Contrary to the overtly one-sided and dominant representation of male sex workers as depressed, depraved, dissolute and violent sociopaths in popular Chinese culture and media representations, Kong has found that the option of sex work has offered new possibilities for survival, livelihood and self-development for young migrants in a class-stratified society confronted with massive tensions between rural and urban developments.

LBGTIQ scholarship filtered through an upper middle class lens and elite sensibilities tends to overlook communities of migrant workers whose sexuality is commonly assumed to be non-existent. The second chapter studies the ways in which Indonesian migrant workers in Hong Kong, not unlike rural-to-urban sex workers in China, re-configure their sexual identities and behaviours contingent upon the economic-driven contexts of labour and mobility. In studying the *trans* of "transitional sexuality" among female migrant workers, Sim looks at the nature of same-sex relationships that occur during labour migration and focuses on the mutability of sexuality, object choices and sexual behaviours to explain the complex ways in which cultural norms "at home" inform the experiences of migrant workers in the "host country". Sim also explains how geographic mobility enables greater sexual and gender mobility, rendering a mutually constitutive and simultaneous existence of the needs of queer agencies with the demands of straight family norms possible. This chapter explores the conditions within which lesbian relationships emerge and recreate expressions of alternative sexual identities, which Sim coins "neo-heterosexuality". I would suggest it could also be read as "trans-lesbianism", a form of experiencing same-sex desires on the part of transnationalized bodies which not only complicates lesbianism in its variable combination with heterosexual marriage and family norms but also produces multiple possibilities for transitionally gendered embodiments. Echoing other chapters in the book addressing survival problems encountered and creative coping strategies invented by various sexual minoritized subjects (in ways more than one), this chapter investigates the ways in which the social body of migrant workers is heavily disciplined by mechanisms of socio-political control. These Indonesian trans-lesbians are rendered as multiple abjects, yet they simultaneously reconfigure bodies, values, and challenges to lead meaningful lives that go beyond binary oppositions of resistance and co-optation. This chapter also touches upon the ways in which these meanings are informed and transformed by the various spaces sexual subjects enter, produce and manoeuvre in.

Due to the density in population and the lack of physical land space, people in Hong Kong—sexual abjects more than others—negotiate privacy and self-expression in specifically spatially-defined ways. In a contrastable study, but on a more micro scale, Tang maps how lesbian commercial spaces in Hong Kong—including karaoke bars, upstairs cafés, lesbian specialty stores in a high-density shopping hub known as Causeway Bay or Tung Lo Wan—function as sites of community formation for lesbians to escape from heteronormative society, validate their self-images, build and maintain social networks, and/or to perform political subjectivity. Through this study, based on interviews with more than thirty lesbians and space owners/managers, Tang contends that these physical spaces are in a continuously mobile process to transform themselves through customers who take part in the reproduction of social and sexual relations within them; a finding shared by other writers in this section. All three chapters problematize the heteronormative class-biased dichotomy of private versus public that marks the beginning of modern selfhood—the domestication of emotions and privacy within the "home" and rationalized civic engagement and regulation in the public realm.

The chapters in part two articulate narratives which explore strategies in challenging *and* living/thriving with the systematic modern abjection of "deviant" gender and sexual subjectivities, under the shadows of upholding, subverting and/or redefining the respectability and usability of institutions, hence offering *tongzhi* studies channels in understanding the productivity of power relations in specific contexts today. Cheung argues for a depathologization of transsexuality through detailed and contextualized data gathered from studying the operation and limitations of the medical system in Hong Kong and from interactive fieldwork with gender-variant subjects[8] in order to further understand the complex processes of gender identity (trans)formation at work today. Cheung relates how transgender and intersexed peoples negotiate with medical institutions demarcated by handbooks, definitions, standards, (mis) information, presumptions, and habits of surgical and psychiatric treatments. This original study investigates and critiques the various ways in which the institutionalization of a gender identity spectrum have been recently taking shape in Hong Kong and recommends a critical paradigm shift in revising current treatment directions and methods. As one of the first academic studies of this silenced topic in Hong Kong, it is significant not only as an account studying the history of contemporary transsexuality but also as a powerful political critique of Hong Kong's specifically modern regulatory apparatus of (inter and trans)sexuality.

Kam's study, based on in-depth interviews with twenty-four *lalas* in Shanghai, politicizes the discourses of standing up (*zhan qi lai*) / coming out (*zhan chu lai*), and examines the negotiational conflicts between the desires for familial recognition of one's personal life and the aspiration for social recognition and political collectivity. As *lalas* in China face not only social prejudice towards sexual non-normativities but also prejudice towards women as a culturally and economically subordinate gender, they are found in this study to feel obliged to outperform their male and heterosexual counterparts in ways that receive greater social recognition ("upward social mobility"): to be filial daughters, productive workers, contributing citizens, and last but not least, married wives, so as to "compensate" for their "abnormal" sexuality, which has been thought to have deprived their parents of "normal" family lives with grandchildren. It is their apparent social hypernormativity that makes their rejection of sexual normativity possible. This "politics of normalization", as argued by Kam, could be seen as a political strategy for maintaining sexual dissidence, earning visibility, recognition and potentially more freedom for a self-identified community in the long run. Would these hard earned new spaces necessarily imply selling out to more regulation through discourses of capitalist individualism? The emphasis on "community" in Kam's chapter seems to suggest otherwise.

Deviant subjects and normative institutions compete in bending each other while they also work hard (and occasionally have fun) in bending themselves accordingly. He's narrative of her performance retraces her unique tactics of setting an admirable example in turning the institution of heterosexual, monogamous *and* monosexual marriage inside out. Her queering of the marriage ritual raises poignant challenges to the limits of the institution as she confronts its discriminatory effects via creative and tongue-in-cheek ways in experimenting towards a programme for change, responsive to the cultural-specific needs of her community and society, "the lived arrangements of queer life, and articulated in queer publics" (Warner 146). Her appropriation and critique of the ritual demonstrates the vitality and pleasure of a possible queer politics and counterpublic which prioritizes non-normative intimacies, coalition building, sex education and advocacy over love, privacy and the life-long couple form of marriage. While the two chapters of He and Kam speak dialogically to the politics of compulsory family, marriage and heterosexual normativity and various diverse strategies for possible subversion and reconfiguration, the playful language that He's essay strategically adopts in documenting her own performance also paves the ways for Chao's readings of performing transvestism in Chinese documentaries. The research of Kong, Sim, Kam and Cheung place more emphasis on the ongoing struggle for a (like-)normal possibility under the overarching shadow of impossibility (closer to normal but never quite there), whereas in He, Yau, Chan and Chao's essays one might be able to see how "normativity" takes on many angelic and contradictory shapes (and / or has been bent) in its giving way to multiple (as-if-)possible lives. These subjects and representations move away from being normal in order to becoming possibly something else, something perhaps closer to accessing normal on their own terms. In this process of moving from one "as" to another, this "normal" might have been bent to create new desires and visions. Possibly as normal as ...

The last part of the book interrogates the symptomatic relations of sexual discourses to modernity and postmodernity, linking contemporary identity positions and performativity through continuities in representation with largely unlexicalized gender- and sexual-variant subjectivities from a past not too long ago. These chapters inaugurate readings of Chinese cinematic texts and cultural icons—from late Ming to post-Mao China, from colonial (1970s–1990s) to post- or neo-colonial (post-1997) Hong Kong—that reconfigure as they reinvent "Chinese" and "sexuality" *vis-à-vis* each other. While "homosexuality" has been positioned rhetorically by official Chinese authorities today as "a decadent ideology imported from the West", the rendering of Ming erotic texts by pan-Chinese film director Li Han-hsiang's (Li Hanxiang) (1926–96) helps to set the historical scene for charting a vibrant yet suppressed trajectory of Chinese sexualities. Li's cinematic explorations yield historical knowledge in multiple ways: it sheds light on the contemporary—in fact, very recent—regulation of sexuality through polarizing categories such as homosexuality and heterosexuality, symptomatic of Western modernity, as well as the rich but much repressed representations and discourses of diverse and malleable genders and sexualities in Chinese culture. If, according to Kong's study, the proliferation of money boys in China today has been significantly re-shaping and problematizing the landscape of normative masculinity, Li helps us gain further insights on the ways in which so-called normative sexualities in Chinese sexual imaginaries have always already been diverse, malleable and undefinable—if you like—queer, thus helping to expose the fragility of contemporary heteronormativity. Extensively drawn from a Chinese literary tradition deemed obscene, Li's "softcore" pornographic films were most popular during the 1970s but continually made until the 1990s, constituting a genre of its own known as *fengyue pian* ("wind and moon" films). These films are often referred to by critics as Li's "cynical" films as they portray a world "morally corrupted by vulgarity" and sexual "perversions". Yau's essay re-traces the radical potential of the *fengyue* porn genre populated by nonmonogamous subjects and *yinfus* (licentious women or women "who have seen a lot of life", as defined by Li) in dialoguing with Li's own historical epics—primarily narratives of shrews and abject men—as well as "talking back to" (and laughing at) the increasingly normalizing times that through regulatory privatizing apparatuses privilege the modern monogamous marriage. This body of work, according to Yau, should be reread as political as these films communicate a precious sociability and sexual equality—an abjection intimately shared by the pornographic gaze and the heterogeneous, commonly denigrated as "pre-modern" sexual subjects on screen.[9] Yau explores the various ways in which Li's *fengyue* complicates the genre of pornography through subverting the sexual hierarchies assumed by film critics, inventing Chinese pornography as a *different* modernity than the colonial-Western, and seducing the audience—including men, women and in-betweens—through strategies such as recentering women's and polygamists' sexual and cross-gendered agency, use of multiple perspectives and self-reflexive devices.

Although the focus of this collection is on the contemporary, I hope to also emphasize that what is "contemporary Chinese" sexuality needs to be reunderstood in terms of the region's territorially differentiated relationships to the representations and disavowal of a "Chinese past". This collection cannot even begin to include the varieties of relations to the "past" that distinct Chinese locales have (whether or not a part of the PRC at a given historical moment) because each of these relations is embedded within each place's formation of sexuality. Yau's chapter might allow us to register one way in which renewed readings of "past" texts could enrich our understanding of present formations—including their desexualizing and normalizing processes in their complexity and quandaries. Research of the past in light of non-normative sexualities is even more difficult in the scholarly communities in Chinese Asia itself. The difficulty could be explained in terms of the specific formation of communities of knowledge of sexual politics in Asia, which has been unequally developed and heavily skewed toward disciplines of the contemporary, most notably literature, sociology and anthropology.

For *tongzhi* studies scholars, rewriting history and its interconnectedness to the present is an urgent political necessity. Leslie Cheung, hailed as one of the most important queer icons in pan-Asian popular culture in the past two decades, jumped off the balcony of the twentieth-fourth floor of the Mandarin Oriental Hotel in Hong Kong in 2003. While Li's cinematic representations demonstrate the abundance of nonnormativity in the historical trajectory of Chinese popular imaginary, Cheung used his life (and death) to illustrate the extreme lack of room outside normal in a contemporary Chinese society. Would these two conditions be mutually constitutive of each other? Rewritten from a small part of her appraised Chinese book on Leslie Cheung, Chan's chapter re-contextualizes Cheung's (sudden) suicide in light of Cheung's cross-dressing gender performativity, his "bisexuality"/"androgyny" and "intersexuality", and the polarizing reception and consumption of his work both locally and internationally. As opposed to the dominant ideology of Cheung as a ghost-haunted freak who miscalculated the reception of transgressive sexuality in the society he lived in, Chan's work provides the first sustained study of Cheung's gender and sexual representations as consumed locally, while she maps his suicide as a result of various forms of stigmatization he had suffered from Hong Kong's own inadequacies in negotiating its contradictions embedded in glocalized consumer culture. The fact that Cheung ultimately used his own death to perform a critique of life impossible, hetero- or homo-sexual, speaks to the immensely oppressive gap between the global discourse of (promising) compulsory happiness[10] circulating in the post-identity neoliberalist world, and the local dominance of queerphobic normativity. Through detailed textual analysis and focusing on debates within existing local discourses, this chapter carefully interrogates the ways in which a cultural icon with his various non-normative behaviours and expressions, struggled to negotiate with mainstream media. While such struggles might have increased his marketability for queer reception, they more overtly and with relatively little resistance aggravated the destructiveness of normalizing forces.

What are the strategies of queer representation currently circulating in non-mainstream culture in China? The last chapter, "Performing Gender, Performing Documentary in Postsocialist China", addresses representations of transgender and male queerness found in the prolific underground documentary genre, also known as the "New Documentary Movement". By focusing on two recent documentary films, *Tang Tang* (Zhang Hanzi, 2004) and *Mei Mei* (Gao Tian, 2005), Chao examines how the film's reflection on queerness could be seen as parallel to its reflection on realism and how the two embody and foreground each other. Reading transgender performance as a means of survival and a negotiation strategy with capitalist mechanisms *and* the normative tradition of *jingju* (Beijing Plays a.k.a. Peking Opera) in (post)modern Chinese contexts, this chapter resituates forms of boundary-crossing (from gender-crossing, genre-crossing to translocal/glocalized imaginaries and consumption; between "failures to repeat" and "refusals to repeat"; between heterosexual and homosexual; between the urban and the rural; between reality and fiction, etc.) *vis-à-vis* the emerging queer and popular subcultures, in enabling nonessentialized dissident subjectivities-in-the-making. Further expanding the inquiry begun in the first two chapters of this book, the analysis of Meimei and Tangtang's transgenderism as labour and the construction of new intimacies by this form of labour facilitates deeper understanding of the multiple ways in which gender and sexual identities are being reconfigured and negotiated within hierarchies of political and capitalist class struggles in contemporary (post-socialist) China. The controversial representation of Tangtang's realistic suicide *as* fabricated foregrounds and critiques the power dynamics between queer subjects, media control and audience expectation, helping to reflect on forces that inform suicides of subjects beyond the screen like Leslie Cheung's. These forces contribute to aspects of Cheung's suicide that have gone beyond representation, the limits of which Chan's chapter passionately engages with. Chan analyzes how Cheung pushed limits in his representational life that are intrinsically in Hong Kong unpushable for an out queer public figure. The multiple possibilities of queer desire as publicized and evoked through Cheung's representations are also actually not realizable in public in Hong Kong people's experiential life. Since the source of impossibility and the hold/regulation of the private lies in the limits placed on the public, the only way to unravel this is to commit an act of suicide bombing—on one's public self. Cheung's suicide amounts to a form of social protest against an unspeakable contradiction that, as Chan argues, needed then to be recontained in the normalizing media discourse of privatizing sexuality and gay pathologization.

Challenges

I was invited to contribute a short essay to an issue of *GLQ* in 2005 focusing on perspectives from film critics and scholars working with queer film festivals and media. I concluded my essay by outlining some challenges "facing us in Asia today", which I would like to rewrite as follows: to strengthen LGBTIQ writers access to knowledge production and distribution resources in Asia; to foster an interest by writers and readers to reconnect current issues with repressed histories, however obscene and/or colonialist; to develop the willingness and courage of LBGTIQ constituencies and communities in building coalition with other sexual dissidents and minoritized peoples in order to fight ghettoization and stigma, discuss the interconnectedness of all sexual marginalization and advocate *real* structural change; and to relocalize LGBTIQ issues and strategies within and against the global gay economy. It is not fortuitous that Li Han-hsiang, with audiences in Chinese communities worldwide, chose a modernized Hong Kong after all as the base for most of his work of rewriting historical texts, and that one of the sites where a project like this one in its attempt to carve out and formulate a publicly queer critical space is also Hong Kong. Organizing and editing this anthology in this late-colonial city where global Christian and paternalistic Chinese forces are miraculously working hard to join hands (despite tensions and contradictions) in systemically defining normal and possible for us in certain parts of Chinese Asia, I hope this volume can contribute to the long march of registering and learning from the subjects analyzed, experiences and feelings lived and documented which speak of survival, authenticity, courage and hope. This can only be an introduction.

Acknowledgments

I would like to thank the Department of Cultural Studies at Hong Kong Lingnan University for providing me a safe and supportive space to work on this project, Hong Kong University Press for its continual commitment to academic freedom and intellectual pursuit in spite of the "controversial" nature of the project, the two anonymous reviewers for insightful comments, Liang Xiaodao for not giving up on me in offering editorial assistance most needed, and all the writers in this collection for their trust and hard work. I am deeply indebted to Denise Tang, Kathy High and Laurie Wen who took care of me when my health was in crisis. Last but not least, my apologies and deepest gratitude go to dnf who serve as my reader, therapist and companion through hard times as well as to my two cats, Dimdim and Suensuen, for their tolerance and unconditional support.

Spring 2010

I

Travelling Bodies

1
Outcast Bodies: Money, Sex and Desire of Money Boys in Mainland China[1]

Travis S.K. Kong

> ... the construction of self-identity for the prostitute is an embedded process, one which is shaped by the institutions surrounding the profession, the social and moral climate of the time, the contemporary nature of sexuality and prevailing understandings of business activity, health, consumption and education. (Brewis and Linstead 2000b: 177)

> A sea-change has swept through China in the last fifteen years: to replace socialist experimentation with the "universal human nature" imagined as the essential ingredient of cosmopolitan worldliness. This model of human nature has the desiring subject as its core: the individual who operates through sexual, material, and affective self-interest. (Rofel 2007: 3)

Initiated by the then General Secretary of the Communist Party of China, Deng Xiaoping, in 1978, many reforms have changed China's economic, political, social and cultural landscapes over the past few decades. This series of reforms has included agricultural decollectivization, the creation of a market economy, the enhancement of social mobility, modernization and internationalization. Crystallized as the "opening up", the reforms have privileged liberal market principles, emphasized money and other material rewards, encouraged consumption and personal choice, intensified social conflict, widened inequality and created the massive growth of a floating migrant labour underclass population, among other effects. This apparently revolutionary yet contradictorily multifaceted process has affected every single citizen and has re-positioned China in the world (Solinger 1999; Perry and Selden 2000; Liu, L.H. 1999; Blum and Jensen 2002).

All these changes have resulted in a lessening of state monitoring of private life, and have created a new social environment for (especially young) people to engage in sexual and romantic interaction. Values and norms associated with love, intimacy and sexuality have all been given new meanings by the neo-liberalization process, which has opened up a new sexual space for young Chinese men and women (Farrer 2002; Pan 1993; Jeffreys 2006; Rofel 2007; Kong 2010). It is in this context that prostitution is said to have re-emerged as a serious social problem.

Prostitution has been visible, and quite tolerated, throughout Chinese history (Hershatter 1997; Ruan 1991; Van Gulik 1961). Academic studies and public discussions of prostitution mainly focus on female prostitutes (Hong and Li 2007). After the Chinese Communist Party (CCP) gained political power in 1949, great efforts were made to eradicate prostitution, as it was depicted as a remnant of imperialism, the sexual exploitation of women and a sin from the West. The government claimed they had been successful in this effort. However, accompanying the economic reforms that began in 1978, the government was forced to acknowledge that there had been a widespread resurgence of prostitution (Hershatter 1997; Cohen et al. 1996; Gil et al. 1996). At present, third party prostitution (e.g., organizing, inducing, introducing, facilitating, or forcing another person to engage in prostitution) is a criminal offence in China, punishable by a number of years of imprisonment, with possible fines. First party prostitution is not criminalized but is regarded as socially harmful, and both female prostitutes and their clients are subject to periods of reform detention, with possible fines (Jeffreys 2007).

Male prostitution has been evident throughout Chinese history, but it has been discussed mainly in the context of homosexuality, since the majority of clients are males (Hirsch 1990; Samshasha 1997; Ruan 1991; Van Gulik 1961; Tong 2006, 2007). The PRC has no written laws explicitly criminalizing same-sex prostitution. Likewise, there are no specific laws prohibiting homosexuality in China. The 1997 revised Criminal Law deleted specific reference to the crime of hooliganism, an umbrella term that refers to a wide range of social misbehaviours but was often used to penalize same-sex sexual activities. Homosexuality was also removed from Chinese psychiatric texts as a form of mental illness in 2001 (Wu 2003). Although there are no laws against same-sex sexual acts, homosexuals in China are still subject to strong social disapproval from society and can be penalized on the basis of the Chinese system of administrative and Party discriminatory sanctions (Li 2006, 1998).[2]

Since the 1990s, male homosexuality and male prostitution have caught government and media attention, partly because of the rapid increase of visible gay consumption venues like bars, clubs, massage parlours, saunas, karaokes, etc. (Rofel 2007; Kong 2010) and partly because of the upsurge of HIV infection among the MSM (men who have sex with men) population (China Ministry of Health et al. 2006; Zhang and Chu 2005; Kong 2009a). In 2004, 34-year-old Nanjing City native Li Ning was sentenced to jail for eight years and fined

60,000 yuan for organizing male-male prostitution services. Since this case and similar cases, the government has tended to treat same-sex prostitution in the same manner as heterosexual prostitution and has implemented a "strike hard" campaign against same-sex prostitution as a result of the rapid rise of HIV/AIDS infection in the commercial sex industry and as a way to regulate the "inappropriate" range of same-sex sexual activities (Jeffreys 2007).

Prostitution in modern China is thus affected by two compelling but contradictory forces, probably due to the state's endeavour to balance "material" and "spiritual" civilization. On the one hand, it is perceived as a leisure activity. The hedonistic morality of the neo-liberal climate encourages the idea of the commodification of the body as an object for consumption. An emphasis on material rewards and severe economic hardship provide justifications for some, especially rural or semi-rural, young men and women to enter the sex industry. On the other hand, prostitution is perceived as an offence against morality. The Chinese government exercises strict prohibition measures against prostitution and makes special efforts to crack down on sex-related businesses and parties. Male prostitution further complicates the situation, as the organization of the male sex industry always entails the element of homosexuality, and is negatively stigmatized by society.

It is against this background that this research to understand "money boys" (MBs, the local term for male sex workers who serve men) in Mainland China, presenting various aspects of their lives through a qualitative study of 30 such individuals, was carried out.[3] It is an attempt to understand the relationship between routes into sex work and homelessness, poverty, unemployment and migration; and to identify how some men might be discriminated against or treated unequally due to their interlocked identities along the lines of gender, sexual orientation, class, education, migrancy, work, etc. In the following, after a brief discussion of the methodology and findings, I will discuss the pathological and public health threat paradigms, which have dominated the discussion of prostitution in the West as well as in China. I will then discuss an approach which is sensitive to worker's agency and structural constraints and which suggests that some young men rationally choose to engage in sex work in the context of personal and structural constraints; and to negotiate the risks, harms, and gains within their work settings. I will argue that my findings tend to refute the pathological and public health threat paradigm approach and to encourage the adoption of the latter one. Secondly, I will examine the difficulties of the working experiences of most informants that result from their triply-stigmatized identities—as rural-to-urban migrants, prostitutes and homosexuals in the process of urban subject formation. The informants seem to have put much effort into maintaining boundaries between their work and their private selves—at the two sites of contestation at which they negotiate risk and harm, excitement and love, under the complex web of domination such as familial pressure, social discrimination and neo-liberal state governance.

Methods

Drawn from a continuing research project on the male sex industry in greater China (major sites: Hong Kong, Beijing, Shanghai, Dali, Guangdong and Shenzhen) since 2003, this chapter focuses on field visits made in Beijing and Shanghai from 2004 to 2005. Participants were all Chinese in origin, at least eighteen years old, who reported having had sex with at least one other man in exchange for money in the previous six months. During the period, I conducted thirty in-depth face-to-face interviews with Chinese male sex workers in Beijing (n=14) and Shanghai (n=16), the two cities believed to have the highest number of homosexuals (or MSM) and male sex workers. The formal interviews ranged in length from 1.5 to 3 hours, making up a total of approximately 47.5 formal interviewing hours. Apart from formal interviews, I engaged in casual conversations with different individuals related to the male sex industry—including workers, agents and clients—in order to make sense of this occupation.

The interviewees were recruited mainly through a non-governmental organization (NGO) whose mission is to fight HIV/AIDS and to strive for acceptance of sexual diversity and equality and who had established rapport with some of these individuals; as well as through word-of-mouth referrals from workers (i.e., the snowball technique). Interviewees were recruited who were as diverse as possible in terms of backgrounds (e.g., age, education, sexual orientation, place of origin, marital status, etc.) and working experiences (e.g., full time/part time, and occupational settings such as street/brothel/massage parlour prostitution) in order to grasp a fuller picture of the industry. The interviews were conducted at hotels, workers' homes and the NGO's office.

The nature of the study was carefully explained, and confidentiality and anonymity were emphasized. Participants were told of their right to end the interview at any time if they felt any psychological discomfort. Consent was sought before the tape-recording of all interviews, which were later transcribed from Putonghua, in written Chinese. Interviews were free-flowing in style but focused on these men's identity formation in relation to their working experiences. Guided by a grounded theory approach (Strauss and Corbin 1997) and following Ryan and Bernard's (2000) framework, data analysis consisted of different procedures, such as identifying themes, building codebooks, marking texts, constructing models (relationships among codes), and testing models against empirical data (see also Miles and Huberman 1994). Coding themes were initially based on the interview guidelines, which had been derived from the existing literature on male prostitution. New themes emerged during the interviews and the coding process. Findings and analyses were then compared to existing local and international literature.

Findings

All respondents in this research were ethnic Han Chinese, the dominant ethnicity in China. They ranged in age from 19 to 32, but clustered in their early twenties. Three identified themselves as heterosexual, seven were ambivalent about their sexuality (but showed interest in men), whilst the rest identified themselves as homosexual (or self-labelled as "*tongzhi*", "gay" or "*quan'nei ren*"). All of them were single except one; four claimed to have steady non-paying affective relationships with men and three had such with women. More than half of them had attained average or higher levels of education (three had primary education, eight had attended junior middle school, thirteen had attended senior middle school, and six had post-secondary or university education). They were all born in Mainland China and were from different regions, but they mainly came from villages in rural or semi-rural areas. No one was homeless. Very few reported having suffered from sexual abuse or violence in childhood.

There are many types of male sex workers in the world (Aggleton 1999; West and de Villers 1993), but four are reported among my samples. The first type of male sex workers is the full-time independent worker (or "street hustler"), who mainly works on his own, hustling in public areas such as parks and bars and through the increasingly popular cyber channels of the internet. These venues usually provide opportunities for workers to meet potential clients. Sex normally takes place elsewhere (e.g., hotels) after negotiation has been made. Nine respondents belonged to this type.

The second type is the full-time brothel worker, who usually works under an agent in a sex venue (e.g., male brothel or massage parlour). Clients can choose boys, and sex and/or erotic massage may take place in a room or cubicle inside the venue, or clients can buy the boys out (*chutai*) for a few hours and even stay overnight with them elsewhere. These boys usually live in the venue and are kept by an agent, and cannot freely go out without permission. There were eight respondents of this type.

The third type is the part-time worker, including the worker who has "quit" the job but who freelances occasionally when he is short of money or is requested by old clients. Eleven belonged to this type.

The final type is the houseboy (or *beiyangde*)—i.e., a boy kept by a sugar daddy. Two respondents belonged to this type.

Their work histories were complex. Before entering the sex industry, most had worked at other jobs, such as manual work in manufacturing or heavy industry (e.g., as car mechanics, factory workers), or in service work (e.g., as chefs, waiters, hotel bellboys, security guards, salesmen, barbers). The respondents, like other rural migrants, had come to Beijing or Shanghai mainly for work, but also for independence and excitement. They had chosen these two cities, which for them represented modernity, sophistication and freedom, where they could earn more money and experience a new world that did not exist in their hometowns.

Ah Yang was only 22 and had worked full-time for a brothel for six months:

> I came to Beijing because it is one of the four municipalities of China, you can earn more money here. That's why I came here. (Ah Yang, 22, ambivalent about his sexuality, full-time brothel worker, 6 months)[4]

I met Xiao Jin through his former brothel manager. He was twenty-seven, older than other workers, and very well-mannered and articulate during the interview. He came to Beijing because he wanted to forget about his lost love (who had passed away a few years previously) and also because of the charm of Beijing City:

> This city (Beijing) is big, with a very long history. I found it a very tolerant city. And there is something behind this city, behind modernity and sophistication, behind those walls and bricks, there is something that I can't tell but it's liberating. (Xiao Jin, 27, gay, freelancer, 6 months)

Interviewees had entered the sex industry through friends in their hometowns or through contacts with agents whom they met at gay bars, in parks, on the internet or in shops. Most of the interviewees treated sex work as a source of income and engaged in it for this specific purpose—i.e., money was the primary reward:

> I never treated it as a job, it's just a tool to earn money. (Ah Hao, 25, straight, freelancer, 3 years)

Apart from money, however, interviewees mentioned other aspects of satisfaction, which related to their sexual orientations and the job nature. For those who were gay or interested in men, sexual pleasure from work and ensuring gay identities were frequently mentioned:

> In this job, I can work as well as enjoy the sex! (Dou Dou, 22, gay, full-time independent, 6 months)

> I can be relaxed and say that I love men! I am a tongzhi! (Ah Dong, 26, gay, freelancer, 6 months)

The flexibility and freedom of the job was also emphasized:

> Freedom! For other jobs, you have to work and be on time; for this job, you can sleep whenever you want, eat whenever you like. It's quite free, really. (Ah Wei, 25, gay, full-time independent, 8 years)

They also argued that sex work could act as a springboard to achieve a larger plan—a sort of self-development for upward mobility:

> I knew a lot of people through this job. They came from all sorts of classes, they are helpful to me ... I was a very ordinary, average *dagongzai* (working son). But since I entered this industry, I have known a lot of things... the change was fundamental ... and I know this social networking will be very useful for my future ... this is my major gain! (Xiao Yu, 26, gay, freelancer, 6 months)

> Maybe you would meet someone in this circle, and he could help you get something that you want. (Ah Tian, 20, ambivalent about his sexuality, full-time brothel worker, 1 year)

As with other migrant workers, job mobility is common. The length of time interviewees had been working in the occupation varied from 6 months to 8 years, but most of them had been working for 1 or 2 years. By mobility, here I mean mobility within the sex industry. They had worked for more than one place, or in different occupational settings in the same city, or had moved among cities. For example, Ah Tao was 32. He first started to hustle in parks when he was 24. He later moved to work in different brothels and massage parlours and in different areas (e.g., Shenzhen and elsewhere in Guangdong, in Chengdu, etc.). He had been working as a sex worker for 8 years and was now working on his own and was settled in Beijing.

Mobility can also mean moving in and out of sex work. Some had started small businesses (e.g., a fashion boutique) but freelanced as sex workers if they were short of money or were requested by old clients. This tendency can be explained by the nature of the industry. The career life-cycle, in fact, is short-lived. The sex industry is constantly looking for "fresh meat", so that the longer one is in it, the less money one can make. The "prospectus" of the job is also rather limited, leading only to the position of a manager, which involves totally different skills. As mentioned, third party prostitution is a criminal offence in China.

The Prostitution Debate

Much of the international sex work literature has focused on the female experience, and unconventional female sexual behaviour has been understood in relation to the psychological state of the actors. Pathological views of female sex workers (e.g., Glover 1960; Davis 1976) have gradually been replaced by concern for public health in relation to the HIV / AIDS epidemic (e.g., G. Scambler and A. Scambler 1997; Weitzer 2000). The rise of the sociology of emotions has resulted in a renewed interest in the interactionist concern with the fragility of interpersonal exchange and identity negotiation (e.g., Brewis and Linstead 2000a, 2000b; O' Neill 2001; Chapkis 1997; Sanders 2005; Kong 2006).

Studies of male sex workers have followed a similar pattern. Most either adopt a pathological view (e.g., Coombs 1974; Reiss 1961) or have approached the subject from the viewpoint of health, particularly as concerns the prevention of HIV / AIDS (e.g., Davies and Feldman 1997; Aggleton 1999), but recently some have brought identity, emotion and body into the discussion—e.g., Browne and Minichiello (1995, 1996a, 1996b) (on male sex workers in Australia); Escoffier (2003) (on straight male actors in the US gay porn industry); Pruitt and LaFont (1995) (on Jamaican beach boys in "romance tourism"); and Ronai and Cross (1998) and Tewksbury (1993) (on male strippers).

For Mainland China, studies of male sex workers are scanty, and, as in the West, predominantly adopt pathological and public health threat paradigms, according to which male sex workers are usually portrayed as young "innocent" men, with little or no formal education—rural male migrants who provide same-sex sexual services solely for money. They are perceived as the highest risk group among the MSM population, as they are most likely to engage in high-risk behaviour and to have a serious problem of substance abuse (e.g., Zhang et al. 2004; Choi et al. 2004; He et al. 2007; Wong et al. 2008). A small literature is emerging which offers a more sociological / anthropological understanding of the issue at stake, bringing identity and body, migration, class and other socio-cultural factors into consideration (Jeffreys 2007; Rofel 2007, 2010; Tong 2007; Kong 2009a, 2009b, 2010).

To begin with, the dominant representation of money boys in China studies is still very similar to the traditional account of male prostitutes in the West. Coombs (1974: 784) depicts:

> a drifter, [who] has a poor work history, possesses no vocational skill, is of low to average intelligence, comes from a deprived socioeconomic background, and is below the average in educational attainment. He is a drop-out and comes from a broken home or a home in which his parents were poor models. His was a shattered family in which there

was a dearth of warmth and an excess of violence and rejection. He was the victim of indifferent mothering. Most hustlers have been found to be irresponsible, immature, unstable, and neurotic, with a strong dislike for authority.

Reiss (1961) also described a group of young men who identified themselves as heterosexuals who engaged in commercial homosexual transactions with men but emphasized material rewards of the work, denied sexual pleasure from the sex, performed only as a fellator and disdained or even had physical violence to clients.

Similarly, Choi et al. (2002) reported that money boys in China engaged in "survival sex", that rarely involved using condoms, in order to please their male clients. Zhang et al. (2004) reported that MSM who were young, unmarried, poorly educated, and with no, or low, incomes, were more likely to engage in sex work and that male sex workers had engaged in high-risk behaviour. Wong et al. (2008) and He et al. (2007) showed that the major motivation for becoming a money boy was economic survival. Their respondents had engaged in high-risk behaviour, suffered from depression, were dependent on substance use, and were exposed to past or current sexual abuse and violence.

The following assumptions seem to underlie these accounts. First, no young man would rationally choose to become a sex worker. It is not a voluntary choice, or at least not a right choice to make. Second, having a broken family and a history of sexual abuse is a precondition for engaging in sex work. Third, sex work is only a means of gaining monetary rewards; there is no sexual pleasure in it at all or, if any, it should come from certain sexual practices defined as masculine, such as insertive penetration. Fourth, there is a general negative feeling about the clients, especially the male clients, as they are the "real" homosexuals. Finally, the implication of this traditional picture is a social need to "help" these young men give up prostitution and return to some other way of life. As in the case of the female prostitute, the male prostitute is portrayed as "a powerless prostitute … trapped by personality defects, childhood traumata or economic destitution in a cycle of penury, prostitution and self-loathing" (Davies and Feldman 1997: 33).

However, a newer picture has been emerging in the international literature. Although studies in the 1980s continued to discuss the reasons and motivations for entering the industry and to refer to "deviant" socialization (e.g., Allen 1980; Luckenbill 1985, 1986), work since the 1990s has been shifting slowly away from the socio-pathological model. These later works have acknowledged male prostitution as legitimate work and have discussed men's engagement in sex work to be a result of rational calculation of a number of factors, such as migration and considerations of financial gain, sexual pleasure, affection, and freedom in the context of personal and structural constraints (e.g., Calhoun and Weaver 1996; West and de Villiers 1993; Browne and Minichellio 1995, 1996a, 1996b; Davies and Feldman 1997). The working experiences of sex workers have been documented, with different degrees of victimization, exploitation, agency and control found in different cultures (e.g., Aggleton 1999). However, the dominant concern has been the relationship of sex workers, safer sex practices and HIV/AIDS infection, in a public health paradigm (e.g., Vanwesenbeeck 2001).

Therefore, in the discussion of male prostitution, one view is that it is a survival strategy enforced by poverty, homelessness and powerlessness—a form of slavery arising from economic, social, and cultural deprivation. The other view is that prostitution is a "rational" choice for men who are constrained by their marginalized positions in a highly class-stratified social structure.

The results of this research seem to refute those of the first view, and they convince this researcher of the validity of the second one. First, the young men in my research were part of the rural-to-urban migrant population and had come to cities for survival, work and excitement. They were from ordinary family backgrounds and had average education. Very few reported having suffered from sexual abuse or violence. Although one might be cautious about the possible underreporting of such traumatic experiences, it is also fair to regard such experiences as unnecessary for becoming sex workers. Most of my informants self-identified as "gay"; some were ambivalent about their sexuality but had personal (sexual) interests in men. They enjoyed the sex from work (even those who identified themselves as straight). They did not privilege certain sexual acts (e.g., insertive penetration). They also had good relationships with clients.

Second, the informants had not been forced to enter the sex industry. Becoming sex workers seems to have been one of the options that had opened up for these young men to deal with the difficult overall employment situation for migrants. They had all made conscious choices to engage in sex work. They had realized that their bodies could be a means to gain economic rewards. Their main reasons for entering the industry were instrumental—to earn money, pay debts—but other reasons included exploring gay sexuality, having fun and finding romance. Thus, although monetary reward was the primary satisfaction, they enjoyed other aspects of the job, such as sexual pleasure and expression, flexibility and freedom, and self-esteem and self-development, all of which seemed to be difficult to attain in other jobs they might get, for which the remuneration would also be poor.

The findings seem to conform to those of other international studies, which suggests that male sex workers' engagement in sex work is a result of rational choices made under particular conditions of possibility and constraint (e.g.,

Calhoun and Weaver 1996; West and de Villiers 1993; Browne and Minichellio 1995, 1996a, 1996b; Davies and Feldman 1997; Aggleton 1999). The findings also conform to present migration studies in China which suggest that rural migrants are desperate to move out from their rural or semi-rural hometowns. They are caught in a specific subject formation of citizenship under the reconfigured rural-urban distinction in the post-Mao development discourse (Solinger 1999; Guang 2003, Zhang 2001; Pun 2003, 2005; Yan 2003a, 2003b). Likewise, although money was a major reason for these young men to engage in sex work, the desire for a cosmopolitan life in big cities—for them symbolically representing freedom, money, opportunity and upward mobility, a place where they could find work and love—was equally important. The men were highly mobile, transient and temporary, and moved back and forth from one occupational setting to another, from sex work to other jobs and from one city to another. It is under the neo-liberal market process of subject formation in China that my understanding of money boys exemplifies a specific urban Chinese formation of sexual identity (Kong 2010).

Being a Money Boy

So how did they work? What problems did they encounter? What were the risks and dangers, as well as the gains and pleasures, of the job?

The job certainly entails a lot of risk and danger. For example, sex workers may encounter bad clients who rob, steal or cheat, or who are violent. They are also constantly exposed to the risks of contracting sexual diseases and of being caught by the police. In the following, however, I would like to discuss the ways the workers manufactured work personae, as this requires boundary maintenance between their work and personal selves; and the problems that may result in the process.

Sex work entails both physical and emotional labour. Giving massages, performing oral sex, engaging in anal penetration, taking certain sexual positions, and "finishing" a client within a certain period of time all involve skills and techniques. Providing services and offering smiles and care are equally important, and these can be seen as emotional labour. By consciously offering smiles, care and concern, as well as their bodies, male sex workers suppress or falsify feelings and actively manufacture work personae in order to control their work and to prevent their work selves from collapsing into their "real" selves. Their lives seem to confirm the statement that they are "selling the body, keeping the soul". In attempting to separate personal selves from work selves and emotions from bodies, boundary maintenance is of paramount importance (Kong 2005; Browne and Minichiello 1995; for a similar discussion of female sex workers, see Brewis and Linstead 2000a, 2000b; Sanders 2005; O'Connell Davidson 1996; Ho 2000; Kong 2006).

Two principles of boundary maintenance were frequently referred to by the respondents. Boundaries seem easy to draw, but difficult to maintain.

Boundary one: Work versus leisure

Sex workers sell something which has not been fully commodified. What do they put into the "market"? What do they sell and what don't they? Which areas of their bodies are allowed for clients' access and which are off limits? Although sex is regarded as "work" that should be performed by the sex worker, it is regarded as "leisure" that is enjoyed by the client. But when is a worker off limits and "at play" (Brewis and Linstead 2000a, 2000b)?

First of all, all informants had (hetero/homo)sexual experiences at early ages (12 or 13) in their hometowns, in which none had used condoms. Not until they migrated to the cities and entered the sex industry did they start to use condoms at work. This information not only reflects their limited knowledge about AIDS before leaving their hometowns but also reveals the fact that they did not differentiate sex from work and leisure. It was only after they entered the sex industry that they tended to develop good knowledge about AIDS, to hold good attitudes towards using condoms at work and to have perceptions of their own high risks at work, causing them even to derive different strategies to negotiate condom use with their clients. In short, they picked up the "occupational" discourse of prostitution and fashioned themselves as sex "workers". This tended to contradict the common sense that money boys are the highest-risk group among the MSM population, as it was in fact their entrance into the sex industry that had led them to begin using condoms.

Second, a derivative of this occupational discourse of sex work is the separation of sex from work and from personal love. Most informants told me that sex at work was different from sex at home. Like the participants in Browne and Minichiello's study of male sex workers in Melbourne (1995, 1996a, 1996b), they separated "work sex", which was regarded as "meaningless" and with affection shown only as a performance, from "personal sex", which was regarded as passionate and intimate, engaged in only with their non-paying affective partners.

> Big difference. With clients, if he wants anal intercourse, I will lay down and let him do me. If he wants a blow job, I will give it to him. But with my boyfriend I will be very active. Even if he doesn't request anything, I will do it for him ... and even if we hug each other, you will feel the passion. (Ah Wei, 25, gay, full-time independent, 8 years)

With my boyfriend, it's pleasure; with my clients, it's work—you just want to do it quickly, finish it, cum and go. (Ah Lin, 22, gay, kept by a man, 2 years)

Great efforts have to be made to maintain this boundary. But what if they "cross" the boundary? Ah Ji was a university graduate who had entered the industry partly for money and partly because he wanted to try out gay sexuality. He was in great pain when he encountered a client who could be regarded as "heaven trade" (c.f., Browne and Minichiello 1995)—i.e., a client who represents the worker's fantasy and symbolizes a "potentially happy future". These clients represent something more than just money. They are special encounters for the worker:

> Well, at one time, I met a guy … he came to Beijing for business. When I opened the door, I said to myself, oh my God. He was so gorgeous, I was instantly attracted to him. I worked very hard that day … ha ha … the next few days, I so missed him … I called him out for dinner, I could sense that he also liked me … But … then I asked him why we couldn't go out … he admitted it (that it was because I was an MB), that's why we couldn't (go out then) … I felt terribly sad and disappointed. I still keep the money that he gave to me, I didn't use it, just kept it … oh, it was really hard for me … (Ah Ji, 24, gay, freelancer, 6 months)

Quite a number of respondents reported similar experiences, which they considered "tragic"—when love had entered the work relationship. The emotional damage could be something unbearable, but a more serious outcome would have resulted if they blurred the boundary between work and friendship.

Although they all reported condom use at work, they sometimes broke this rule, especially if they treated the client as a "friend".

> I did it once (unprotected sex), I didn't use it (condom). I was a bit drunk, and the feeling was quite good, and he was an old client. (Ah Gang, 22, ambivalent about his sexuality, full-time brothel worker, 1.5 years)

> I have known him for a long time, more than half a year, and he is my regular client. He said he didn't like condoms and he tested negative so we didn't use it. (Ah Wei, 25, gay, full-time independent, 8 years)

Ah Lin was 22 and had been working in the industry for two years. He was now being kept by a man, his ex-client. The conversation below reflects his double standard concerning using condoms for his present boyfriend/ex-client and his ex-boyfriend:

Ah Lin:	... yes, of course I always use it (condom) when I am working. But the year when I was living with my boyfriend, we didn't.
Interviewer:	But he was also an MB right?
Ah Lin:	Yes ... when he was working, he used it, he just didn't use it with me.
Interviewer:	Why?
Ah Lin:	Because we treated each other as BF (boyfriends).
Interviewer:	So, you don't use condoms with your boyfriends?
Ah Lin:	He said that if we didn't "mess it up", we didn't need to use a condom.
Interviewer:	But how do you know that he didn't "mess it up" himself?
Ah Lin:	Well ... I ... trusted him.
Interviewer:	So do you use a condom with your present boyfriend?
Ah Lin:	Oh, yes, because I always treat him as my client ... although he treats me as his boyfriend.

(Ah Lin, 22, gay, kept by a man, 2 years)

The condom holds a special symbolic meaning for these workers. It is the way to demarcate their work and private selves. Although condom use at work seems to be the norm, they broke the rule when the client was a regular client who was more like a friend. They seldom used condoms with their wives, girlfriends or boyfriends. Information about the sexual behaviour of their partners is unknown, but it is doubtful that all their non-paying affective partners had had no sex with others or practiced safer sex all the time.

Unprotected penetrative sex in the context of affective relationships seems to have a significant symbolic meaning for these workers, for whom the underlying operative logic is work=risk=unsafe and love=trust=safe. Having unprotected sex with love, ironically, thus becomes the most dangerous sex act. This finding conforms to those of other studies: sex workers may be more at risk of HIV infection in the context of their private sexual lives than in their work lives (Joffe and Dockrell 1995; Browne and Minichiello 1996a, 1996b; Minichiello et al. 2002; Vanwesenbeeck 2001; Kong 2009a).

Boundary two: Public versus private

Being a prostitute is a role in which radical contempt, compassion, support and opposition are mixed (Pheterson 1996). However, many of my respondents viewed their engagements in sex work differently. Some adopted a sexual-victim identity, saying that they were losers. Some argued that this was not a job, just a way of earning money. Some stressed that it was simply a way of meeting "friends" and having fun, downplaying the basic logic of exchange of their bodies for material rewards. Some treated it as an ordinary job, stressing the monetary and other rewards that they got. Some even viewed themselves as career professionals who treated sex work as a business and a means of upward mobility. Their diverse interpretations of sex "work" destabilize the apparent binaries of public/private, work/leisure, love/sex, client/friend, etc., that underline the logics of production, consumption and intimacy. Their ambivalent work identities can be seen as coping strategies for disassociating themselves from this highly stigmatized job and its intense emotional toll (Kong 2010).[5]

However, no matter how they viewed themselves, most of them had to bear three stigmatized identities: those of rural-to-urban migrants, prostitutes and homosexuals. Like other migrants, Ah Tao (32, gay, full-time independent, 8 years) left his home village because of economic difficulty. However, he also emphasized that migration was the way he coped with first homosexuality and later prostitution.

> My family was very poor. I had no other options to earn money apart from leaving home ... And I desperately wanted to leave (my hometown). My home village is very rural, small and conservative ... There is no such a platform (*pingtai*) for you to survive. The whole atmosphere is very repressive. They don't understand you ... They would think that it (homosexuality) is a sickness, a perversion, they would take me to see doctors! ... Now it's even more difficult for me to go back because of this (working as a MB) ... I haven't gone home for more than 4 years ...

Although moving out from his hometown had been a dream for Ah Tao, he, like other rural migrants, realized the difficulty of living in a city. He could not enjoy various social and medical benefits due to his rural *hukou*.[6] More importantly, his rural status, which was embodied in the way he looked, the accent he had, and the assumed low quality (*suzhi*) he possessed, marked him off from the cultural formation of an urban citizen. His work as an MB thus served him as a rural-urban dividend:

> The living standard is very high in Beijing. As a rural migrant, you have to rent a room, buy clothes, etc ... and if you don't know how to dress, how to act ... it reflects that you have low *suzhi* ... people would look down upon you ... you have to live up to this urban ideal ... and also you cannot enjoy a lot of benefits, the basic costs are larger than those of a local ... like when you are ill, you have to pay extra.

Second, the social stigma of sex work seemed to be a big issue for them. They were very reluctant to tell others about their work. They could easily hide their work identities, as they had moved out of their home villages and went home only occasionally. When they did so they usually lied, saying that they worked at other jobs.

> No, none of my friends and my family know what I am doing ... I lied to them. I said I was working as a waiter in a restaurant ... I won't tell them (what I am doing) ... they will definitely discriminate against me. (Ah Tian, 20, ambivalent about his sexuality, full-time brothel worker, 1 year)

Like Ah Tao, they thus use migration as a strategy to hide their work identities.

The discrimination sometimes is not just from outside, but also from within. The gay community tends to equate rural migrants and money boys with thieves and blackmailers, and puts them all in the category of those with low *suzhi*. They are thus alleged to contribute to the overall chaotic (*luan*) situation of the gay community (Jones 2005; Rofel 2007, 2010; Kong 2010).

As for those who were homosexual, most had not come out to their friends or families. They were very worried that their friends or family members would not accept their homosexuality, as they thought people considered homosexuality to be abnormal, sick or perverted. They were scared that the news would break the hearts of friends and family and worried that it would distance themselves from them.

> The history seems to suggest a man with a woman - there is no man with man. If you are one of them, you are sick, you are a pervert ... (Ah Dong, 26, gay, freelancer, 6 months)

They were constantly pressurized by their families to get married.

> Family! My parents always want me to get married. If I won't, my mom will die! (Ah Wei, 25, gay, full-time independent, 8 years)

> In the small village where I was born, it's too remote. For them, not getting married means you are not a good son. (Dou Dou, 22, gay, full-time independent, 6 months)

> The family pressure is very high ... maybe I will just find one to get married to and then secretly go out with a man. (Ah Lin, 22, gay, kept by a man, 2 years)

> I am facing a big problem, my family wants me to get married, this is their expectation. But for me, this is a pain. If I think from their point of view, I think I should, but for myself, I don't want to, definitely not! (Ah Dong, 26, gay, freelancer, 6 months)

Because of the government's "hard-strike" campaign against same-sex prostitution and the social stigma against rural-to-urban migration, prostitution and homosexuality, the participants have to bear the triply-stigmatized identity of "rural-to-urban migrant", "prostitute" and "homosexual". As migrants, they are deprived of many social welfare and other benefits of living in a city (Li et al. 2007; Amnesty International 2007; Zhu 2007). Although rural-to-urban migration was their dream, and also the way they coped with homosexuality and prostitution, they had to pay a big price to live up to the urban ideal. As sex workers, they were constantly worried that they might be caught by the police, as well as other physical risks and threats, psychological tolls and discomforts. Lying was a common way of hiding their work identities. In both work and personal identities, they had to face discrimination from both straight and gay communities, due to their "low *suzhi*". Workers who identified as gay found it very hard to live as gay people in China. They struggled to find male partners to live with without offending their families; rather than expressing "pride" in their homosexuality, they sought family acceptance and behaved discreetly in order to avoid the shame that they might bring to their families. They sought to find "suitable" gay identities that could be reconciled with the institutionalized neo-Confucian family setting (Kong 2010; Gil 2002; Li 1998; 2006; Wong et al. 2006; see also Kong 2002, 2004 for my discussion of gay men in Hong Kong). Hiding their work, living in the closet and getting married thus seemed to be common strategies for dealing with social discrimination against prostitution and homosexuality. They lived in secrecy and received little help from those in their social networks unconnected with their work, and this subsequently led them to live rather solitary lives or be confined to a "closed circuit" (i.e., their worlds became tightly connected with their occupation and / or sexuality).

Conclusion

I understand that there are certain limitations to this study. First of all, as male sex workers are difficult to interview, normally hiding their work identities and being reluctant to talk about their lives, interviews in this study were made according to non-probability, convenience sampling. Secondly, as this study is part of a larger study of the MSM population, male sex workers who mainly served men, or who served both genders, were chosen, and male sex workers who exclusively served women were excluded. Moreover, transsexual or transvestite sex workers, common in other places, did not appear in the sample, and it is believed that such male sex workers' life experiences may be different. Thirdly, this is a qualitative study with a rather small sample size and so cannot claim to be representative of the larger male sex worker population, which is believed to be a highly stratified and complicated community rather than a monolithic one. Fourthly, this study, carried out in two big cities, may reveal different characteristics than one concerning male sex workers in small cities or rural areas would do.

This said, this research contributes to the scanty literature on male prostitution in China by presenting the lives of 30 money boys in Beijing and Shanghai through qualitative research. The traditional portrait of the male prostitute depicts him as a powerless young man trapped by personality defeats, childhood traumas, and family dysfunction in a cycle of self-loathing, poverty and cultural deprivation. However, my findings show most respondents to have been rural-to-urban, young, single homosexuals who had made rational choices to come to big cities to engage in sex work, for identified material incentives as well as for non-material reasons, within a fantasy of cosmopolitanism. Although the job was regarded as risky, short-lived, unstable and tedious, most of them cited a number of job satisfactions besides money, such as freedom, flexibility, and enjoyment, which might have been difficult to attain in other jobs they might get, given their social backgrounds. Their engagement in sex work can thus be seen as a process of urban subject formation in the neo-liberal regime of modernization.

Male sex workers have to create work personae to fulfil their clients' fantasies and needs. Their work requires both physical and emotional effort. Boundary maintenance is important in their work lives, involving two major principles: that of "work versus leisure" and that of "public versus private". The boundary established according to the first principle is a site of contestation for deciding which part of their "selves" can be "sold", as well as when work is not work, but leisure or love. This distinguishing of "work sex" from "relational sex" seems to be important for the production of work personae derived from the occupational discourse of prostitution throughout the whole process of sexual transaction and when workers "cross" the boundary, they encounter trouble. Those who put too much "love" into their work may end with broken hearts, and those who blur the boundary between work and friendship may practice unprotected sex. Some reserve room for intimacy—yet this, ironically, puts them at greater risk of HIV/AIDS. Far from being a matter of moral condemnation, the notion that the "whore is heartless" is indeed a "professional ethic" that needs to be upheld (c.f., Ho 2000). However, maybe it is this hard facet of life that drives these young men to run the risk of crossing the boundary over and over again.

Then, too, the second boundary is one of contestation, as they must negotiate how much they can disclose of their work and sexual identities to friends and family, as well as how much they can "perform" as urban citizens. With punitive measures for prostitution and general social stigmatization against rural-to-urban migration, prostitution and homosexuality, choosing to live in a closet or a solitary life seems to be the common strategy.

For a number of reasons—state laws restricting access to permanent urban residency, the hard-strike government policy on same-sex prostitution, the short life-cycle of the sex industry, and the rural homophobic culture—money boys are transient labour: they move back and forth from one occupational setting to another, from sex work to other work, and from one city to another. Moreover, money boys are transient queer subjects. They live in "queer time", "outside of reproductive and familial time as well as on the edges of logics of labour and production" (Halberstam 2005: 10) and in "queer places"—parks, brothels, massage parlours, clients' owned flats—that do not and never will belong to them and which others may have abandoned.

Male prostitution is thus a contested but negotiated arena of power, and the identity of the male sex worker involves a strategic self that constantly negotiates risks and dangers, excitements and gains, in the process of sexual transaction. My case of money boys exemplifies such an urban formation of strategic self in contemporary China, which is undergoing a rigorous process of liberalization, modernization and cosmopolitanization in the global era. In this multifaceted process of development, work is hard, whether it involves sex or not!

2
Lesbianism among Indonesian Women Migrants in Hong Kong[1]

Amy Sim

For the casual visitor to Hong Kong who stumbles on Victoria Park in Causeway Bay on Sundays, what becomes immediately obvious is that it is occupied almost entirely by migrant women, and more strikingly, that heteronormativity among them is not an unquestioned norm. In the park, fashionably attired Indonesian women migrant workers in Hong Kong as same-sex partners share a day of rest together after a week—and sometimes more—of not having seen each other, both working as foreign domestic workers in their employers' homes.

There are about 129,505 as of 30 June 2009[2] Indonesian women domestic workers in Hong Kong, now almost equal in numbers to Filipina domestics who have been arriving to work here since the 1970s. It was in connection with Filipina domestics that the first mention of lesbian relationships surfaced in letters in the press in the mid-1990s and created awareness among the Hong Kong public of an emerging form of alternative sexuality among its foreign women workers. The highest estimates for Filipina domestics who are either involved in or had been involved in same-sex relationships with other women while in Hong Kong was cited at 40% (Constable 2000).

When an Indonesian staff member in a non-governmental organization in Hong Kong, working with Indonesian migrant workers, first learnt that there were Indonesian lesbians among the foreign domestic worker population from Indonesia, she immediately attributed this phenomenon to the influence of Filipina domestics because she was convinced that such relationships do not exist and could not have come from Indonesia. She is not alone as such views are common among Indonesians ashamed of what they perceive to be sexual deviance, contributing to a bad reputation for Indonesian women in general. However, earlier studies (Murray 1999; Blackwood 1999; Oetomo 1996; Wieringa 1999) testify to the existence of same-sex romantic love and sexual relations in Indonesia.

This chapter is about the emergence of a phenomenon in Hong Kong of lesbianism among Indonesian migrant women. It examines the nexus of sexuality shaped through practices and ideologies embedded in nationalistic and patriarchal constructions of women, and the opportunities and constraints presented by labour migration within which migrant women move. Most of the research for this chapter was conducted from 2002 to 2005 in Hong Kong with lesbian Indonesian women migrant workers between the age of seventeen and twenty-five using ethnographic methods. Most conversations took place in public parks, restaurants, coffee shops, during public rallies, in NGO offices, etc. All discussions were immediately translated into fieldnotes either through note taking, audio-recording and transcribing or through recall after each event.

This chapter documents issues and conditions in migrant women's lives, linking the micro-politics of individual lives to the impact of existing powers on individuals' social lives, and examines the repercussions of the cultural regime in Indonesia that affect women migrant workers, in regards to their sexuality, in terms of materiality, processes, strategies and embedded ideologies. This chapter looks beyond the fragmented differences among individual women to examine the sources of power that pervade their lives in and beyond labour migration.

Butch-Femme Relations in Context

The commonly used term in much of Western literature referring to homosexual relations between women, "lesbian", is a highly contested one with some arguing that it is not applicable to non-Western sexual relationships between women because of its Euro-American origins and connotations. It is a moot point whether women who love women could possibly have been "lesbian" or "same-sex oriented" or even "homosexual", given that these terms are Euro-American in origin and do not exist in other languages. Precluding the requisite equivalent lexicon to be "lesbian", the use of identical, parallel or corresponding terms in different languages, even in oblique references, included an awareness that theirs was a choice that did not conform to categories of normative sexual behaviour.

In the lesbian scene among Indonesian women in Hong Kong, however, masculinized women are commonly referred to as *tombois* (Indonesian spelling), which conflates with "butch" women in earlier Western discourses, just as feminine women who seek out *tombois* are known as "femmes". Other equivalent terms that originate from Indonesia are *sentul* and *kantil*,[3] meaning butch and femme respectively. The term "lesbian" is hardly ever used among them and would be a label of last resort, if no other option were available. Sometimes, the term *lesbi* is used to refer to women's same relationships in discussions, as in a type of relationship, but never used on a personal level to describe or label someone. One reason there is some disdain and avoidance of the term "lesbian" among Indonesian lesbian women can be attributed to its foreign origin and also to its negative association with stigma and deviance.

The definition of female homosexuality which I will refer to as "lesbian" henceforth in this chapter is taken at its broadest to include:

> [W]omen who love women, who choose women to nurture and support and to create a living environment in which to work creatively and independently, are lesbians.[4]

Compulsory Heterosexuality

Relations of love have always existed between women from intimate friendships to physical acts of love. Despite attempts to camouflage or deny them, these relations are important when understood in tandem with theories of kinship and family that tend to emphasize women's roles as wives and mothers because they capture an alternative view of women's lives that includes a range of social relations not confined to social and biological reproduction. But are all lesbian relationships to be understood only in terms of Rich's conception of "compulsory heterosexuality" (1981), that explains the existence of female homosexuality as resistance to heterosexuality? Despite the criticism by Blackwood (with Saskia E. Wieringa 1999) that attributing same-sex desires simply as a response to heterosexuality reveals an ignorance of the range of female sexuality and the inability to imagine women's same-sex desires as anything else but resistance to heterosexuality, Rich's central thesis that many societies are characterized by systems of compulsory heterosexuality, which represent underlying conditions of patriarchy remains unchallenged. But how salient are these foregoing debates to Indonesian lesbian women in Hong Kong?

Indonesian women's lesbian relationships in Hong Kong are divided into masculinized and feminine women, with the former playing the social role of men. The case of Indonesian lesbian women in Hong Kong cannot be understood as one of simply resisting heterosexuality because of deeply embedded gender hierarchies that become manifest on the bodies of women who love other women "as men", or of femme women who seek out *tombois* with whom they can behave "as women". In this lesbianscape, the principle of heterosexuality prevails. It is one where women "become" men, in dress and demeanour, in order to love other women, and where femme women find masculinized women to love. It is possible that role playing, which is a crucial aspect of lesbian women's identities, stems from the absence of other known models or alternatives for understanding and locating their relationships in their given social universe.[5] On the other hand, the process of butch- and femme-making becomes a social process that requires the collaboration of their partners as well as their communities, which accept, endorse and validate the emergent identities, making space for these to become real and rooted in the interactivity of social practice.

While their motivations could very well have been an aversion to heterosexual prerogatives, butch women assume male social roles in public and in some cases, they also assume what they perceive to be the privileges of men, such as dominating their femme partners, gaining sexual access to different women as in male polygamous behaviour, etc. Androgyny as it is practised in Westernized lesbian communities where there are seemingly no distinct male-female roles is rare among Indonesian lesbian women in Hong Kong. The study of this group of women does not provide for Rich's thesis (1981) that lesbianism is a result of the rejection of compulsory heterosexuality because what is evident is that these women actively recreate conditions of what I would call, neo-heterosexuality, in which they can enact their romantic/sexual scripts for meaningful relationships during labour migration.

The notion of neo-heterosexuality highlights the development of two earlier theoretical paradigms on the butch-femme role-playing with a third proposed by Goodloe (1993, 1996). The first of these theorists, Butler (1991), Case (1993), and de Lauretis (1988), examined lesbian butch-femme role-playing as deconstruction of gender categories—a challenge to the "natural" relationship between sex and gender—and as a symbolic rebellion against male hegemony. The second, espoused by Ruth (1991) considers that the cultural configurations of lesbian sexuality, and especially butch-femme roles, are much more "complex, contradictory, and diverse "than the above theorists admit. The data found in this study among Indonesian women in Hong Kong supports Roof's (1991) position that while lesbian butch-femme theory offers a critique of binary heterosexuality and the sex/gender system and represents a subversion of patriarchy, "lesbian sexuality is already too completely intertwined with cultural constructions and configurations to comprise more than a partial perspective in any politics premised on identity" (Roof 1991: 251).

Hence, in the work towards redefining lesbian identity politics, the configuration of butch-femme according to Roof (1991: 245) rests on "a resolution of the 'inconceivability' of lesbian sexuality in a phallocentric system, recuperating that inconceivability by superimposing a male/female model on lesbian relationships". Lesbian role playing in this light, according to Goodloe (1996) is "a construct of the dominant culture, imposed on lesbians in order to make sense of female sexuality in the absence of a phallus, and therefore not a self-empowering move on the part of lesbians themselves". "Neo-heterosexuality" thus represents an attempt at liberating the butch-femme relationship from an unwitting disempowerment emerging from a reification of heterosexism in defining lesbian identities.

In Hong Kong, there is some evidence that political lesbianism from Western discourses[6] is influential in shaping young local women's awareness of their rights as lesbian women, as they access feminist/lesbian theories through higher institutions of learning (Sim 2004). However, this awareness remains limited to a small group of educated local women so that among Indonesian migrant women in Hong Kong—even those who have been living there for years—their level of understanding about their rights as women to have romantic relationships with other women, is almost non-existent. They do not generally conceive of loving other women as a right that they could or should possess as women. So unlike discontinuous approaches to lesbianism which emphasize geographically rooted and historically developed forms of women's liaisons that discount commonalities in universal structures of male domination, or notions of resistance, this study, like postmodern feminism, affirms divisions among lesbians on issues of race, ethnicity, class, etc., (Ferguson 1990).

There are no simple universals in characterization of lesbian women, as there are no simple configurations of what "causes" lesbianism among women, but the common element among lesbian women in different places and time is their rejection of male-bodied persons as sexual/romantic-life partners. But the search for a cause is ironic because arguments about the cause of homosexuality reifies heteronormativity while "othering" homosexuality as deviant, or as an unequal alternative, even further. What is probably more useful is to examine the conditions and realities in women's lives where despite the given norms, taboos and ideologies built into supporting heterosexism, and the oppressive conditions that go into exploiting women's productive capacities, women are able to find footholds to disagree, resist and protest, and importantly, to stake out the space to choose differently.

At the same time, gender as "situated accomplishment", conceptualized by Fenstermaker et al. (2002: 29), frames this study in which butch lesbian drag becomes understandable through the related conception of gender accountabilities. This far exceeds "gender performativity" (Butler 1990) in accounting for the experiences of the respondents in this study because "doing gender" is certainly not a set of performances or a combination of various factors in display but "an ongoing interactional accomplishment" (Fenstermaker et al. 2002: 206).

Women and Labour Migration

Sassen showed in "Women's Burden" how larger economic transformations have come to shape women's lives on the ground from rural women's shift towards commercial agricultural production, to the feminization of labour in the international division of labour, and to the most recent phase, on women as migrants in the integration of global systems of trade. This last phase of feminist studies captures the cultural and structural features of women's mobility in internal and overseas migration in niche sectors such as factory, domestic, care and sex work.

Many of these have traced the transformations in women migrants' lives, their behaviour, values, aspirations and worldviews,[7] showing how distance from home and reduced familial supervision can destabilise cultural constructions of women's bodies for migrant women and their communities. Migration is hence never just an export of raw labour power (Bourdieu 2000: 175) and the migrant body, especially of migrant women, becomes the focus of discipline and concern in both sending and receiving countries, as biologically reproducing bodies—symbolic of and, for that reason, a threat to group identity (Bourdieu 2000: 180).

With little exception,[8] attention paid to women's sexuality in migration has focused almost exclusively on women's sexual abuse, disease or sex work. In destination countries where they work, sometimes for years, they are perceived as a source of sexual threat and competition for female employers, reflecting nationalistic and ethnicized anxieties of foreign women's sexuality in recipient countries.[9]

Missing from most existing studies on migrant women's sexuality are representations of how they experience and respond to their needs for sex and love during labour migration in sexual activity and choices surrounding their sexuality that fall beyond the formal scope of work. Beyond the supervision of their employers, Indonesian migrant women workers in Hong Kong live, enact and expand their roles and notions of self and identity during their rest time through relationships that allow for individual expressivity versus the instrumentality embedded in formal work relations.

In Indonesia, Robinson (2000) recounted the public outrage from the mid 1980s over the sexual abuse of Indonesian women migrants working as domestic workers in Saudi Arabia. From leaders in parliament to religious Islamic leaders, pressure was put on the Indonesian government to protect its migrant women with calls for limitations to women's freedom to work overseas. The government, caught between its economic agenda and the need for moral accountability, scapegoated several recruitment agencies in Indonesia and put the blame on the migrant women themselves for being lacking in skills.

With estimates of nearly four million (Loveband 2004) Indonesians overseas and more than seventy per cent being women, labour migration from Indonesia was set to double to a million workers each year in 2009,[10] because the Indonesian government is unable to create sufficient jobs for twelve million new entrants into the job market each year, resulting in a deficit of one million jobs annually (Hugo 1995). Unemployment, marginal livelihoods based on agriculture and broader structural developments have intensified the shift away from resource-based livelihoods, with increasing emphasis being paid to the export of labour. In 2003, there were a total of 9,132,104 jobless people in Indonesia, among them 5,659,715 were graduates with diplomas and bachelor degrees with many looking simply for temporary jobs just to get by.[11] Apart from reducing unemployment, increasing remittance flows[12] from its overseas workers offset the effects of poverty for their dependents at home.

Under the New Order government[13] women's participation as citizens was based on their difference from men as "reproducers of the next generation of workers" (Robinson 2000: 250) and socially as wives and mothers. So even while women were recognized in the state's development plans as workers for the first time in 1993,[14] State sponsored ideologies of womanhood, of what is acceptable and desirable, are powerful[15] in relegating women to their heterosexual and biological roles, which are deemed the primary, legitimate functions of women's bodies. These ideologies are normalized through public institutions and discourse, making intimate areas of women's lives grounded in heterosexuality, marriage and reproduction (Atkinson 1990; Bennett 2005; Suryakusuma 2004).

In 1995, Hugo (2000) found that the levels of knowledge about issues of sexual relations were consistently low among migrant workers from Indonesia but despite this and the Indonesian government's incorporation of labour migration into national development agendas, sex education in connection with women's reproductive health is not a mandatory component in migrant women's pre-departure training. Women's mobility is premised on the protection of the State[16] but its lack of capacity for managing labour export has meant that the State delegates the care and welfare of its migrant women workers to profit-driven private sector recruitment agencies (Komnas et al. 2002; Wee et al. 2004), in practice leaving sexually naïve migrant women open to considerable exploitation.

There were 116,000 Indonesian women, mostly from the island of Java, employed as domestic workers in Hong Kong in 2006,[17] constituting the second largest ethnic minority in Hong Kong after Filipina domestic workers. Most Indonesian domestic workers are young, under thirty,[18] single and with a secondary school education. The most common problems amongst them are underpayment, the lack of rest days, problems with employers, recruiters, employment agencies, Indonesian officials and with discrimination in Hong Kong.[19]

Coming out in Hong Kong

Until 1996 foreign workers with same-sex orientations had gone relatively unremarked and were seen as sexually unthreatening by their female employers in Hong Kong. But, as noted by Constable (2000) this changed with hostile letters to the press. Other Indonesians expressed shock that Indonesian women in Hong Kong had become lesbians. They found this to be unbelievable and attributed it to the "bad" influence of Filipina domestic workers. There is historical evidence, however, that shows that homosexuality did exist in Indonesia even in Islamic schools among both sexes (Oetomo 1996: 264). In Hong Kong today, they are a common sight, especially at the weekend, identifiable instantly by what appears to be the generic wear of Indonesian *tombois*: baggy pants, large shirts and baseball hats.

The dress code of *tombois* becomes the main statement of sexual orientation. By putting on this "uniform", Indonesian lesbians immediately make visible their sexual orientation and community. The *tomboi* dress code shows their belonging to particular groups, helps them attract girlfriends, and at the same time, deflects male attention. In Hong Kong, the Indonesian lesbian calendar is always full, with lesbian birthday parties, dance classes and even weddings.[20] Places of refuge in the weekends include discos and "love" hotels. Despite the consternation that many Hong Kong employers had of employing lesbian domestic workers, noted by Constable (2000) earlier, an increasing number are openly lesbian and accepted by their employers on those grounds.

For Indonesians who found the fact of openly homosexual liaisons among Indonesian women in Hong Kong startling given the strong heterosexist culture and near invisibility of lesbians in Indonesia, they would be more startled to know that lesbian practices among these migrant women did not always start in Hong Kong; on the contrary, the acculturation to alternative sexuality often began in the labour sending processes in Indonesia. Without exception, all potential Indonesian women migrant workers to Hong Kong, would have spent time, from several months to a couple of years, in training centres in Indonesia. These take the form of penal-like institutions severely limiting the rights of its trainees in most cases while violating basic human rights in others. Various explanations have been suggested for the existence of this system of incarceration. One of these as mentioned earlier, stems from the limitations of the Indonesian government to manage labour migration in a way that is morally responsible. This has meant a hands-off approach to women's labour migration in practice while promoting it as one pillar of national development. Delegation also ensures that its responsibility to this migrant population is kept to a minimum and costs for labour migration are "outsourced", while flak can be deflected—as in the case noted by Robinson—when public outrage demands official accounting. At the level of national policy, the government has mandated a "one-door exit" policy for all migrant workers which entails the use of a highly monopolized, non-transparent system of labour export where all potential migrant workers are required to use agencies licensed by the State, from recruitment, to training, deployment, employment and return to Indonesia.

Another reason given for migrant women's incarceration prior to their departure is mainly for the protection of the recruiting agent because poor Indonesian women who register with agencies to work in Hong Kong do not have the resources to pay a deposit to the agent for finding her employment. This is to ensure the availability of the women when a job is found, the time when their agencies can begin to collect on the "fees" owed for training and housing them. These non-negotiable fees for migrant women coming to Hong Kong are equivalent to four to seven months of salary deductions totalling up to HK$21,000 each (approximately US$2,709).

Yet another reason for the incarceration of potential migrant women workers suggested by the workers themselves as to why they are not allowed to return to their families once they register with an agency, is to ensure that women workers sent overseas are not pregnant. Incarceration in these detention camps is indefinite until a job offer is received from the destination countries. For those lucky enough to have families living near these centres, they get to see their families once a week during visiting hours, but for most whose families live hours away by bus they may not see their families for years. The cost of transportation over long distances is beyond the affordability of most families where the average take home wage is Rp300–600,000 (US$29–59) a month.

The journey from home to the training centre is often overlooked in studies of how labour migration processes can traumatise young women migrants. For example, one nineteen-year-old related how the overnight ride in the passenger seat of her recruiter's car on the way to the training centre became a nightmare. The recruiter while driving, and despite the presence of three other passengers in the back seat, relentlessly molested her until she threatened to throw herself out of the moving car in a suicide attempt.

Pre-migration experience for new inductees in Indonesia is often traumatic and amidst very poor living conditions in the camps, such as extreme conditions of overcrowding, shortage of food and bathing facilities, abuses, exploitation, etc. Inductees were often packed in tight rows on the floor, where they spent months sleeping skin-to-skin with the next person. Baths were taken communally with one bucket of water each. Moreover, research conducted on a hundred such training camps found that incidents of physical and sexual abuse were rampant. Minimum standards set by the Indonesian Labour Department to regulate practices within these camps were rarely enforced, restrictions were placed on inductees' movements, and poor camp conditions resulted in health problems with little medical care.[21]

A number of Indonesian women migrant workers in Hong Kong have reported that their initiation and awareness of same-sex relationships began in these harsh conditions. It is in these conditions that deep friendships develop, providing comfort and companionship. Are these merely "deep friendships", "romantic friendships" or situated somewhere on what has been called the "Lesbian continuum" (Rich 1980)? These conditions resonate with studies of homosexuality in total institutions like prisons, boarding schools and so forth. Intimacies involve holding of hands, hugging and kissing.

In the camps, another source from which same-sex relationships arise is from returned migrants who have worked overseas. On their return home, they are required to go through the entire process of living in training camps again when seeking new foreign employment from Indonesia. It is through some of these relatively sophisticated women familiar with urban lifestyles in cities elsewhere that same-sex relationships become something of a "fashion statement". One respondent said that "Being a lesbian makes a woman 'powerful' ". By this she meant attractive to other women, in terms of their strong identity statements, as rebellious and independent especially where it relates to their sexuality. Apart from fulfilling the physical needs for sex, she believed that this form of behaviour is common because it is perceived as trendy.[22]

It is in oppressive conditions of labour export that young women's experiences contribute towards creating conditions where social norms of behaviour are temporary dislodged by needs for comfort and self-validation. In labour migration, physical distance from home and financial independence have the effect of destabilizing previously unquestioned arenas of power, definitions of symbolic boundaries, and social and moral codes that govern behaviour. However, transformations in notions of sex and gender roles are not always indicative of anomie, rebellion, resistance or sexual adventurism. At times, as I will show below, these are attempts to preserve the moral order connected to standards of women's sexual behaviour in their community of origin.

From Friends to Lovers: Holding Hands and Intimacy

In Indonesian society, holding hands between adult members of the same sex is rarely construed as sexual and is understood to be merely companionable. Holding hands with one's opposite sexed partner before one is married, is however deemed taboo in Indonesia, even among university students I spoke with in Jogjakarta, a major university hub in Java in Indonesia. While the role-playing evident among Indonesian women same-sex couples in Hong Kong may suggests a lack of alternative models to the heterosexual prototype, it could be experienced by migrant women in Hong Kong as liberating precisely because holding hands with a social male, i.e. the butch partner, is something that they would not be able to do back home. Butch women migrants in Hong Kong *become* butch or *tomboi* when they show that they are capable of taking up the social role of males in the company of other women.

It is interesting to note that none of the butch women described themselves as men trapped in women's bodies, nor aspired to be men by undergoing sex reassignment surgeries. When asked, they replied that it had not crossed their minds that it is something they want to do. Masculinized lesbians, butches or *tombois* are admired; they draw attention and are accorded high status in their communities by non-masculinized women who seek their affection. They are dressed to reflect a lack of concern to their physical attractiveness and affect a public style that says it is "hip" to be a "mess". These experimentations are not, however, completely unrelated to an individual's personal history and must be understood as consistent with their narratives of self, even during states of dislocation. As I have indicated above, some attempts at alternative sexuality stem from women's anxieties about relationships with men and their desire to stay beyond reproach as good daughters, but for others, it is a means of redemption.

Redemption and Purity

One of the places I frequented in the course of this research was the shelters or boarding homes provided by NGOs for foreign domestic workers who need help. After one such visit, Eli, one of my respondents, showed me a photograph of her girlfriend, Binte, who had to return to Indonesia. For nineteen-year-old Eli, her story with Binte began in a shelter in Hong Kong. They met when Eli moved into the shelter where Binte was living and their relationship blossomed in the three months that their stay overlapped. When Binte's dispute with her employer was settled she returned to Indonesia with the intention of coming to Hong Kong again.

This was Eli's first lesbian relationship and while she was clearly in love, she had had an unfortunate encounter several years earlier when she became pregnant by her boyfriend in Indonesia when she was sixteen. She had undergone an illegal abortion, bringing intense shame, regret and a sense of failure towards her parents. She had promised herself that she would avoid intimacy with men until she was married. Well-built and attractive, Eli was extremely popular in the shelter as a *tomboi* with the women there who were vying to become her girlfriend. Eli viewed her homosexuality as a temporary aberration and she was vehement that she would not get involved with men in Hong Kong because "all they want is money and to get the girls pregnant".

She took great pride in her own transformation and that her father had been moved to tears when she started sending money home. She had redeemed herself by showing that she was a useful and dutiful daughter who loved her parents. Remittances from labour migration had redeemed Eli's status within her family as a worthy daughter, and in this sense, there is no change in gender relations back home. In fact, the same relations are reinforced because the use of remittances is often subject to the male head of the household's authority. Gender relations in Indonesia, are thus not being challenged through women's labour migration and economic independence.

Disappointment and Betrayal

Polygamy is tolerated in Indonesia but most Indonesian women today expect nothing less than monogamy. The reality for absent migrant wives, however, is often quite different. Noora became a migrant worker to support her husband and their child when he could not find a job in Indonesia. While living on her remittances, her husband remarried, supporting his new wife on Noora's earnings. Noora's relationships with women began after she learnt that her husband had acquired another wife. She became aggressively male, usurping the sexual rights of men through having a series of concurrently ongoing, clandestine relationships in Hong Kong with other Indonesian women. She became a social male —enjoying their sexual access to women —which carried no stigma but on the contrary, brought an increased status as a *tomboi*.

The above serves as a critique of the sexual conventions among Indonesian men and the ideologies that underwrite them, and illuminate the socio-historical context in which sexual identities are de / constructed, discarding biological and cultural determinants. Femme identities are created out, too, of a resistance to the dictates of patriarchy embodied in culture and the gender ideology in Indonesia.

"Straight" Women, Femmes and Wannabes

Feminine women are attracted to Indonesian *tombois* because they offer an alternative lifestyle to what is otherwise a prescribed path to adulthood, through marriage with a man and child-bearing. In one case, Yanti, who had been in Hong Kong for seven months, returned home to find that her husband had married another wife. Yanti's best friend in a shelter in Hong Kong, Susanna, a pretty 21-

year-old, was outraged at Yanti's husband and that nobody had warned Yanti about it before her return. She raged at the injustice and wished that she could live without men. The others agreed.

Susanna was one of several women who had on more than one occasion expressed the desire to have Eli as her partner. The obstacle to this pursuit seemed to have been Binte, Eli's partner, who had returned to Indonesia but who was "calling and checking on Eli all the time". There is more evidence about "femme fever" in Hong Kong where heterosexual feminine women would pursue a *tomboi* because "she is so cool, just like a boy!"

In general, there is a latent sense of feminist consciousness that "women are not treated equally, they are required to do the cooking (and) have babies" in Indonesia. In terms of reproductive rights, one woman summed up what she perceived as the Indonesian male's prerogative as: "I am a man, you must take care of yourself" and "serve me"; and where it relates to birth control: "if I want a baby, you must have a baby"—a description of the gender relations in Indonesia as women see it.

In many cases, parents' concern for the sexual reputations of their unmarried daughters has translated into tremendous pressure for single women in labour migration to marry. Susanna's strategy for dealing with parental expectation was to stay in Hong Kong for as long as possible to avoid the pressure to marry, but this strategy has backfired for some women who find on their visit home that well-meaning families have arranged their marriages as a surprise for the migrant woman on her return. The motivation for familial intervention in expediting these marriages rests in the desire to safeguard young women's sexual purity in migration, especially when the latter have intentions of repeating and extending the migratory experience.

Conclusion

Among Indonesian migrant women in Hong Kong, there is a strong sense of morality attached to the women's sexual purity. Shame—which underlies gender constructions—is instrumental as a tool of discipline even when women are far from home. They are the harshest critics of other Indonesian women who get involved with men during their stay in Hong Kong, and those who become pregnant outside of wedlock. Some of their criticisms are:

> ... they even do sex freely;

> ... they have sex with Indians, Pakistanis, Chinese;

> Sex is their own business but this is the culture ... at Star Ferry Terminal, you can see them dancing all day because of the burden [stress] with employer and their family in Indonesia;

> ... they enjoy, they don't protect themselves, they fall now from the sky (when they find themselves pregnant), they are not ready to be mothers.
>
> (Eri, personal interview, 30 June 2003)

Given the shame attached to premarital failures at sexual restraint and the alienating conditions in labour migration, same-sex relations with other women that at first glance appear to transgress mainstream norms can be attributed to migrant women's desires to conform to gendered expectations back home of women's sexual purity—meaning not having sexual relations with men. On another level, as a site for transformation, migrant women who become involved in lesbian relationships do push the boundaries of their sexual identity in ways that cannot be imagined at home. By doing so, femme women resist and question expectations of gender roles by having relationships in which the main elements of women's subordination to patriarchal control are absent. Butch women on the other hand, who seem to impersonate Indonesian men, make a mockery of the entire edifice of gender structuration and bring into question the double standards in morality by usurping male social and sexual privileges. While this is so, as products of history and culture, the assumption of lesbian identities far from home does not immunise them from replicating the same heterosexist and mysogynistic attitudes that they resist, among themselves.

A common element that this particular case study has with other works on lesbian women is the recurring theme of patriarchy which could suggest that all women's same-sex relations based on the rejection of men are responses to persistent patriarchy. It is likely that for patriarchial practices to have become "normalized", other forms of sexuality that existed side by side, like women's same-sex relations, had to be marginalized and made "deviant". Despite massive efforts by the State, religion and cultural mores, there are still cracks in heteronormativity that allow the light through and it is interesting that it is in the processes of labour migration that young Indonesian women are able to lift the lid on the gendered exploitation of women through cultural and political ideologies, and better still, to give voice to it and act on it.

3
Tung Lo Wan: A Lesbian Haven or Everyday Life?

Denise Tse Shang Tang

Lesbian spaces as sites of resistance have been studied in the last decade with social geographer Gill Valentine urging geographers and urban sociologists to map lesbian neighbourhoods "from nowhere to everywhere" (Valentine 2000: 1). Notions of resistance have taken on multiple meanings within major theoretical strands such as postcolonialism, feminism, cultural geography, postmodernism, Marxism and queer theories. A mapping of resistance points to the interrelations and competing influences these theoretical strands have on each other. In this chapter, I will investigate how lesbian commercial spaces function as temporary sites of resistance for Hong Kong lesbians to validate their lesbian identities, to form social networks and to question their political subjectivities. I define lesbian commercial spaces as businesses that cater to lesbians through their marketing strategies such as posting on lesbian websites or passing out flyers at lesbian events. These spaces include lesbian bars, upstairs cafés catering to lesbian customers and a lesbian specialty store.

Geographically, resistance can be charted at a particular place over a period of time in overt terms such as protests, marches, riots and candlelight vigils. But resistance is also present on cyberspace such as guerrilla websites and online petitions, or with other forms of new media as in film and video. Resistance can be practised through our daily decisions when lesbians choose to meet friends at a lesbian bar or log online to chat with other lesbians. Minute as they seem, these decisions signify a need to bond with other women who have same-sex desires. A space of resistance points to a critique of structural relations of power manifested through spatialities, being global or local places.

To speak of resistance is to acknowledge the nature of power. Structural relations of power affect the way we live our daily lives as gendered bodies, social beings and political subjects. Steve Pile asserts that resistance is not as easily pinned down to "political subjectivities which are opposed to, or marginalized by, oppressive practices; whereby those who benefit from relations of domination act to reproduce them, while the oppressed have a natural interest in over-turning the situation" (3). In other words, marginalized groups have more vested interests in engaging themselves as political subjects fighting "over access, control and representation" (Tonkiss 59). It is not surprising that most informants have stressed the importance of lesbian businesses being lesbian-owned and operated.

When power is defined through the spaces it aims to occupy, architectural design of buildings or public spaces come quick to my thoughts. Government buildings, streets, housing, schools, prisons, parks and shopping malls, just to name a few, signify institutional power both in and out of the spaces. The city of Hong Kong is widely known for its density in spatial terms and in population figures.[1] Yet it is important to understand such density in both historical and economic terms, more specifically, a British colonial history in conjunction with a dominant real estate market narrative. Shortly after the occupation of Hong Kong island by the British Empire on January 25, 1841, the British government declared all land to be British-owned Crown land. This declaration allowed the colonial government to immediately organize an auction of 34 pieces of land within six months in order to generate operational expenses for the colonial government. Land sales since then has been a primary source of revenue for the government. As the population of Hong Kong increases overtime, land was purposely left undeveloped in order to formulate an excessively high demand for land and hence, to create profitable businesses for landowners. As a result, only 22% of Hong Kong's land has been developed for human inhabitation (Chen Cui'er et al. 2006: 14). It is widely understood that intense negotiation processes and structural planning were involved in making land sales viable, profitable and sustainable throughout the colonial era and in continuation for the current Hong Kong Special Administrative Region (17). In other words, geographical limitations may not be a sufficient answer to the high density of Hong Kong. Apart from the changes in government from a British colonial government to a Hong Kong SAR government under China, the stakeholders in land sales have also evolved from British merchants and a small community of Parsi merchants to a handful of land developers owned by Chinese tycoons (Feng 2001: 16). Land usage and urban development in Hong Kong has always been jointly regulated by the government and market forces with minimal community consultative processes.

In the context of Hong Kong lesbian spaces, one needs to look at the nooks and crannies between buildings or walk up the narrow stairways leading up to cafes to make sense of how hegemonic power enacts itself through marginalization of lesbian spaces. Not only am I concerned about the physicality of spaces, but the human aspect of who has access to these spaces is critical in the analysis of power relations. Michel Foucault, by bringing up the notion of "heterotopia", suggests that heterotopias are "counter-sites" that challenge spatialities and social arrangements by inverting the common order of space (24). Fran Tonkiss further suggests that "women-only spaces" can be read as a modern version of the heterotopia, "as heterotopias of separation that escape the eyes and the order of men" (133).

On the notion of multiple discourses, Marxist geographer David Harvey links postmodernism with Marxism through his analysis on urban issues and his notable observation on a contested public space such as Tompkins Park in New York City. Harvey believes in order to understand the composition of park users adequately, one must take into account the "multiple discourses" and "contradictory codings" among park users, such as students, young artists, yuppies, squatters or motorcyclists (201). Harvey's study on Tompkins Park reminds us to view public spaces as a field of rendering discourses in its own positionalities. He also points out how park users have used Tompkins Park as space of protests against various notions of power as defined by themselves. Similarly, lesbian spaces can also be a gathering place for women with different class backgrounds, levels of education, occupations, health status, ethnicities, gender and sexual identities. Although lesbian spaces in this case, are not public arenas comparable to open spaces such as parks and streets, the reasons for lesbians entering into a lesbian space can differ from curiosity to familiarity, offering a myriad of explanations specific to each person.

Gender, Sexualities and Space

A discussion on gender and space often refers to the public/private dichotomy. The public/private dichotomy and its practices are nonetheless gendered. Home has been relegated as a domestic site primarily for women and hence, situates women's emotions and identity formation processes firmly out of public view. The idea of privacy is a deep-rooted tradition within Western political theories of autonomy, private property, patriarchal family structures and personal freedom (Duncan 128). One particular concern surrounding privacy is what constitutes as personal freedom. Modern liberal concepts of individual freedom and rights within familial structures situate an individual within state and private households that are heterosexual and depoliticized in nature. Therefore, being private, in essence, is to abstain not only in the public sphere but to be domesticated in a heterosexual reproductive unit. An ideal private realm would point to notions of domesticity, embodiment, nature, family, property, intimacy, passion, sexuality, emotions, unwaged labour and reproduction. On the contrary, an ideal public sphere encompasses principles of disembodiment, rationality, citizenship, justice, economy, waged labour, the state and valour. As a result, women have been historically treated as belonging to the private realm, and incapable of asserting objectivity through emotional detachment.

Moreover, lesbians have been marginalized in the wider discussion of women and spaces due to a heterosexist bias in the field that leads to more emphasis on nuclear family units. Earlier women's liberation movements in the West start to problematize the notion of women as housewives and private subjects, yet it failed to recognize working-class women, women of colour and lesbians. In addition, the discussion on sexualities and space had not often included lesbian spatialities. Manuel Castells' (1983) explanation on lesbians not having sufficient financial resources to own property and hence, not being a vital part of San Francisco's urban landscape in the early eighties have drawn criticisms from others, most notably, Maxine Wolfe (1992), who asserts that lesbians do play a major role in the city by renting homes and going to other places, like social gatherings or commercial establishments. Mapping lesbian spaces requires "social contacts and insider ethnography, rather than via the architecture of cultural and public life" (Tonkiss 107).

I conducted participant observation, informal interviews, and thirty in-depth interviews with Hong Kong lesbians between 2003 and 2006. By snowball sampling, interview participants were identified through personal contacts and referrals from individuals whom I have gotten to know through my community involvement with local organizations. All interviews were taped and consent forms were signed. Interviews range from one and a half hour to three hours. Interview subjects identified as female, expressed erotic interests or have had romantic relationships with women. Interview subjects range from fifteen to fifty-one years of age. Apart from one subject who is biologically male and in transition to become a woman, all interviewees identified as female.[2] Interviews were conducted in venues chosen by the participants or mutually agreed upon by the participant and myself. These venues include lesbian cafes, restaurants, homes and the university's postgraduate student office.

Tung Lo Wan: A Les Hub

One of the basic premises in arguing for the existence of lesbian spaces is the demand for visibility and in essence, the enactment of a space of resistance (Kennedy and Davis 1993; Valentine 1995; Ingram et al. 1997). Lesbian-only spaces can be defined as spaces reserved for women who express interests in same-sex desires. Entering a lesbian space does not presume one's identity to be a lesbian per se, but imply an interest in same-sex relations. Lesbian commercial spaces in Hong Kong are best recognized as bars and cafes, primarily in Tung

Lo Wan and followed by Mong Kok and Tsim Sha Tsui.[3] Established in 1990, two lesbian bars, H2O and Red, also known as Circus, were located in the upper floors of commercial buildings in Tung Lo Wan. H2O, in particular, has often been mentioned by informants with fondness and a sense of nostalgia. Both bars have since changed ownership and do not function as lesbian exclusive sites. Franco Yuen-Ki Lai's thesis on lesbian masculinities and TBs in Hong Kong highlights three bars in particular: Virus, Oasis and Chatroom. Lai (41–42) describes the setting of these pubs vividly:

> Inside the pubs, the light was dim and the environment was very noisy. Customers had to speak very loudly. The size of each pub was not large (about 700 sq. ft.), and each could accommodate 80 customers. There were around ten tables, and each table could hold eight customers. The pubs were almost empty on weekday nights. Friday night and Saturday night were the golden times, especially on Saturday night. A set of Karaoke equipment was placed in a corner, and customers could take turns to sing Karaoke. Pub games such as *chai mui* and *sik jung* were very common.

Lesbian cafés, on the other hand, have gained interests recently through the popularity of an upstairs café culture. Rents are usually lower compared to ground level businesses and licensing regulations tend to be more relaxed. Upstairs cafes have sprung up in virtually every possible trendy location in both Hong Kong and Kowloon. At time of writing, there are approximately six cafes and six bars consistently listed on lesbian websites. Although the area adjacent to Tung Lo Wan known as Happy Valley is also a common place for lesbians to hang out in Hong Kong, its significance as a lesbian neighbourhood remains pale to that of Tung Lo Wan. One of the reasons can be its inaccessibility via one major public form of transportation such as the underground Mass Transit Railway and its limiting bus routes. The bars and restaurants in Happy Valley also cater to customers with higher class status as reflective in their décor and food prices.

Tung Lo Wan is one of the areas frequently mentioned by informants as a neighbourhood for everyday activities.[4] These everyday activities may take on a leisurely nature such as shopping and dining, watching films in cinemas, singing in karaoke boxes, purchasing street food off corner kiosks or hanging out at cafés. Putting activities aside, the everyday spaces tend to be ordinary establishments that we pass by without any particular observation. If Tung Lo Wan is constructed to be an everyday location where ordinary citizens engage in common activities, it is by no chance also a place of convenience and an attractive location for businesses. It is not surprising then to find an emergence of lesbian spaces such as bars and cafes in the same area. According to a real estate industry report titled "Main Streets Across the World 2006" released by a global private real estate firm, Cushman & Wakefield, Tung Lo Wan remains second most expensive after New York's Fifth Avenue.[5] It is worth noting that Tung Lo Wan has also been historically expensive as a locale with colonial trading companies Jardine Matheson & Co. and others establishing their offices in the area once known as East Point (Feng 16).

Jean-Ulrick Désert points to the shifting nature and erotic possibilities in queer spaces:

> Queer space is in large part the function of wishful thinking or desires that become solidified: a seduction of the reading of space where queerness, at a few brief points and for some fleeting moments, dominates the (heterocentric) norm, the dominant social narrative of the landscape. (21)

Translated onto a project to queer Tung Lo Wan, same-sex couples can hold hands and display physical affection to disrupt heteronormative social relations (Ingram et al. 1997).

On the political front, local lesbian and gay activists have chosen Tung Lo Wan as the site for the International Day Against Homophobia March in two consecutive years. March organizers have chosen a pedestrian area behind a Japanese department store, Sogo, to assemble march goers and to put up tents for community outreach activities. It points to visibility and to the queer use of space for asserting lesbian, gay, bisexual and transgender rights in an open space (Ingram et al. 1997). Although pride parades and political marches have been held in the downtown core of many Western cities, it is still a struggle for many Asian cities to hold highly visible marches raising the banner on affirmative sexualities or human rights for lesbians, gays, bisexuals and transgender peoples.

Spaces for Everday Resistance

Cultural theorist Ben Highmore (2002: 16) suggests:

> The everyday offers itself up as a problem, a contradiction, a paradox: both ordinary and extraordinary, self-evident and opaque, known and unknown, obvious and enigmatic.

In the case of Tung Lo Wan, it is both known as a shopping mecca and yet also a lesbian hub for the number of lesbian establishments both past and present within its gridlines. Can it be summarized as a lesbian enclave or is it better understood as an everyday space with queer possibilities? The area conjures up an imaginary landscape where families would go about their normal business along with lesbians holding hands freely without fear. To use Highmore's words, it can be "both [an] ordinary and extraordinary" place. As a message from the Hong Kong Tourism Board, there is something for everybody when one shops or dines at Tung Lo Wan. By appropriating the area, lesbian spaces can be read as sites of consumption and function as a part of the formula that fits into the Hong Kong capitalist ideology. Yet the nature of the businesses and the clientele they strived for denote their resistance to normative values embedded in gender and sexuality. Lesbian spaces and the socialization processes that happen within constructs the cultural identities of Hong Kong lesbians. As I asked the informants questions related to what they did as leisure, I have come to understand more about the conflicting meanings of lesbian spaces within their own interpretations of what accounts as a Hong Kong lesbian.

Marxist philosopher and sociologist Henri Lefebvre, in his foreword to *Critique of Everyday Life*, asserts that a worker looks to leisure for "the non-everyday in the everyday" (40). Everyday life to a worker is the mundane daily grind of labouring for the capitalist. Leisure holds an illusive nature similar to an escape from both work and family life. As labour becomes fragmented in modern times, the worker becomes alienated from the production process and hence becomes part of an industrial process. Where labour is an unfinished project, the worker develops "a new social need" for leisure (Lefebvre 32). Therefore, Lefebvre calls for a commitment from sociologists to study the interrelations between work, family and leisure as a "totality" of "the concrete individual" (31). Similarly, my study on how Hong Kong lesbians view lesbians spaces as both sites of consumption and places for socialization points to their resistance towards heteronormativity in their everyday life. It is this notion of everyday resistance that is present in the way they negotiate their lesbian subjectivities, transform dominant narratives, and assert their temporary claim on spatialities.

Lesbian Bars and Cafés

Lesbian bars have a long history in many lesbian communities. In the 1920s and 1930s, many women who have desires for other women entered the public sphere to socialize and to find potential lovers in certain Western cities (Faderman; Wolfe; Kennedy and Davis). Cultural anthropologist Antonia Chao stated in her research on *T*-bars in Taiwan that Wang You Gu (Forget-sadness Valley) first opened its doors in 1985 in the red-light district in Taipei (Chao 2001: 192). The word *T* was first used by gay men in Taipei in the sixties to describe tomboys (186). As mentioned earlier, the year of 1990 saw the openings of two significant lesbian bars in Hong Kong, namely H20 and Red in Tung Lo Wan. Ji-eun Lee in her study on teenage *Iban* girls in Korea mentioned the popular emergence of lesbian cafes in Seoul (Lee 2006: 50). *Iban* is a local term used by Korean young women who identify as lesbian or bisexual (51). Similar to the situation in Hong Kong, Lee mentioned that a lot of general cafes in Seoul may not exclusively market themselves as lesbian-specific, yet their clientele are primarily queer girls and lesbians.

Through the gathering of lesbians in public places, lesbian identities were formed and communities were developed to foster these identities. A shared identity slowly emerged among women who frequented these bars. The bar, then, was a space not only for gathering, but a space for public interactions. The lesbian bar became symbolic for public lesbian lives. The reasons were simple, and one might say, these same reasons can still ring true currently in many urban centres. It was difficult for lesbians to meet other lesbians in their own neighbourhoods. Public streets, parks, beaches and street corners were more dominant of a heterosexual and homosexual working-class male presence (Chauncey). Kennedy and Davis were quick to point out that:

> The concentration of lesbian social life in bars derives from the danger lesbians faced as women in a patriarchal culture based on the sexual availability of women for men. (65)

The importance of lesbian bars has been clear throughout American lesbian histories.[6] The existence of these bars is crucial to many lesbians who have just come out or who are in search of a community. These designated lesbian or gay spaces can be perceived as "safe" spaces for many (Rothenberg 1995; Valentine 2000). Sheila Jeffreys, writing as a lesbian feminist scholar, recognizes lesbians' attraction to "seedy" lesbian bars. Much discussion on lesbian bar culture points to the complexities of lesbian visibility, public lives, social and cultural experiences in the past and in our current times. Lesbian bar space is not exclusive to lesbians, bisexuals and queer women. Kelly Hankin (2002) prompts us to take note of heterosexual voyeurs, hate bashers and police officers that are also present in these spaces. Many scholars have also challenged the perceived "homogenized myths" of lesbian bars. Butch-femme identities are embraced by some and questioned by others (Lorde 1993; Nestle 1992; Kennedy and Davis 1993). Rochella Thorpe (1996) problematizes the "whiteness" of lesbian bars in Detroit. I find the accessibility of these histories primarily lies in its medium of publication being English. Whereas there must be abundant meeting places for lesbians and bisexual women in many Asian cities, the diversity and cultural differences within Asia or more boldly, the concept of Asia as a geographical entity remains to be critically examined and not generalized. Even with that said, as more scholars work with local queer knowledge, I believe the availability of such scholarship will vastly contribute to our current limited understanding of sexualities.

Lesbian bars and cafés provide physical spaces for women to gather, to develop friendships and to seek potential erotic interests. These experiences may not be the only place to assert one's lesbian subjectivity yet lesbian bar cultures have continued to exist in many cities within different countries. As Maxine Wolfe puts it, lesbians have continued to be "active creators of their own identities and environments, rather than mere bearers of dominant social relations or passive absorbers of dominant ideology" (302).

Elizabeth Lapovsky Kennedy and Madeline D. Davis' pioneering study on lesbian bar culture from the 1930s to 1950s demonstrated that bars "were truly the only places that lesbians had to socialize; but it was also more dangerous, bringing lesbians into conflict with a hostile society—the law, family, and work" (29). Antonia Chao in her influential work on Taiwan's *T/Po* ('Tomboy' and 'wife') communities has shown that lesbian bars are crucial to our understanding of "queer histories, identity formations, and body politics" (369).

The existence of lesbian commercial establishments can be best summarized as temporary sites. High rental rates and unstable income forces bar and café owners to close down and to relocate to other commercial buildings. Histories associated with physical spaces are often erased and customers proceed to the new bar or to find other places for socialization. Yet, I continue to find lesbian bars and cafés located around commercial buildings in Tung Lo Wan, Wanchai and to a certain extent, Mong Kok. Kennedy and Davis suggested that lesbian bars used to be located in more seedy areas, such as red light districts since women were traditionally not allowed entry into male territories such as bars. Going out alone at night for women was dangerous enough. Similarly, I have been to lesbian bars and parties in Vancouver and San Francisco where their locations are not exactly the best parts of town. Lower rental rates can be one explanation but also "moral permissiveness" within these particular locations leads to an easier emergence of lesbian and gay bars (Kennedy and Davis 1993). Police authorities have been less controlling in these areas, and in some cases, accepted bribes for smooth operation of these businesses. This is not to say that police raids are not common but maybe lesbians were not the main targets in this case.

Responses from Informants

I have asked informants to describe how they feel about lesbian spaces and what concerns them the most in these spaces. Their responses centre on their past experiences in visiting bars and cafés. Most informants found the locations of these businesses on lesbian websites such as Blur-F.com and relez.net or through word of mouth from friends. During my research period, tabloid magazines have also started a barrage of coverage on sensationalized topics such as where les girls hang out, why do young women become lesbians, or TBs as the assistants to teenage bopper music artists.[7] More than once, these magazines publicized the locations of les hangouts such as bars and cafes. Although such media coverage tended to be sensational at best, and a peeping tom to say the least, it made lesbian spaces seem real, tangible and local. The range of responses from the informants can be divided into the following themes: the issue of comfort in women-only spaces, a sense of camaraderie, gay bars as an entry point, to have or not to have lesbian spaces, and a matter of accessibility.

The issue of comfort in women-only spaces

Informants often mentioned the issue of comfort in their choices to be in lesbian spaces. This comfort zone is characterized by being first and foremost, women-only and secondly, by its identification as a lesbian space. Comfort is often linked to the absence of men—hence a lesser chance of being sexually or verbally harassed. Safety is a serious concern for lesbians who come to these spaces as an affirmation of their sexual identities and erotic desires.

Ah Lok was fifteen years old at time of interview and attended a secondary school in Tung Lo Wan. Her tomboyish looks had often attracted unwanted attention from boys in schools as well as in other social environments. Smart, articulate and quick on her feet, Ah Lok divided her time up by attending school, hanging out in video arcades and upstairs cafés. She had no qualms holding her girlfriends' hands in areas such as Tung Lo Wan and Mong Kok. I asked her how she felt about having heterosexual men in a lesbian space, in this case, a lesbian bar:

> If I sit together with my friends and we keep to ourselves, it's fine. There were times when I was with other friends and some of their young male friends came and I felt okay about it. I don't like those who hit on you. It's easy to have this kind of situation. But if they are brought in by my close friends, I don't have a problem with that. The other kind of situation is embarrassing. Don't know what to do when they come over and hit on you. At Home [a lesbian bar], there are men in the upper and lower floors. I've gone up to use the washroom on the twentieth floor and had men hitting on me a few times. He would say, "You're chilling out downstairs? Which floor?" "Eighteenth floor." "I'll come by to find you." "Oi! Downstairs is only for women." "Ok. Have fun." Then nothing happened. Some men have class.

Being stared at or under "the homophobic gaze" is one of the many reasons for women to seek out lesbian spaces for solace (Corteen 260). These sites function as a buffer zone from homophobia in the wider society. Karen Corteen has investigated how lesbians define and perceive safety in two public spaces: one is a visibly gay village and the other one is a small local town. Her findings have shown that lesbians internalize homophobic violence and hence experience a kind of "interior harm" from their "localized management of their sexual representation and demeanour" (276). In other words, homophobia takes a daily toll on their everyday lives and lesbian spaces can help to temporarily alleviate some of these painful reminders. Eileen, a butch lesbian in her fifties, opened an upstairs café in Wanchai not exclusively for lesbians, but for community groups to hold meetings or workshops. The place resembled a queer-friendly environment where people from all genders and sexualities are welcomed. Eileen believed that starting up a café was a result of her own lesbian identification:

> If I opened up a space like this one, for people who are like me, we can go to a very relaxed place. You don't have to be all tensed up, don't have to be stared at by people who think you're odd. One can just be relaxed at my place. One can be flirty, can talk about love, just anything, approach someone you like, even cruising, anything goes.

As a twenty-year-old student, Bik Bik is politically active and well-versed in social issues that affect marginalized groups in Hong Kong. She started going to the bar, Virus, when she was around fifteen or sixteen years old. Bik Bik did not think of going to the bar as a particularly exciting experience which might be indicative of how the younger generation perceives such spaces. For example, Bik Bik and her peers pick and choose between various social spaces and change their preferences in accordance with their social activities:

> The first time I went with my classmates ... er ... it was nothing special, that is, I expected what it's like to go with my classmates. It's heavy drinking, it's not like I haven't drunk before and it's not like I haven't smoked before. Nothing special, really, but it's a relatively safe space because I will not bump into my family. You will if you're on the streets. You also won't bump into people you don't want to see, for example, family friends or your relatives. It's really troublesome. These networks are huge because of my extended family.

Yet, it can be uncomfortable for some lesbians to enter lesbian bars whether it is a first time for them or a regular night out. One might feel intimidated entering a public lesbian space for the first time not knowing what to expect. Even though the location is more obscured and less likely to be of interest to most heterosexuals, the possibility of heterosexual peeping is not unheard of in both gay and lesbian bars. Therefore, it is still possible for lesbians to run into colleagues or friends. Moreover, the particular culture of a bar can make one feel anxious and hence, deter one from entering the space again. Kitman was twenty-seven years old at time of interview and worked at a non-governmental organization. She started logging onto the Internet to make lesbian friends and to hang out at lesbian bars when she was nineteen years old. She recalled her eagerness in going to lesbian spaces and her level of comfort in different sites:

> At that time, I really wanted to go [lesbian bars]. But when I got there I didn't know what to do. Everyone there was playing and drinking hard. I don't like approaching others or *chai mui* [a dice game]. I feel I cannot fit in. But still, lesbian bars are considered to be a form of *tongzhi* space, sometimes I do have the urge to go to these spaces even though I don't feel comfortable there. But I still want to go. … There is no place like *Joca* then. If there was such a space, I would like it better but I would still feel a bit weird. That is, if you go to a bar for *tongzhi*, it's like going to *yum cha* [drinking tea and eating small dishes]. It's odd to go just with the two of you but if a whole gang goes for *yum cha*, it's okay.

The age factor figures prominently in the discussion of lesbian bars with most of their clientele being younger women from late teens to mid-twenties. Most informants who are older mentioned how they felt disconnected from the younger generation when they were in these venues. Their comments on the younger crowd tend to take on a negative approach where they described them as "rowdy", "heavy drinkers" and "with attitude". At first I had doubts whether it was associated with class background, however, my interview data did not allow me to make a general claim as such. It occurred to me that a disapproving reading of these spaces has more to do with the physical environment of these bars such as the location, the décor, the karaoke music and the people who work there. Regardless of their negative assessment of lesbian bars, all informants except for one respondent have been to either a lesbian bar or café.

A sense of camaraderie

Some informants have expressed feeling a sense of camaraderie in exclusively lesbian spaces, such as bars and cafés. This sense of solidarity can be associated with the need to find solace and as one informant has said, "a common language". This "common language" denotes an imagined community and refers to customers who are in the lesbian space regardless of whether they know each other at all. Essentialist as it might seem, the assumption that each woman in a lesbian space is potentially a bisexual or a lesbian is already enough to conjure up notions of commonality. As Alison Eves puts it cogently in her study on butch/femme negotiation of spatialities, "the strongest expression of essentialism took a spatial form and involved defending the boundaries of 'lesbian space'" (486). Alex, who visited lesbian bars occasionally, witnessed a marriage proposal among women:

> I go with friends, that is, they like to go everywhere [lesbian bars]. It's very common now to just approach the people sitting at the table next to you and say something like "Hey, let's play together." ... Some people will suddenly propose [at the bar]. One person will come over and say, "I'll propose marriage later, can you come over and be the witness?" I said, "Sure! Sure!" Then I'll hang out with another new group of people.

A night of hanging out at the local lesbian bar turned out to be a group affair where Alex took part as an observer for a marriage proposal. The fact that they were in the same space at that particular moment already bodes possible moments of casual camaraderie among strangers. Since same-sex marriage is forbidden in Hong Kong, lesbians find other ways to enact marital vows for each other. The lesbian bar then becomes a space to "validate the reality of their world and their lives as social and sexual beings" (Wolfe 315). The bar becomes a safe space where forbidden acts were performed to subvert dominant heteronormative narratives in public settings, for this instance, a marriage proposal between two women. The marriage proposal, as a precursor to a same-sex marriage, if they indeed choose to proceed, is a temporary matter. Once they stepped outside of the bar's door, their status as a lesbian couple is challenged by heteronormative social relations.

Easy bonding among women in a safe space is a primary criterion for Hong Kong lesbians to venture into these spaces. Phil, a thirty-three-year-old who identifies as a TB, left school by sixteen and had worked at various jobs, enjoyed the casual atmosphere in lesbian bars:

> I like going to les bar because I would approach anyone and doesn't matter what identities they have. That is, I can just stand around or when I see someone coming back from dancing on the dance floor for a sip of her drink, we can chat casually to see if we click. I go to les bars two or three times in a month. I went with my friend for the first time to a les bar. I thought, wow, there are bars just for les!

Needless to mention, socializing at lesbian bars or cafés requires one to have some sort of financial resources. There are many possible connections between a consumer subject and a social subject (Pellegrini). A consumer subject, let's say, a lesbian consumer subject can purchase visibility through participation at queer-friendly cultural events (as in film festivals, theatrical productions and concerts) and through sipping a drink at the local hangout. A social subject might push for political and social rights, in pursuit of social acceptance via market visibility. Both subjectivities intersect and rely on each other to establish an effective relationship for queer visibility. But this form of queer visibility is class-stratified and not affordable for all. Seventeen-year-old Miki is a secondary school student who mentioned spending money as a deterrent factor—"hanging out at cafes usually takes money". Instead, Miki often hung out at video arcades or walked around in shopping areas such as Mong Kok and Tung Lo Wan.

Gay bars as an entry point

Lesbians have continued to seek out bars and cafes as symbolic of physical spaces that offer a certain degree of safety and comfort. The lack of visible lesbian businesses has prompted others to find gay bars as a possible venue to meet gays and lesbians for the first time in their lives. Two informants went to gay bars specifically for this purpose. When Nikki was a first-year student at a local university, she remembered how lesbians were not often mentioned in the media. Now in her mid-thirties, she could still remember her quivering experience in entering a gay bar:

> I thought there are only gay men in Hong Kong because the newspaper only mentioned gay men. Did not mention women, but I checked out some foreign magazines on the web, they are written in English and contains the word "lesbian", that is why I thought lesbians only exists as foreigners. I thought there are none in Hong Kong. Then one day at the university, I was bored and was walking around then I noticed a poster advertising a group called Hong Kong 10% Club with a contact number on it. Then I suddenly remembered that I have heard of this group on television or in newspaper. I know it's a gay group. I copied down the number and called them up and found out there are also lesbians in the group.
>   Before I noticed 10% Club, I don't know whether it's from television or from magazines, that there are a lot of gay men in Lan Kwai Fong. … There is a night club called Yin Yang, I've heard that only gay men enter the club. But I still went there by myself once … It took me a long time to find out where it is. I have heard of a YY Disco and don't know where Yin Yang is. I found out that YY means Yin Yang when I got there. I did not know how to *po* [Cantonese slang for clubbing] then and I went there at nine. The guide I was reading said there would be more people later at night, so I went at nine. I waited for almost an hour downstairs from the club, almost forty-five minutes.

There isn't anyone there. It's quite expensive, 50 to 60 dollars per drink. I went on a weekday as well. I didn't know much then. I just know it's a well-known place, so I went. I was very nervous. I kept asking myself like what to wear, will people kiss with each other freely, will someone [a girl] come over and flirt or talk with me, what should I do? I thought about these things for a very long time downstairs. Then I drum up my courage and walked in. There weren't many people there. Many of them are men, so I got scared and walked over to the bar to buy a beer because I don't know what else I can drink. [Laughter] Then I hid by the bar and just watched what's going on … I drank very slowly, looked around and stayed there till around 10. Nobody came over to talk or flirt with me, then I left by myself. At that time, I thought so this was it.

Beatrice, on the other hand, travelled from Macau to Hong Kong to visit Yin Yang Disco as well. Born and raised in Macau, she described the adventure as a significant experience in finding out whether or not she was attracted to women:

I told myself, I need to find out the truth! Then I approached a gay male friend, who is working in the hotel and he said, "Let's go over to Hong Kong for that gay bar called YY. Go there and see how you feel, then you'll find out for yourself!" So I went with him and when I just walked in, wow! It felt like I belong here and then when I saw the people there, it felt great and very compatible. Just that moment, I was quite sure of myself. I became a regular guest going there every weekend. Then I made more friends and met my first girlfriend … Macau doesn't have the same market and it's too small. I don't know a lot of people in Macau but some people are closer to me. There isn't a place I know of. Hong Kong is much better, then I think it would be better for me to go over to Hong Kong and see how I feel … YY is very nice then, it's a place to see and to be seen, I felt very comfortable there.

Gay spaces have always been easier to find since gay consumption has been a primary driving force in gay male culture (Bouthillette 1997). Indeed, this aspect of consumption is not limited to gay men but is indicative of a more established economic status than women in general. One can easily pick up a gay magazine or newspaper and find out which bar to go to or which area is more dotted with gay businesses. In most cities, there have been longer gay publications than lesbian ones, especially where advertising and marketing is concerned. So it is not surprising at all that both Ah Wing and Beatrice would locate a gay bar prior to finding a lesbian one even though Beatrice was introduced to Yin Yang Disco through a gay colleague.

In a comparative study on a lesbian neighbourhood and a gay male enclave in the city of Vancouver located within the Pacific Northwestern part of Canada, Anne-Marie Bouthillette finds that the blurring of boundaries between these two cultures has been occurring as a result of changing material realities that have led to spatial choices. For example, middle class lesbians can now afford to live in the gay area, the West End. At the same time, gay fathers and their children have been attracted to "the leftist political street culture" of the Commercial Drive, also known in the queer community as the Dyke Drive for its affordable family housing (Bouthillette 1997: 231).

To have or not to have lesbian spaces

Most informants have different opinions on whether there is a need for lesbian spaces. There seems to be a general agreement that these spaces are necessary for a political reason such as lesbian visibility or a social reason such as a space for building support networks or socialization. Yet the need for lesbian exclusive spaces is often translated into a question of whether these same spaces isolate lesbians and hence, prohibits the normalizing of lesbian identities into broader society. Beatrice echoes the same concern about the need to just be yourself and most of all, "to behave":

> When I go with a large group of friends to a restaurant, any restaurant, I think the people know who we are. You can tell. I don't feel ashamed of myself but the point is, I won't tell people that I am one [a lesbian]. I don't need to say it. We're not fifteen or sixteen years old, taking drugs and drinking too much. We are normal people and we behave. As long as we act maturely, we don't need to say it.

When asked about whether there is a need for lesbian-specific places, twenty-seven-year-old Jo expressed her opinion on the irony of these spaces in comparison to straight-identified sites:

> There is a need for lesbian-specific places. But for myself, I may not go there. What I mean is that there should be, I mean, on a societal level. I think there should be spaces for sexual minorities, but I also think that these spaces isolate us. For example, if I go out with my girlfriend or lesbian friends for dinner or for a drink in a straight space, I think it is important to show them that we exist. If we only go to lesbian spaces, we are isolating ourselves and confining ourselves to our own spaces.

What the respondents meant by normalizing often point to positive representations of lesbians in everyday situations, a visible consumer culture and an affirmative discourse on sexualities. It is as if when one talks about lesbian and gay politics, one needs to think of assimilation tactics in order to be a part of the social milieu. I have asked myself whether a ground-level business would facilitate more visibility or would it be contrary to its purpose, limiting the number of lesbian-identified women entering such a visible space. Thirty-four-year-old Lik Lik had been very active in organizing social events through local lesbian groups. Always dressed impeccably for the occasion and sociable beyond description, I had often found Lik Lik to be the perfect host and event organizer. She offered a political way of looking at lesbian spaces; she questioned whether ground-level businesses would make a difference in terms of visibility:

> Does not seem to make a difference for me. It is more about the culture whether it is located upstairs or on the ground level. It is difficult to conduct business either way. I think it is more important for it to survive financially. There is no point if the business cannot survive even if we have ten similar establishments. I have friends [lesbians] who asked me why we have to support them, why we are boxing ourselves in, why I cannot be more like the mainstream. I don't think the same way. I learnt from community organizing that there is a thing called pink money. I think there is a value for these [lesbian] businesses to survive. We [the organizers] do when we pick the venue for events. We would pick a business to support in order to build up its value as part of the community. I'm making it sound like it is very political ... I know there are gay streets in other countries but Hong Kong does not have one ... I feel that if Hong Kong has such an area, it will prove that the society pays attention to this community.
>
> It doesn't matter whether it's boys or girls but it has to be a non-heterosexual space. This is very important. It is also important for it to survive as such a space, for people to enter freely and for others to know that such a space exists! Also for people [lesbians and gay men] are not afraid to be seen. Hong Kong does not have such a space for long time.

A matter of accessibility

At the point of the interview, Nick was twenty-five years old and the owner of a specialty store selling products catering to lesbians. These products included DVDs, books, Pride souvenirs and TB vests.[8] The store was not easy to find as one had to wander through a maze of small shops within an underground shopping mall. Most shops sell street fashion which has made Tung Lo Wan a magnet for young shoppers and trendsetters. This particular shopping mall has been known for its speciality in finding limited edition sneakers. Commenting on various spaces for lesbians, Nick had much to say in regards to how these spaces functioned as lesbian sites:

Actually when I was studying in Australia, I thought I may not be able to afford continuing my studies; I thought I should come back and open a les café. When I returned, others have done it. Then I don't want to compete with others by doing the same thing, so I started to think what else I can do. I have just been to Taiwan and saw how well Gin Gin [a well-known queer bookstore in Taipei] is doing. A big shop would be too expensive, so I opened a smaller one. It's not enough of a gimmick if I open another les café. There are already three cafes in Tung Lo Wan, four cafés if I open another one! I think that might be too many cafés.

On why she chose the specific shop location:

Because Mong Kok is too expensive, I'm afraid I cannot afford it. Have to open one that I'm okay with and if I cannot afford it, I cannot ... It [the rent] is about ten thousand. Actually it's considered cheap in Tung Lo Wan ... I like Ginza Plaza. People might think it's hot to open a shop like mine and I worry that people won't come in. Ginza Plaza's environment is darker or more low-key, customers will come in more easily ... I have a friend who is also a les opened another shop there ... [Tung Lo Wan] is *nui gai* [women street] Girls' street! (Laughter)

Similarly, café owners like Felix and Anne, also chose Tung Lo Wan as the prime location for their businesses. Other contending locations are usually Mong Kok or Tsim Sha Tsui, with high rental rates and the kind of customers as primary criteria for choosing business locations. Felix, aged forty, reinforced the notion of Tung Lo Wan as the central location for young lesbian socialization. Her café, Restricted Entry, has since been closed. I have been to the café many times for community meetings, social functions and research interviews. Regular clientele tends to be younger in age and wearing school uniforms. Unlike chain operations, it is much harder for lesbian café owners to break even not to mention making a profit just by selling cups of coffee or fruit tea.[9] Therefore, café owners are caught in a dilemma where situating one's business in an attractive physical location in order to capture a wider market is often the reason for generating higher rental costs, hence leading to temporary sites. The owner of Restricted Entry explained her struggle with choosing a physical location to open up her café:

It's not a bad idea to group them together. The chances increase for people to come up [to a lesbian café]. ...Yes, I actually wanted to try it out in Mong Kok but my partner did not want Mong Kok. She wanted Tung Lo Wan. Sometimes I am not the only one to call the shots ... I felt that Mong Kok is better because there is less competition and also, those lesbians, they also go to Yau Ma Tei or Tsim Sha Tsui or Mong Kok! They are also hubs.

For Anne, aged thirty, her choice of location denoted another concern that involved stereotypes of customers who frequent different neighbourhoods:

> I thought of Tsim Sha Tsui at the beginning because I live in Taipo. To come all the way every day is a deadly chore! That is why I thought of Tsim Sha Tsui but there is no available spaces and it's expensive. You think about it, we are not opening a bar for *pek jao* [Cantonese slang for binge drinking], we will not lose money if everyone puts down over a hundred bucks once they walk in. But we are not [opening that kind of space] and that's why it's difficult. That's why if we don't look for upstairs space and cheap space, we cannot operate. That's why we cannot find a space in Tsim Sha Tsui.

When I posed the question of whether she had thought of another location apart from Tsim Sha Tsui or Tung Lo Wan, Anne exclaimed:

> Not in Mong Kok! So disgusting! Those people are not appropriate. I mean I feel they don't drink, that is, I feel for those who knows how to drink coffee or want to find a quiet place to have a cup of coffee are not the kind of people you'll find in Mong Kok ... Because there are lesbians everywhere in Tung Lo Wan, and lesbians usually hang out in Tung Lo Wan. ... Yes because it's very central. Les bars are all in Tung Lo Wan. It makes sense for them to like coming to Tung Lo Wan.

Apart from the overall emphasis on Tung Lo Wan as a lesbian enclave, other informants had similar opinions on other districts in terms of lesbian visibility. Ku Tsai, in her early twenties, worked in a trendy clothing store within a shopping arcade located in Mong Kok:

> I feel it's true in the past. In the last few years, I still think it's more visible in Tung Lo Wan, that is, you will not see as many [lesbians] in other areas but now there are a lot, actually. Mong Kok, Tsim Sha Tsui have a lot!

For two younger informants like Ah Lok, Miki and Ah Ying hanging out at Tung Lo Wan became an issue with their parents. Ah Ying's mother had expressed disapproval at Ah Ying loitering in Tung Lo Wan:

> I'm used to going out at night. My mom asked me why I go out at night all the time. Where do I go? What kind of troubles am I into? Are you hanging out with improper folks? Because she knew that I'm always in Tung Lo Wan.

Ah Lok interjected and laughed at the matter:

> Tung Lo Wan is improper (*laughs*). The impression, for parents, the impression is that people in Tung Lo Wan is improper, just like those people in Mong Kok.

I tend to read the obvious split between Tung Lo Wan and Mong Kok that resonates among many informants to take on a class dimension. Tung Lo Wan tends to be more of a trendsetting shopping area and undoubtedly more expensive in product prices, whereas Mong Kok is considered to have cheaper products and ideal for finding pirated goods. The extent of Mong Kok as a shopping mecca for bargain hunters and a place for cheap entertainment has even contributed to the creation of a slang term "MK look" referring to young people who dress in cheap, tasteless clothing with gangster dyed hair. Mong Kok often appears on news media as a troubled area with plenty of police raids for illegal gambling activities in bars, underage drinking and prostitution in bars or upstairs flats in both residential and commercial buildings. Eric Kit-Wai Ma in his study on "the hierarchy of drinks" observed that Mong Kok bars are generally considered "inferior because they only sell draught beer and 'simple cocktails'" (Ma 2001: 128). His informant was concerned about his personal safety as a customer in Mong Kok drinking holes. The negative reading of Mong Kok can also be taken as a post-colonial thought since Mong Kok is associated with tourists from Mainland China and Southeast Asia. Therefore, it is rendered as an inferior part of town and substandard in moral values. Recently, the area has been gentrified to include condominiums and a luxurious shopping mall, Langham Place. Informants had also mentioned going to a lesbian bar in Yau Ma Tei, a few blocks down from Mong Kok, and had complained about the bar charging them extra to clean up the mess they made. Instead, the young informant cleaned up the mess that her friend vomited, which saved them five hundred dollars.

Lesbian spaces as in lesbian use of spaces

Apart from lesbian exclusive spaces, many informants had hung out at spaces otherwise known to be more straight-identified, such as video arcades and billiard rooms. There is also lesbian use of spaces in every facet of their lives, for example, going to any common restaurant with a group of lesbian friends who on the outside might look suspicious for being ambiguous, androgynous and slightly queer, yet as insiders would know, as one of our kind. Lesbian use of spaces is prevalent in Hong Kong as a sense of lesbian community is not often aligned with political causes; therefore, social networks are often built around lesbians and their friends which translate into queering everyday spaces for their own use. In addition, the Internet has created other ways for women to meet other women and to organize net meetings. Lik Lik, a veteran lesbian event and party organizer, offered insights into lesbian organizing:

I feel that now is very different than before: the social atmosphere. What is most obvious is that there used to be a lot of people coming out for events, anywhere from thirty to sixty for bbq. Everyone would come out to play but it's different now. I mean before 1997, before the handover. When we used to organize activities, people would all come and they don't come to know people [potential romantic interests]. They would come to have fun with a group of friends. It is obvious now that you don't need to organize these events since people can meet others by themselves. One can meet others on the net. It's really obvious ... honestly, those who come to join these activities are good friends. For others, they won't feel that there is a need to join activities, to join events [organized by lesbian groups].

Conclusion

In this chapter, I have outlined how lesbians have been marginalized in the field of gender and space and how notions of resistance can offer a theoretical framework to understand the spatial decisions made by Hong Kong lesbians. I attempt to position everyday resistance in the city of Hong Kong as lesbians negotiate with capitalist ideologies as entrepreneurs or as customers to lesbian spaces such as bars, café or a specialty store. Informants had pointed to Tung Lo Wan as the hub of lesbian activity yet lesbians were increasingly visible in other locales such as Mong Kok and Tsim Sha Tsui. They had also raised concerns about the comfort of lesbian spaces, accessibility and whether there was a need for such spaces. Moreover, lesbians had also used gay bars as an entry point to learning about the lesbian and gay scenes.

II

Communities

4
GID in Hong Kong: A Critical Overview of Medical Treatments for Transsexual Patients

Eleanor Cheung

When the general public in Hong Kong hears the word "transsexual", crime, cabaret, suicide[1] and mental illness are some of the notions that often spring to their minds—as that is often the kind of news that get covered when transsexuals and transgendered people[2] are mentioned in the media. During the summer of 2007, for example, there were sensational news coverage about a young FTM who was convicted for stealing his elder brother's Identity Card and using it to apply for a job,[3] and around the same time that year, there was also the news about the infamous Zung Kai-leon[4] who has been arrested several times over the last few years for loitering and trespassing while wearing various kinds of female uniforms.[5]

Meanwhile, cabarets and entertainments are some other prominent impressions that Hong Kongers have on transgenders, as can be seen by the pervasive use of the derogatory term *"renyao"* which is often used by Hong Kongers to describe the transgendered cabaret performers in Thailand. The association between transgendered people and the "human monster" cabaret performers can be seen from the result of a 2006 random sampled telephone survey conducted by Mark King from which 54.2% of his Hong Kong respondents used the word *"renyao"* when they were asked to provide a word they would normally use to describe a transgendered person. This kind of association is a form of stigmatization, because while some Hong Kong tourists may enjoy a *renyao* show when visiting Thailand, it is certainly not the kind of industry they would like to have in their own backyard, as could be seen by the complaints made by Aberdeen residents against the Bangkok Golden Dome Cabarets performing in their neighbourhood.[6]

Apart from the kind of stigmatization mentioned above, transgendered people are also being perceived by the general public as mad, a layman view which has, ironically, been backed up by the medical community. According to the said survey conducted by Mark King, 24.2% of his respondents believe that transgenderism results from "a mental disorder and/or psychological problem" (King, Winter and Webster). Nevertheless, it is unlikely that the general public knows much about the relevant mental health condition, namely, Gender Identity Disorder (hereafter GID) that many transgendered people are being diagnosed as having.

In this chapter, I shall write briefly about GID, the Standards of Care advocated by Harry Benjamin, the treatment transsexual patients have been receiving in Hong Kong since 1986, discuss whether or not GID should be regarded as a mental illness, and my recommendations for the future.

Gender Identity Disorder

There has been a very long history recorded in many countries of some men having desired to become women and of some women having wished to become men.[7] The medical term "transsexual" was first coined around the 1920s by Magnus Hirschfeld and later became a clinical category to be distinguished from homosexuals (1923: 14). Benjamin also used the term "transsexualism" in a lecture before the New York Academy of Medicine in 1953 (4), and the term became part of the English language around that time, being listed in the Index Medicus since 1967 (Raymond 1994).

The first reported sex-change operation took place in Germany in 1931 (Pauly 1968). But the procedure was not well known until the 1950s when the case of Christine Jorgensen, who had a male birth-gender and had undergone surgical gender reassignment in Denmark, was published (Hamburger, Stump and Dahl-Iversen 1953). Meanwhile, the notion of gender identity, which had been deployed to distinguish it from the concept of gender role (Money 1995), had also started to surface at around the 1960s.

Not before long, the phenomena of cross-dressing and sex-changing had become a medical problem to be understood, managed, and treated. For instance, the diagnosis of transsexualism was first introduced in the DSM-III in 1980 for gender dysphoric individuals who demonstrated at least two years of continuous interest in removing their sexual anatomy and transforming their bodies and social roles. In 1994, the DSM-IV committee replaced the diagnosis of transsexualism with Gender Identity Disorder (GID). The diagnostic criteria for GID in the DSM-IV-TR includes:

1.   A strong and persistent cross-gender identification (not merely a desire for any perceived cultural advantages of being the other sex).

2.   Persistent discomfort with his or her sex or sense of inappropriateness in the gender role of that sex.

3.   The disturbance is not concurrent with a physical intersex condition.
4.   The disturbance causes clinically significant distress or impairment in social, occupational, or other important areas of functioning.

Treatments in the West

Since it is hard, if not impossible, to change a transsexual's sense of gender identity to match their anatomical sex,[8] attempts to alter the body seems to be the only successful way to treat transsexuals to make their gender and body to be as congruent with each other as possible, such as through hormonal therapy and Gender Reassignment Surgery (also known as Sex Reassignment Surgery). In the UK, Gender Reassignment Surgery will only be performed with recommendations from two psychiatrists and the patient has to undergo the "real-life experience" for at least one year. According to Harry Benjamin's Standards of Care for Gender Identity Disorders (the 6th version), which is used by many psychiatrists in many countries as a guideline to treat transsexual patients, the real-life experience is "the act of fully adopting a new or evolving gender role or gender presentation in everyday life".[9]

The real-life experience is essential to the transition to the gender role that is congruent with the patient's gender identity, because change of gender role and presentation can be an important factor in employment discrimination, divorce, marital problems, and the restriction or loss of visitation rights with children. These represent external reality issues that must be confronted for success in the new gender presentation. These consequences may be quite different from what the patient imagined prior to undertaking the real-life experiences.

Treatments for Transsexuals in Hong Kong

In Hong Kong, the first documented case of Gender Reassignment Surgery was performed in 1981 in Princess Margaret Hospital (Ng et al. 1989). In 1986, a Gender Identity Team (hereafter GIT) was established as part of the sex clinic of the University Psychiatric Unit of Queen Mary Hospital to address the growing number of transsexual patients seeking Gender Reassignment Surgery. The treatment provided by GIT was quite consistent with the Harry Benjamin's Standards of Care which is used by many psychiatrists in many countries as a guideline to treat transsexual patients.

GIT was an organized multi-disciplinary team consisting of psychiatrist, clinical psychologist, gynaecologist, endocrinologist, urologist, medical social worker, lawyer, geneticist and reconstructive surgeon (Ko 2003; Ma 1999). Its aims and functions were clinical services for transsexual patients, education for professionals in the allied mental health fields and research (Ng et al. 1989). Between 1991 and 2001, 34 cases were referred for assessment relating to Gender Reassignment Surgery, and 28 of them were found to fulfil the DSM-IV diagnostic criteria for transsexual (Ko 2003). Thus, on average, there were about two to three patients being referred to the GIT per year, and all patients had to be referred by a practising physician or a paramedical professional such as a social worker, clinical psychologist or mental health worker.

According to Ng et al., assessments by the GIT included asking the patients to write about their life story, interviews with various professionals in the GIT, patients undergoing a battery of standardized psychological and laboratory tests. After the diagnosis of transsexualism and a decision to undergo gender reassignment was made, the patients would then be expected to establish their cross gender identity and live and function in society in their chosen gender. The patients would then be re-evaluated after about one year of establishing their cross gender identity, and if they had shown sufficient emotional stability, they would be placed on hormone therapy. After a further twelve month period, the patients would be re-evaluated with a view to possible Gender Reassignment Surgery. Patients also received psychological treatment which served both exploratory and supportive functions; for example, to determine whether the wish for reassignment was mutable and to help patients cope with negative feelings, such as alienation and social rejection, that were associated with cross-gender identity.

Despite the achievement made by GIT, in Spring 2005, the Hospital Authority announced, to the disappointment of many transsexual service users, the closure of GIT, and that the health service for transsexuals was being regionalized, viz. from then on transsexual patients have to seek the health service in their own regions which often have no or very little experience in treating transsexual patients. It was believed that the decision was made because the public health service was facing a huge deficit and the medical professions in Hong Kong did not take this mental health condition seriously, as reported by the *Ming Pao Daily News* on 8 March 2005.[10] Dr. Kwok Ka-Ki, who was a Legislative Councillor representing the Functional Constituency of medicine, was reported to have said that it was reasonable to reduce the services for transsexual patients by shutting down the GIT, because he thought the GID that transsexuals suffer was a "general mental illness", and was quoted from the same newspaper saying that:

> Compared to cancer and other major illness, [counselling transsexuals] is only a minority's service, it takes up a lot of time for treatment. When

there is not enough resources to treat some general mental illness and cancer, one must choose to treat the kind of illness that is more important. (Chinese to English translation mine)

Before I comment on the remarks made by Dr. Kwok, I would like to evaluate the current mental health service received by transsexual patients in Hong Kong.

Trranssexuals' Experences with the Health Service in Hong Kong

I started my fieldwork with transsexuals in Hong Kong around September 2005; I met some of my informants through TEAM (Transgender Equality and Acceptance Movement) and some through my own personal contacts. Overall, I have met about twenty people who identify themselves as transsexuals, and over half of them have had or are currently undergoing GID treatments either through the GIT or the regionalized health service respectively. I have had formal interviews with four of my informants about the treatments they have received regarding their GID condition, and had informal conversations with the rest of my informants on this topic.

Although the GIT consisted of such a large team of professionals, all the professionals worked only part-time for the GIT, and a GID patient might not have seen all the professionals in the GIT. For example, one of my informants, Ms. Y, who is a male-to-female transsexual and has already received her Gender Reassignment Surgery through the GIT, said that she was never referred to see a gynaecologist or endocrinologist during the five years when she was being treated by the GIT, and when she asked for such a referral in order to get a prescription of estrogen (a female hormone), her surgeon told her to buy her own from some local pharmacies because it is not very costly. Many medical professionals in the West may think that it is unreasonable to ask patients to administer hormones for themselves without doctors' prescription. In the UK, for example, transsexual patients would not only receive prescription of hormones if deemed appropriate, but would have regular blood tests in six months' intervals to determine whether the hormonal dosage is appropriate, because hormonal treatment can cause impairment of liver function, hypertension and increase glucose tolerance.

Even though the service provided by the GIT was not 100% satisfactory, all of the transsexual informants I have personally come across who have been served by the GIT seemed to be happy with its service, especially when it is compared with the service provided by the regional psychiatrists.

At least two of my transsexual informants complained about the regional psychiatrists for not having the knowledge or expertise to treat GID. Mr. K, a post-operative female-to-male transsexual, told me about two unpleasant incidents with regional psychiatrists, one before he was referred to the GIT and one after the closure of GIT. Before Mr. K was referred to the GIT, he had been showing symptoms of depression because of his gender dysphoria, and in 2001, he decided to go for the gender reassignment surgery and went to a regional psychiatrist for help. The psychiatrist told Mr. K that he did not know if there was any service for transsexuals in Hong Kong (even though that was before the closure of the GIT). After going through various routes (including getting relevant information from some local transsexuals), Mr. K was eventually referred to the GIT and had his gender reassignment surgery after going through various assessments and real-life experience. Apparently, Mr. K was not the first transsexual being turned down by regional psychiatrists because of their ignorance of the service provided by the GIT and their lack of knowledge of GID; several other transsexual informants had similar experience too with regional psychiatrists before the closure of the GIT. Moreover, the judgement of some of those regional psychiatrists seemed to be coloured by their own values of gender-norms, and instead of referring their patients to the GIT, some had attempted to persuade their patients to abandon their cross-gender behaviours and to give up their intense wish for gender reassignment surgery. This suggests that many regional psychiatrists were ignorant of GID and were not briefed about the service provided by the GIT.

After the closure of the GIT, Mr. K went to see a psychiatrist at a hospital in his region for some GID related psychological problems. The psychiatrist told Mr. K that he did not know what he could do for him because he had already had his gender reassignment surgery and did not offer any other support.

Meanwhile, Ms. C, a male-to-female transsexual, said that she did not manage to be referred to a psychiatrist until after the closure of GIT, and during the first meeting with her regional psychiatrist, he confessed to Ms. C that he did not know much about GID and could not tell her about the procedure for treating GID. However, during the second consultation, the psychiatrist appeared to have gathered some information on GID and was able to refer her to a medical social worker and a psychologist for further assessments. Ms. C found that although the psychiatrist and the social worker showed understanding of her situation, they do not have any guidelines or individual treatment plans for the service users. For example, they have different opinions in relation to the use of hormones.

The experiences Mr. K and Ms. C had with their regional psychiatrists indicated that the Hospital Authority has not, since the closure of the GIT, briefed regional psychiatrists about GID treatment guidelines, such as Harry Benjamin's Standards of Care and post-operative care.

Is Gid a Mental Illness?

Some people may say that GID is a mental illness right away simply because they think it is abnormal and sickening for an otherwise physically healthy individual to have the intense wish to get rid of his or her genitalia and to live the life of the opposite sex. Similar to the now out-dated opinion of homosexuals being abnormal and mentally ill,[11] this way of thinking about transsexuals has a lot of value and cultural judgement in it (e.g. thinking that transsexuals violate the gender norms) rather than thinking solely in terms of, say, whether an individual has any impairment in their cognitive, emotional, or behavioural functioning.

One of the diagnostic criteria of GID is related to distress and impairment, according to the DSM-IV, "[t]he fantasies, sexual urges, or behaviours cause clinically significant distress or impairment in social, occupational, or other important areas of functioning" (1994: 531). It is true that transsexuals tend to be under more emotional distress and have higher suicidal rates compared to the general population. For example, a 2005 study conducted in Philadelphia found that about one-third of their transgender respondents had attempted suicide (Kenagy 2005). This raises the question regarding whether transsexuals are inherently emotionally unstable or whether their distress is mainly due to a combination of the dysphoria with their birth genders and their experience of discrimination and hostile socio-cultural environment. Ma suggested that it was the latter by stating that in Hong Kong three out of forty-four transsexuals surveyed had attempted suicide and in Singapore the rates were even lower, whereas in China 85% of the forty transsexuals in a study were reported to have attempted suicide.

All in all, as in the case of homosexuality (Hooker 1957), there is no evidence that the distress and impairment of the respondents are inherent to transsexualism. Although some transsexuals suffer from depression and may even be suicidal, this seems to be the consequence of the prejudice and discrimination they encounter in our society. Many transsexuals are disowned by their families and friends, and lose their employment because of it. It is hard to imagine not feeling distressed living under such harsh conditions.

Meanwhile, not all transsexuals are distressed and suffer from functional impairment, according to Katherine Wilson, "[p]sychiatric studies of clinical populations, like those of clinical gay and lesbian subjects in previous decades, failed to consider the incidence of functional, well adjusted transgendered people and couples in society". Many of the post-operative transsexuals that I have personally come across live a very well adjusted life in their chosen genders. Indeed, all, except one (who regretted having undergone sex reassignment surgery), told me that they feel happier now living in their chosen genders. Nevertheless, there are always some cases of very difficult or even traumatic transitioning experiences and a few anecdotal cases within and outside Hong Kong about regret after transitioning. The difficult or traumatic transitioning experiences are often related to: problems with family members who are against their gender reassignment decision; loss of employment as the employers and/ or co-workers react negatively after being informed about their decision to transition or about their previous gender; not being able to "pass" (i.e. to be able to assume successfully the gender role of their chosen gender when interacting with society and function in public situations as a member of that gender) very well which often leads to public ridicule and harassment; and being rejected for health care treatment for gender reassignment.

The regret issue is often related to rushing for surgery without sufficient psychiatric/psychological assessment. From the regret case that I have personally come across, the said informant had been self-medicating female hormones for some years and went abroad for gender reassignment surgery without going through any proper psychological/psychiatric consultation beforehand, and he did not go through any real life experience as suggested by Harry Benjamin's Standards of Care. It seems to me that it would have helped eliminate the possibility of regret if the patient had followed a procedure akin to that stated in the Standards of Care.

According to a preliminary analysis of the information I have gathered from my informants, it seems to me that the main instigations of emotional distress, severe depression and other psychological disorders, and even suicide attempts/ completed suicide are from the way transsexuals are being treated by those who react very negatively to their gender expression and gender reassignment, not being informed about the Standards of Care, and being deprived of gender reassignment treatments when needed.

If my analysis of the sources of distress and other psychological problems many transsexuals often experience is correct, then it seems more accurate to say that distress and impairments some transsexuals experience do not originate from their transsexuality per se, rather, it is a kind of sexual minority stress, namely, an additional stress since the "stigma, prejudice, and discrimination create a hostile and stressful social environment that causes mental health problems" (Meyer 2003: 675).

A lot of ink has been spilt for several decades challenging the medical presumption of gender essentialism (namely, exactly two natural sexes being determined by chromosomes and/or genitalia). It is beyond the scope of this paper to go into the socio-cultural literature that supports the view that gender is a social construction as opposed to a biological imperative (Beauvoir 1993; Kessler and McKenna 1985; Butler 1990; Lorber 1994; and Garber 1992), nevertheless, it is worth pointing out that it is about time Hong Kong people have to shift the question from what is wrong with a transgendered person to the question of what is wrong with our society which is imprisoned in this rigid gender norm. The issue is akin to those wearing sun glasses complaining that the room is too dark. It is time for our society to be critical and to examine our own schema of the world, and to come to the realization that the problem does not lie in transgenderism. It rather is our prejudicial and discriminatory perception, derived from the problems and limitations within our rigid gender norms, that is causing a lot of unnecessary heartaches.

As in the case of gays and lesbians lobbying for homosexuality to be deleted from the DSM-II in 1973, one may assume that transsexuals may prefer to be free from the stigmatized label of mental illness if GID is being removed from the DSM. However, some of my transsexual informants told me that they worried that such a move would also remove the justification for them to receive gender reassignment surgery from the public health service or to claim it from medical insurance. Thus a transsexual person seems to face a dilemma of either fighting to remove a stigmatized label of mental illness or preserving this diagnostic label in order to justify the continuation of receiving public funding for relevant treatments. I shall come back to this dilemma at the end of this chapter.

After the Closure of the GIT and Recommendation for the Future

The news about the closure of the GIT has been very distressing to the transsexual community in Hong Kong, and it has also been very disappointing to hear Dr. Kwok's view on transsexuality in public.

Firstly, Dr. Kwok showed total disrespect to minorities, saying that service to transsexuals was "only a minority's service", implying that it was not worth serving those patients simply because they were minorities. There is certainly something inherently illogical in this kind of reasoning because even when some physical or mental health conditions are rare, they could be very severe and even deadly, and hence are entitled to treatment.

Secondly, it is quite misleading the way he referred to GID as a "general mental illness" and said that one must choose to treat the kind of illness that was more important, such as cancer. Dr. Kwok, and perhaps many other medical professionals in general, showed a tendency to disregard mental illness and treat it as something less important than physical illness. He was perpetuating the message that mental illness is unimportant and was overlooking mental health patients' suffering and lack of quality of life which is often as severe as, if not more severe than, many serious physical illnesses, and could lead to suicide which is as deadly as other terminal illness. Additionally, by saying that GID is a "general mental illness", he showed total ignorance of the severe distress GID patients have been going through when being forced to live the gender role that is incongruent to their own gender identity. It is not uncommon for GID patients to commit or attempt suicide if they could not see any possibility in crossing gender. At least two of my informants had told me that they had attempted suicide in the past, and an informant also told me that one transsexual had committed suicide a few years ago as a result of being told by a medical professional that she was not suitable to continue gender reassignment.

The issue regarding the misunderstanding or the "minimization" of the severity of GID by the public as well as the medical professionals ought to be addressed, because they are often the main source of distress to transsexuals as already discussed.

There is also a fear among transsexuals in Hong Kong that the closure of the GIT is just a way for the government to refuse service to GID patients. While this fear may be irrational, as we have witnessed gender reassignment surgery being performed on a transsexual patient who went through the regionalized route (as opposed to the GIT route), it is clear from some transsexual patients' first-hand experiences, as discussed earlier, that many regional psychiatrists do not have the knowledge and expertise to treat GID patients. Thus, the Hospital Authority is obliged to give clear guidelines and support to medical professionals and the professionals in the allied mental health fields regarding treatments for transsexuals, otherwise tragedies, whether suicide or regret after surgery, might easily repeat themselves when a GID patient is not treated appropriately.

Last but not least, psycho-education to the public about transgenders is also very important, as most, if not all, transgenders experience discrimination in all sorts of ways, including being victims of hate crimes.

The GID Dilemma

The consideration of prejudice and discrimination loops us back to the dilemma about whether or not we should de-pathologize transsexualism. An in-depth discussion of this dilemma will constitute a paper of its own, thus, instead of going into the details of the pros and cons, I would like to throw in a suggestion that some of my informants have made as a way to break through this dilemma, namely, to regard transsexualism as an intersexed condition. Such a reasoning of intersexuality involves understanding a transsexual as someone having the psychology of one sex but the biology of the other sex, and it requires medical intervention to realign the mind and body of those who find it too dysphoric to live in such an intersexed condition (and as numerous medical findings have told us, such an realignment can only be done by altering the physical body). In other words, this "mind-body intersexed" condition is a medical and not mental disorder, and as such one can avoid the stigma of mental illness while being justified to receive public health service for the condition.

5
Opening up Marriage: Married *Lalas* in Shanghai

Kam Yip Lo Lucetta

This chapter is part of the research I did during 2005 to 2007 on *lala*[1] individuals and communities in Shanghai. I carried this research during the formative period of identity-based *lala* communities in China. It is one of the first extensive qualitative studies of *tongzhi* communities in contemporary urban China. Tracing the development of the inaugurative period in Shanghai, it documented the struggles and strategies of *lala* women who are the founding members of this emerging community. This chapter can provide ethnographic information to future *tongzhi* studies in China, especially to lesbian studies in China which are much needed at the time being.

During my several field visits from 2005 to 2007, I interviewed twenty-five self-identified *lalas* in Shanghai. Most of them were introduced to me by a local community leader or by mutual referral between informants. They were women who were in various degrees involved in the local *lala* community. All of them are citizens of China and are ethnic Chinese. Their ages ranged from early twenties to mid-forties. Nearly all of them had white-collar jobs (or have had white-collar jobs but were studying for a second degree at the time of interview) or self-employed. Most of them lived and worked in Shanghai. A few of them were staying temporarily (e.g., studying a full-time course) and a few worked in nearby cities but came to Shanghai regularly either for home visits or community gatherings. Five of them were in heterosexual marriage and two had children. One of them was in a "co-operative marriage" (or self-arranged marriage with a gay man who is under similar familial pressure to get married). Two informants were about to have co-operative marriage at the time of interview. In this chapter, I will focus on these seven married or about-to-get-married *lala* informants.

Face-to-face in-depth interviews and participant observations were conducted. The interviews were conducted in Mandarin, Shanghainese or Cantonese. On average, interviews lasted one to two hours each time. For some of the informants, a second interview was conducted to gather updated developments of their lives and to follow up topics that were unfinished in the first meeting. In a few cases, I interviewed couples together. Sometimes it was because the couple approached me or were referred to me together and they expected me to interview them together. The other time I did couple interviews because I wanted to invite discussions between them on topics that were related to their relationship. I also carried out individual interviews of each partner in advance to or after the couple interview for more personal or private information.

One recurring theme that always came up in the interviews is the conflicts between family and marriage, and my informants' same-sex desire and relationship. The pressure of family and marriage has been mentioned in many studies of lesbians and gays in China or in Chinese societies elsewhere (Zhou 2000; Li 2002a, 2002c; Zheng 1997). In this chapter, I will demonstrate the dual lives that many married *lalas* in Shanghai are living now and the ways they used to accommodate their same-sex desire and relationship in a heterosexual marriage, or for some, to survive the ever increasing pressure from their family when they are approaching the so-called suitable age for marriage. Other social groups such as relatives, peer groups (ex-classmates or close friends), and co-workers can also be major players to pressure unmarried informants to find a mate. Or in many cases, informants' parents would be questioned by relatives, friends, or even neighbours if their daughter remains single for too long after university graduation. It is not unusual for them to demand the parents concerned to take a more active role to find a suitable mate for their daughter. Yet the pressure to get married and to remain in a heterosexual marriage is undoubtedly most felt by the daughters. Not only do they need to cope with the expectations of parents, but also the challenges of performing the role of wife (and mother) if they are married and the social stigma of homosexuality. I will detail the sources and forms of pressure that married *lalas* are facing, and in this context, to discuss the emergence of "co-operative marriage", a new form of intimate union and family formed by *lalas* and gay men in contemporary urban China.

The City

According to one local community leader in Shanghai *lala* circle, the city has long been a vibrant site for both gay men and lesbian women. Since 2000, *lalas* have become increasingly visible, first in chatrooms and bulletin boards on the Internet, later in some gay or mixed bars, and more recently in social gatherings organized by lesbian groups in the city. The cyberspace continues to be the most popular meeting place for *lalas* in the country. In 2005, the founder of one Shanghai-based local Chinese lesbian website told me that her website has more than 45,000 registered members since its inception four years ago. They started to organize offline gatherings in 2004 and a community working group was established by volunteers to carry out different community projects and regular monthly gatherings in 2005.

The city has also become the most desired destination for job seekers all over the country. Half of my informants are not Shanghai natives but are working or studying in Shanghai. The reasons for the increasing visibility and community networking of *lalas* in Shanghai in recent years are numerous and I will not be able to have a full discussion in this chapter. But it is certain that the increasing geographical mobility of job seekers in the past two decades have contributed to the emergence of visible lesbian and gay communities in major metropolitan and economically more developed cities in China. Individual mobility, either geographically or socially, has been significantly heightened during the economic transformation since the late 1970s (Lu 2004). The implication of this policy change is that the social control on individuals, which has been long carried out through a centralized job assignment system, has been significantly lessened. In pre-reform period, mobility between jobs was almost impossible and mobility between cities was even more difficult. The work unit (*danwei*) of an individual controlled almost every aspect of her/his social life, from the provision of housing to the regulation of one's private life. Therefore, the opening up of the job market and hence the loosening of state control through *danwei* have created new opportunities for people to live their personal lives more privately. The newly acquired geographical mobility encourages the flow of people from less developed parts of the country to more developed urban centres such as Shanghai. For many people, Shanghai is a place to fulfill their career aspirations and also their desired way of living. For non-natives, the city can provide them a kind of anonymity that they can never enjoy in their hometowns. This is crucial to people who want to live alternative lifestyles. The availability of organized community networks and information, and the provision of relatively safe meeting spaces are another attraction of Shanghai to lesbians and gay men around the country. For some of my non-native informants, Shanghai is where they first put their desires into practice, so to speak. The anonymity in a big city, the freedom to adopt alternative lifestyles, and the vibrancy of the lesbian and gay communities in Shanghai are all pulling factors for people who want to actualize their diverse lifestyles.

Marriage in Contemporary Urban China

During the reform period, there have been significant changes concerning private life and sexual morality in the country. Models of intimacy that deviate from the normative one (heterosexual monogamous marriage) are competing for legitimacy and acceptance. Alternative models such as singlehood, multiple partnership, co-habitation, extra-marital relationship and same-sex relationship have entered public discussion relatively free from the ideological and moralistic condemnation that was typical in the pre-reform era. However, in this social context of changing sexual morality, heterosexual monogamous marriage remains to be *the* normative model of intimacy. According to the official data collected in 2004, 19.5% of the entire population aged fifteen or over were unmarried (i.e. never married), of which unmarried females constituted 16.5% of the entire female population aged fifteen or over, and for unmarried males, it was 22.5% (China Statistics Press 2005). There was no significant change in the size of the unmarried population aged fifteen or above over the previous five years of 2005 in China. In 1999, 18.8% of the entire population aged fifteen or over was unmarried, including 15.3% of females and 22.2% of males who were unmarried (China Statistics Press 2000).[2] The figures for 2004 also showed a drastic decline of unmarried people in the age categories of 20–24, 25–29, and 30–34, which were 69.3%, 21.4% and 5.7% respectively (China Statistic Press 2005). This indicates that the norms of suitable age for marriage still have a tight grip on most people in China. In urban China, 25–29 is considered to be the most suitable age for marriage for both sexes. By that time, people have finished their education and probably for many, already have a stable job. Most people will experience the strongest and also most organized pressure of marriage during these few years before they turn thirty. The pressure is particularly felt by women as they are expected to get married a few years earlier than men. Parents, relatives, or even colleagues and friends will start to introduce possible mates to them and arrange matchmaking meetings. Even in Shanghai, a city which is generally considered to be untraditional in many social aspects, marriage is still held as the norm for most people. The percentage of the unmarried population of the city in 2004 (18.2%) is even slightly lower than that of the country's total (China Statistic Press 2005).

The reasons for the importance of marriage and the high involvement of parents in their adult son and daughter's marriage can be cultural, social and political. While politically there is no law in China which states that everyone should get married, the punitive effects are obvious for people who choose not to marry. Before the introduction of the market economy (before 1979), the central job assignment system, or the *danwei* system, has been the most effective source of social control and resource allocation. Married people in state-run enterprises would get more economic rewards than unmarried people. For example, married couples can be assigned bigger apartments while unmarried people might have to wait years before they can be assigned an independent unit. The marketization of the economy, which affects the supply of housing (commercial housing units have been introduced after the mid-1990s) and other daily necessities, has largely freed individuals from the economic control of *danwei*. However, its control can still be felt on people's private life, especially for those working in state-owned enterprises or government departments. Fang Gang (2005), in his qualitative study of women and men with multiple sex partners in China, also found that people within the job re-assignment system tend to worry more about the exposure of their sexual behaviour at work than people with jobs from the private sector. Although the economic grip of *danwei* on people's daily life has been lessened after the reform period, its political and moral surveillances still constitute a source of stress for people with non-normative sexual behaviour.

There is also the factor of economic inequality of women and men: marriage is still understood as a way for women to attain upward social mobility. In other words, women are expected to marry up to men with higher social status and men who are economically better off. It is materially beneficial for a woman to get married in China. For instance, the contemporary marriage custom in Shanghai requires the male side to provide housing for the new couple. House is always the biggest economic investment in a marriage. There is a popular saying in Shanghai which says to have a daughter now is much better than to have a son. Women may experience pressure of marriage for material reasons. For economically dependent *lalas*, it is more difficult to convince their families that they can support themselves without marrying an economically better off man. It is evident in my research that the importance of economic self-sufficiency is often rated very high for women who have decided not to get married.

Besides economic benefits, married people enjoy much higher social recognition than unmarried people. Marriage is a rite to adulthood. One cannot be a socially recognized adult until she or he gets married and forms her/his own nuclear family. This cultural belief is always expressed through the discourse of social responsibility. To be an adult means she or he needs to take up more social responsibilities and be productive to the country and her/his family. It is every citizen's duty to get married and to reproduce the next generation to the country and the family. Therefore, if a person has reached the age of marriage but refuses to get married, then she or he will be considered as trying to avoid the responsibility she or he needs to fulfill for family and society, and hence she or he cannot be considered as a responsible adult. This cultural belief is also discussed by Li (2002a) and Zhou (2000) in their studies on the homosexual population in China. The force of social conformity is the major reason that causes gay men and lesbian women in Li and Zhou's studies to get married. People over the suitable age for marriage but who are still single are socially stigmatized. In the past decades, *daling qingnian* (overage young people) has been categorized as a social problem. Especially for overage unmarried women, the term *lao guniang* (old girl) is still popularly used in Shanghai. *Lao guniangs* are usually associated with physical unattractiveness, bad social skills, poor health and personality defects. The status of marriage is therefore seen as closely linked to one's internal essence. The politically enforced naturalization of the heterosexual model has led to a discursive erasure of any alternative sexual relationships and subject positions. Those who cannot fit in the dominant model can only survive as sexual deviants or inferior citizens with a lesser share of resources and social respect. For women, the dominant heterosexual marriage model places them strictly in the positions of wife and mother. Evans (1997) explains very well the effect of this discursive hegemony on women,

> The priority the dominant discourse gives to maintaining monogamous marriage as the site and pivot of all sexual activity and experience is overriding. This leaves no discursive space for women—or men—to choose difference, whether this means simply not marrying, having a lover outside marriage, or rejecting heterosexuality. In fact, it leaves no alternatives for representations of a women's sexual fulfillment except in the subject positions identified by the status of wife and mother. The possibility that women may prefer to live separate lives, removed from the dominance of the male drive, cannot be contained within a discourse which naturalizes monogamous marriage as the only legitimate form of adult existence. (212)

Parents will also be affected by this social stigma if they have an unmarried but "overage" daughter. An unmarried homosexual woman is therefore doubly stigmatized and marginalized by the normative heterosexual discourse. There is a hierarchy of social recognition concerning one's marital status in China, in decreasing order, they are: married, single, divorced. Being a homosexual is even more stigmatized than being single or divorced. One of my informants, Jenny (in her mid-twenties), told me that her mother has once said to her, "I would rather that you don't get married for the rest of your life. I will not give you my approval for this kind of matter [*being a homosexual*].

According to my research, parents play a significant role in their daughters' marriage choice, which includes the decision to get married or remain single, when to get married and the choice of husband. Relatives are the second most powerful group in deciding the marriage partner of the younger generations. Although strictly arranged marriages are very rare in urban centres like Shanghai, semi-arranged marriages are not uncommon. Meetings with potential partners introduced by relatives or friends of parents will usually be arranged for younger members in a family who have reached the suitable age for marriage.

After the initial meeting, the young people can decide whether or not they want to further develop the relationship. According to a survey done by Li (2002b), 40% of the two hundred people researched are the major decision-maker of their marriages but also with parents' approval while 13% had their marriage decided by parents and approved by themselves. Only 17% managed to be in full control of their marriage, although 55% said they would prefer to have full control over their marriage.

As state intervention of an individual's personal life significantly decreased in the recent decade, with the opening of the job market and the introduction of consumerism into the country, people are now less reliant on state provision for their daily necessities. In the pre-reform era when centralized job assignments were the norm, marriage was encouraged more by state policies through the *danwei* system and networks of social surveillance over people's daily lives. Now we can see family is left to be most active and effective in the maintenance of the institutions of heterosexuality and marriage. With the power of political intervention fading out from people's everyday lives, contemporary Chinese parents, who have grown up in a uniform society in which any politically or socially deviant behaviour would affect their livelihood severely, are now actively taking up the role of the guard to ensure that their children are leading a normative heterosexual life and do not become a deviant in any sense. Even though there is a growing population of younger urban dwellers who choose to remain single, to most parents of my informants, a life without marriage seems unthinkable. They believe that responsible parents should help their children to find a good match and to establish a new family.[3] This is why many parents are so eagerly involved in the matchmaking of their children and have considerable emotional and economic investments in their children's marriage. How to cope with family and marriage is the biggest challenge for women in China who are now struggling to pursue a life that is deviated from the heterosexual norms.

Pressure to Get Married

The social expectation to lead a "normal" life as everyone else does is very strong in China. The force of social conformity is evident from everyday language (such as the choice of many informants to use "normal" or "not normal" to describe different kinds of lifestyle or sexuality) to real life choices (such as marriage and childbearing). Almost all of the informants have experienced the pressure of marriage. Most of them have attended matchmaking meetings arranged by parents, relatives, colleagues or friends. It seems that most of them have accepted that marriage is not something one can take full control of, either in fulfilling or relinquishing marriage as a controlling social factor. It is more like fulfilling a responsibility to parents and to society. Shu was an unmarried informant in her mid-twenties whose view on marriage is quite representative:

> Since marriage is not a simple matter of love, you need to consider many things. Such as family … society … Since a person's marital status can affect society … a marriage can affect things that one might think does not matter before. It can also well be the reason why someone would attack you. And this will make your parents worry.

Informants always stressed responsibility to parents when talking about marriage. Especially for married informants, marriage is an individual's duty to satisfy her/his family's expectation and to not upset the social order. Yan (married, early thirties) had met her first girlfriend before her wedding and since then she had had a very difficult long-term extra-marital relationship. But even at that time, she had never thought of not getting married:

> I have never thought of not being married. There's no one like that. I felt that everyone has to follow this path. Maybe I thought I was just a bit different from others. But still you cannot upset social order because you're different or special. You still have to bear the responsibilities for others, for your family, for your parents, including for yourself. I didn't see how you can have the ability to challenge [all this]. At that time, both of us [*Yan and her girlfriend*] did not think about this [not getting married]. It didn't seem like an issue. At that time it didn't feel like it's a question that was worth serious consideration because it's simply unimaginable to consider its possibility.

Apart from responsibility, Yan also mentioned the importance of role models. Although she knew there were single women in the country, she had never encountered any positive role models. Similarly, she did not have any idea of what a lesbian's life would be like when she started her first same-sex relationship. Yan did not know if it was possible at all not to get married and have a family with a woman:

> At that time, it was really terrifying to hear people mentioning those three words [*tong xing lian*] (homosexuality). When our friends made fun of us and said, "You two look like you're *tong xing lian*", I and my girlfriend would fight back at once. First of all, it's about not acknowledging your own being. But now I understand the reason why we fought back is also about others not acknowledging your behaviour / … / Both of us didn't know what to do at that time when we got together. We would always cry over the phone when we called each other, and talked about what we should do, because there was nothing to refer to. I thought if we had access to the Internet at that time, we might have gotten together, we might have been with each other … overcome many obstacles. You basically won't think of living this kind

of life. You feel there is no future for this. You think that no one would embark on this road and that this road is impossible to begin with. You feel that everyone should get married / ... / I remembered the night before I got married, she [Yan's girlfriend] went with me and stayed at a hotel. There were many relatives at home and it provided an excuse for me to stay out in order to get a good rest. So she stayed with me at a hotel room. The next morning, I had to return home to put my make up on and to prepare for the wedding. It was really ... together we were crying and crying till four in the morning. That was the night before my wedding.

For many younger informants who are now facing the pressure of marriage, they usually tell their parents they want to stay single. Although staying single is a less preferable and socially recognized lifestyle, it is easier for most parents to understand it than to accept or to gain an understanding of homosexuality. But stereotypical thinking of single women is still prevalent in Shanghai. Chris (thirty years old) told me she thought about staying single after a few frustrating experiences of dating men (so as to please her parents and friends). But she knew her parents would never understand or allow her to be single. And she would never tell them if she really decided to live a life this way. Even her colleagues reacted negatively when she once mentioned to them this idea of staying single:

I am not going to hurt others but I also don't want to hurt myself. That's why even though I may not be able to find a loving relationship, it's all right to be single. Yet this creates more pressure for me because it is a harder fact for families and friends to accept my decision. They will think that you should have a family and be settled that way. I told them that I am not suitable for this kind of life because I prefer freedom and I don't want to be restrained in any form. I have told them before. Of course I did not tell my parents that I wanted to be single. I feel that there is no way for them to accept it. When I told my colleagues and friends that I wanted to be single, they were so shocked! They said, "How can it be!" and immediately told me not to have this kind of thinking.

The popular imagination of single women is still dominated by negative stereotypes. To many, to stay single for life means one has to lead a miserable and incomplete life. Not to mention the communal surveillance (usually in the form of gossips) that one and her family will have to face if she is an overage single woman. Since marriage is the one and only imaginable and socially approved way of life any other alternative life choices will be unavoidably subjected to social scrutiny. The family of the single woman and herself as well will get much unwanted attention that is directed towards the woman's private life. There is a hidden message behind this kind of seemingly good intended enquiries. That is, there must be something wrong about the woman. She and her family might need to struggle against this unwanted social scrutiny as long as the woman stays single. Ling (twenty-seven years old), who had just officially finished the marriage registration with a gay man to form a co-operative marriage by the time of interview in 2007, explained very well the reason why parents are so frustrated if their daughter chooses to stay single and why people will think that they have the right to interfere with the private life of a single woman:

> It is still the power of social pressure. They feel that if their child is by herself and for different sorts of reasons, the pressure is still too much to bear. [...] Also, there were many times that you become the target for much caring if you are not married. Someone might say to you, "Is your daughter still unmarried or does she have a boyfriend?" Or something like that. If you are not married, you will always be the target for this kind of caring. Once you are married, and married off to someone, no one would care about you.

As I mentioned above, there is a cultural belief in Shanghai that a person can only be recognized as a full adult when she or he gets married and has her/ his own nuclear family. To stay single means that you do not have the social identity that allows you to be an autonomous adult. That explains in large why parents, relatives or even friends feel obliged to persuade a single woman in the family to find a mate. It is not anything honourable to the family if they have an overage unmarried daughter. Tan (twenty-seven years old) concluded that it was all about the *mianzi* (face) of parents:

> It is because they [parents] feel they have no "face". You are no longer a part of the family once you get married and you won't be cared after so much. It's like taking care of their "face".

Since a woman can only be independent of her natal family when she gets married, therefore, her parents no longer need to take care of other's inquiry about their daughter when she has officially left the family.

Coping with Marriage

For married *lalas*, the pressure that they need to face is much more severe. The pressure mainly comes from three sources, namely, their natal family, the family of the heterosexual marriage, and their extra-marital same-sex relationships.

We can divide those married or about to get married informants into two groups: those who have started same-sex relationships before marriage, and those who have started them or even realized the desire after marriage. Chris (thirty years old), Ling (twenty-seven years old) and Tan (twenty-seven years old) had same-sex relationships before marriage or were either planning or having co-operative marriage at the time of interview. Yan had same-sex relationships before marriage but she still got married to a man. Mu (thirty-three years old), Coral (early thirties) and Heng (thirty-six years old) belong to the second group. They started same-sex relationships after marriage. Their coping strategies of marriage, either to maintain the marriage or to survive the pressure of getting married, can be categorized into three major ways: 1. Secret dual life: to hide their same-sex extra-marital relationship from their husband and their natal family; 2. Make it open: open or semi-open negotiation with husbands; 3. Fake it: to have co-operative marriage with a self-chosen gay man. It is possible that informants have gone through different stages of negotiation before or after or during their marriage. For example, one might lead a secret dual life at the beginning of her extra-marital relationship and it is only later that she can manage to reach some kinds of mutually agreed settlement with her husband. Or one can struggle between her parents and her secret same-sex relationship for a long time and only after the co-operative marriage that she can get more freedom to live independently from her parents' control. At the time of interview, Yan and Coral were struggling in a stressful dual life. Mu and Heng were managed to have open and semi-open negotiations with their husbands to accommodate their extra marital same-sex relationships. Chris, Ling and Tan, the three younger ones, chose the least confrontational but most experimental way of arranging a co-operative marriage for themselves.

Secret dual life

Yan and Coral, both in their early thirties, chose to leave their hometowns and husbands temporarily and to stay in Shanghai. Physical distance seemed to be very important for them to strike a balance between marriage and their extra-marital same-sex relationships.

Both of them had told me the difficulties of keeping a same-sex relationship outside marriage. Coral was staying temporarily in Shanghai and during these few years she could live with her girlfriend. She told me how she was tortured everyday by this triangular relationship and how difficult it was to get a divorce:

> My husband knew [my extra-marital relationship] within a year ... A person who has never been married will not understand or realize the weight of marriage. In reality, a marriage between two persons is

not only about them; it involves a lot of people, families, even friends and colleagues ... A person who has never been married would not understand ... Now I believe that a married woman should not ... love another woman. If I knew that it would be like this three years ago, no matter how much I loved her, I would have controlled [*my feelings*] because you will end up hurting three persons. All three persons will be in pain. If I knew it would be like this situation now, I would rather have felt a bit heartbroken at the beginning. It's really hurtful to others. Once I went on a chatroom and read an article on how married women do not have the right to love. I felt that it is wrong. I felt that love is a right. It is everybody's right. Why can't I have this right? But now I have experienced it, you can say that it's about having responsibilities, or it's about the other person's gender, you should not really touch this kind of matter ... because she is in a lot of pain now. She feels she has no security. I cannot give her much security and I cannot give her any promises. On the other side, my husband is also suffering because I cannot provide him with what a normal man would have. I have suffered a lot as well. Sometimes I just want to live simply, not to feel any burden when I open my eyes in the morning, to have the simple joy to smile, to work and to read. Now each morning when I open my eyes, I can feel a heavy load, a dead weight.

At that time, I wanted a divorce. I have talked with him about a divorce. He was nonchalant about it. He said, "Don't worry. Just do what you need to do. It doesn't matter. No need to worry about me. I'll be here, forever. When you decide to return just come back." If his attitude were not so accommodating, I would have been more determined to get a divorce, but his attitude has rendered me useless to do anything about it.

Yan's husband did not want to get a divorce even though their relationship had never been easy since the first day of marriage. They still pretended to be a normal couple in front of families and friends. It seems that the cost of getting a divorce is even higher than suffering in a bad marriage. That probably explains why divorce rates are consistently low in China over the years.[4]

Make It Open

Mu, in her mid-thirties and a mother of a son, had a girlfriend living overseas. Her husband accepted her same-sex relationship partly because of the geographical distance that existed between Mu and her girlfriend. Heng, also a mother of a son, was considerably free in her marriage since she and her husband only kept their marriage for the sake of their son. Both of them had extra-marital relationships at the time of interview.

The girlfriend of Mu was also married. Both of their husbands knew of their relationship and for similar reasons both husbands tolerated it. Mu said it was because of the geographical distance and the gender of her lover that had made it easier for her husband to accept it:

> How was his reaction? It's a surprise. Then it feels like, my goodness, how can his life be like this? It's enough to write a story on it. How can this happen to him? But since it happened, even the another party is a woman, being of the same sex poses less of a threat to him. And then, the distance is so far, therefore he accepts it.

When being asked about whether she had considered getting a divorce, Mu named children and economic viability as factors that were of greatest importance to her:

> Children are a very huge reason. If no children are involved, two persons would have gotten a divorce without much to care about. Both parties can figure out their finances and draw the separation. But it would affect the children a great deal if they're involved. We absolutely cannot be too selfish. We cannot ruin a child's future or a child's prosperity for the sake of your own pleasure. Part of it is economic. But the child will be affected personally, that is why it cannot be good for a child's growth or a child's well-being. We cannot impinge upon a child's future only to fulfill your own happiness. This is a very important reason. Of course there is also the economic factor, if, let's say, if it is not economically viable for two people to be together, then there will be a lot of tension. A breakup will happen after fighting. If after spending tremendous energy and so much effort into being together, the end result is still going to be separated, then the stakes are too high. There is no point to it.

Heng also told me the reason she stayed in marriage was not to affect her son too much because of her deteriorating relationship with her husband. And it was also because her husband rejected her request to be the caretaker of their son if there is a divorce. Yet both she and Mu managed to accommodate their same-sex relationships within their heterosexual marriages with different degrees of mutual consent with their husbands.

Fake it: Co-operative Marriage

It seems that co-operative marriage is an increasingly popular option of younger informants in my research. At least for the three relatively younger married or about-to-get-married informants, a co-operative marriage is their way to cope with family and other pressuring social groups.

Co-operative marriage is not new to *lalas* and gay men in urban China. By the time I started my research in Shanghai, I had only been told about the idea of or had word-of-mouth kind of gossip about people who have co-operative marriages. But when I returned in 2006 and 2007, I heard real stories about people having co-operative marriage and later I found that some women that I had met or interviewed earlier were planning or having co-operative marriage themselves. In less than two years the once experimental idea of co-operative marriage had been enthusiastically put into real life test. The rising popularity of co-operative marriage in such a short period of time undoubtedly reflects how desperate *lalas* and gay men are to put an end to the everyday struggle of hiding their desires and same-sex relationships. Also, its popularity can be attributed to the ever expanding cyber community of *lalas* and gay men in China. Both Ling and Chris told me they found their "husbands" on the Internet. They either found the marriage partner from advertisements posted by gay men searching for a marriage partner, or from posting an advertisement themselves on lesbian or gay websites to look for a marriage partner. The process is similar to conventional matchmaking, just in this case, it is about a fake marriage of a *lala* and a gay man. The typical process of a co-operative marriage is that one party will post an advertisement or respond to an online advertisement. Then a meeting will be arranged for both parties. Very often same-sex partners of both parties will also attend the first meeting. As I was told by Ling, Chris and Tan, a co-operative marriage is not only a marriage between the *lala* and gay man involved, but also it is a marriage that will affect their respective partners. Therefore, it is in many cases, a marriage of four people. After the first meeting, if all parties consider it is a good match, then they will start to detail their plan of meeting families of the male and female sides as people will do when dating each other. If both families accept them as their daughter or son's possible mate, then they will plan further their "married life" or marital arrangements such as living arrangements, regular visits of parents of both parties, financial arrangements and so on.

Ling was a Shanghai native and lived with her parents. She had spent over a year "dating" her future husband. During this time her gay co-operative partner spent much time with her family as a boyfriend. Fortunately, her family accepted her gay partner and they had registered for marriage at the time of interview. They would have a formal wedding banquet and make their families believe they would live together in their newly bought apartment, which was actually the home of her gay partner and his same-sex partner. Ling would stay with her own same-sex partner in their own rented apartment after marriage. She told me marriage was the only way for her to move out from her parents' place and to live away from their day-to-day control. Also, after she got married, her parents would not need to cope with her sexuality. For Ling, it would be impossible for them to accept or even to understand homosexuality at all.

Tan and Ling were a couple I interviewed. Tan was also thinking about getting married at the time of interview. She had come out to her mother. Her mother had once implied to her girlfriend Ling that she would rather Tan have a fake marriage than staying unmarried and in a same-sex relationship. Ling recalled this conversation with Tan's mother:

> Actually, her mother talked to me about this problem before. She wished that I can talk to her. Even though they know of the fake marriage, they don't want the groom's side of the family to know this, that is, it's better to have a half-son who can get along with the family and live happily together, and to pretend that we don't know about this or to play a role in not knowing anything about her. Her mother feels that if everyone know it is a fake deal, it's really embarrassing, so why don't we just pretend not to know.

Therefore, Tan was thinking to find a co-operative partner and followed what Ling had done. She thought it was a way to save parents from social pressure:

> They care the most about social pressure. They think of their relations with their relatives. They feel that if this matter [Tan's marriage] can be done appropriately, then a solution can be found. If the problem is solved, then both of you can just move out. No one will bother you anymore and parents can relax.

Chris, one of the first *lala* women I met in Shanghai in 2005, told me two years later she was thinking of having a co-operative marriage. She was almost thirty when I first met her and was under severe pressure from her family to get married. She had found the right gay partner on the Internet and her wedding banquet would be held very soon. It was a relief to her parents since they had been suspicious of their daughter's sexual orientation for a number of years. Yet to Chris, although she had full control of her marriage, it was actually a marriage that she would rather never happen.

Strategizing Marriage

The fading state control over one's private life as a result of economic reform has made family the major gatekeeper of people's intimate life in China. Married *lalas* suffer the most as they are doubly burdened by their natal and conjugal families. Many *lalas* are forced to live a dual life and have their extra-marital same-sex relationships and desires hidden forever under the guise of a heterosexual marriage. The newly emergent form of gay and lesbian union, as in a co-operative marriage between a *lala* and a gay man, is an experimental way for non-normative sexual subjects to survive the everyday intimate surveillance of their families. In the present social and cultural context of China, a co-operative marriage as a fake union of love, is ironically evidence of love that many *lala* daughters and gay sons are expected to demonstrate to their parents. It is also the only "in-ing" (into the heteronormative model) that can make possible the existence of their *real* same-sex relationships.

Married *lala* informants in this research demonstrate how sexually non-normative women in China actively struggle for spaces between the two worlds of heterosexual marriage and same-sex relationship. *Lala* women who feel trapped in heterosexual marriages seek asylum in a foreign city that is away from their conjugal homes and familial obligations. More and more *lala* women of the one-child policy generation are engaging in the self-directed heterosexual performance of co-operative marriage. The new spaces or forms of *lala* household and family they have created constitute an emerging queer private sphere that can offer alternative models and discourses to the heteronormative model of intimacy. The day-to-day operation of this new form of queer family unit, its legal implications and its effectiveness as a form of spatial politics for *lalas* and gay men are yet to be examined.

6

My Unconventional Marriage or *ménage à trois* in Beijing

Xiaopei He

In the 1990s, the lesbian and gay or *tongzhi* movement started in China. I was among those organizing some activities. In 1997, some friends and I set up the first *tongzhi* pager hotline in Beijing. To avoid police harassment, we used a pager rather than a telephone line at a fixed location. Volunteers took turns to take the pager and reply to calls from all over China.

We facilitated a weekly training designed by and for hotline volunteers. The themes were decided collectively, and we all took turns facilitating the forum. Everybody was free to express ideas and opinions on the subject of homosexuality. We did not invite outside "experts". Instead, we were all the experts on our own issues. We shared the joys and difficulties of working on the hotline, and also discussed many other issues, including safer sex, homosexual identities, "coming out of the closet" (making our sexual orientation public), lesbian sex, and dealing with discrimination.

I remember during one of our many discussions some gay men said that they felt much social pressure to get married. They asked whether lesbians had similar difficulties and whether any of us would consider having fake marriages with gay men. Some people suggested that we should organize marriages between lesbians and gay men, so we could take on this pressure together. Other people said getting married would be giving into social pressure and traditional conceptions. There were a few lesbians who had already married gay men, and later on organizers for marriage between lesbians and gays came forward. The question of whether or not gay people should get married, and to whom we should be married, continued to be debated within the gay community.

In 2003, I started working for the International HIV/AIDS Alliance in China. One of our objectives was to work with and develop the gay movement in order to promote AIDS education among gay men. We ran AIDS awareness training for activists and supported them in educating their communities.

In the training sessions, I learnt that some gay activists expressed negative attitudes towards one night stands, casual sex, cross-dressing, bisexuality, and gay men marrying women. Although many people went cruising themselves, some were ashamed of doing so, and did not like to admit it themselves in large group discussion. For example, one activist said "I never visit the train station site [cruising area], but sometimes if I am passing by, I talk to people ... ", but in a private conversation later he admitted that he was into cruising.

Some participants believed that monogamy could prevent HIV/AIDS and therefore should be promoted within the gay community. Indeed some gay organizations and AIDS projects actively encourage gay people to be monogamous and stay in a relationship. During the training mixed views were expressed on gay men marrying women. Some believed that gay men who married women were either cheating them or had simply surrendered to social norms. Others said marriage takes many different forms and that a gay man and the woman who marries him are not automatically less happy than any straight couple. There were also views on discriminating against non-monogamous relationships.

In China, as in many other cultures and societies, marriage is almost compulsory. The institution of marriage not only legitimizes heterosexual and monogamous relations, but also regulates desire and pleasure. In Chinese society, many people get married including gay men marrying women (straight or not), for reasons of convenience and social pressure, but also for reasons of pleasure and through choice. On the one hand, traditional marriage is an oppressive system, and anyone can suffer from it, whether gay or straight; on the other hand, marriage can be the site of a mix of pleasures, affections and happiness.

Heterosexual marriage does not kill homosexual or bisexual desires, neither does it have to be monogamous. Of those who marry and stay married, some are heterosexuals, and some are gays or bisexuals, who negotiate their sexual lives with their partners, explicitly or implicitly, and sometimes through deception. However, the marriage institution is part of a culture which is critical of non-heterosexual and non-monogamous relationships. Consequently, gay men who marry women are often blamed by the gay community for not being gay enough, or by health authorities for transmitting AIDS and endangering society. I know some gay activists who maintain their heterosexual marriages are ashamed of talking about their marriages and thus are reluctant to talk about bisexuality.

Of course, due to gender inequality and gendered constructions of sexuality, husbands may be more likely to have multiple partners than are wives. Women may be more likely to be "faithful" and contract sexually transmitted infections from their "unfaithful" husbands than vice versa. However, this is due to gender inequality, not non-monogamy. Working for gender equality as well as acceptance of a diversity of relationships (whether straight, gay or bisexual, undefined, or a mix) is what is needed, not promotion of monogamy or monosexuality.[1]

Together with some other gay activists, I decided to organize a fake wedding to encourage further thinking about and discussion of these issues. I proposed to a gay activist who was a long-time friend, and a lesbian woman whom I had just met—I would get married to both of them. There would be three of us in a marriage: one gay man and two lesbian women, and we would have a wedding ceremony. They agreed happily.

The idea was to challenge the normative marriage, monogamy and monosexuality. Our wedding ceremony was to claim that bisexuality is not a crime. We accept homosexual, heterosexual and bisexual desires and behaviours, and we also celebrate the diversity of sexualities which might not fit neatly into these categories. Our wedding ceremony was also a call for social recognition for homosexual, non-monogamous, and other non-conforming relationships. Having one man and two women get married challenges the traditional marriage institution, while simultaneously making fun of the institution.

We invited three other people to be our "parents" at our wedding: one lesbian woman was my "father", and two gay men were the "mothers" of my groom and my bride. Over sixty guests came to our wedding. Some were our trainees, some gay activists and some AIDS activists. Others were researchers on sexuality and marriage, and personal friends from non-governmental organizations (NGOs). We wanted the wedding ceremony to be a space to discuss sexual relationships, to understand sexual desires and to communicate sexual needs. We also wanted to use the marriage institution to celebrate and legitimize all kinds of sexual relationships.

On the wedding day, I was totally over-dressed! The wedding gown was borrowed from a drag show team which performed in a Chengdu gay bar every single night and was not properly washed. Although it looked white and shiny on the outside, it was filthy and black on the inside, with lots of stains.

When I put it on, I thought how this was like many marriages—looking nice from the outside, but inside dirty, old and cheap. I also wore a huge hat made from the same material with lots of small flowers and long spikes. It looked hilariously funny! I used many hairpins to make it stay in my short hair. It hurt and was unstable—just like many marriages.

Doudou, a star from the Chengdu drag show team, was the MC (master of ceremonies) for the wedding. He was absolutely gorgeous and did my make-up for me. He made me look like a drag queen: big black eyes, bright red lipstick, and a pink and white face.

I prepared three plastic loops as wedding rings for the three of us. They were different colours and sizes. I put them together with some condoms and

Figure 6.1 Xiaopei He's wedding gown (courtesy of Xiaopei He)

Figure 6.2 Xiaopei He dressing up as a bride or drag (courtesy of Xiaopei He)

lubricant in a see-through plastic bag I found in the toilet at home. Before I left home, I saw a branch of cheap plastic flowers sitting in the corner of my flat. They were covered with dust. I took them with me to the wedding without washing them.

Figure 6.3 Xiaopei He with her wedding accessories (courtesy of Xiaopei He)

Figure 6.4 Xiaopei He's "father": So ready to send her away (courtesy of Xiaopei He)

Our "parents" were magnificent too. My "father", a lesbian woman and close friend, wore leather trousers and a tight black jacket. She also brought a leather whip and kept whipping me in the wedding, which made me sexually over-excited. Doudou's hair was dressed with standing feathers like flying wings. He wore a long black dress and a stylish coat with fabulous furs on the collar, cuff and rims.

The wedding was held in a Beijing gay restaurant with home-style Chinese food. The guests sat at the tables. The three of us—brides and groom—stood and faced the guests, and our "parents" sat in front of us. Our guests were wonderful. The discussion was sincere. People had many questions to put to the brides, groom, our parents, the MC and to each other on the topics of marriage, sadomasochism, gender, homosexuality, and AIDS prevention.

One of my mother-in-laws was a gay community organizer. He called me a "slut" and said the marriage should be stopped. The other mother-in-law was a gay bar manager from Nanjing who told dirty jokes and kept making our guests burst into laughter.

Figure 6.5 Doudou and Xiaopei He's "father" (courtesy of Xiaopei He)

Figure 6.6 Guests at Xiaopei He's wedding (courtesy of Xiaopei He)

Figure 6.7 Question-and-answer session at Xiaopei He's wedding (courtesy of Xiaopei He)

I never thought AIDS training could be so fun and inventive. Although our wedding was fake, our marriage was heartfelt. We had a certificate designed by Jose Abad (an artist and founder of Positive Art Project in China; the project uses art and drawing for people living with HIV to express their feelings and experiences). The wedding certificate was signed by many of our guests who witnessed the wedding.

Figure 6.8 Proud father holding the certificate at Xiaopei He's wedding, with three people's pictures and many signatures (courtesy of Xiaopei He)

After the wedding, I stayed in closed contact with my "husband", and we continued our discussions about sexuality. We even had a "honeymoon" together two years later to deliver speeches at a national lesbian and gay meeting in northwest China. The "mother" of my "husband" has become a close friend, who gets invited to my parties in Beijing and who will soon come to visit me in Delhi. Neither my "wife" nor my "husband" came home with me after the wedding, although my "wife" kept calling and pursuing me to consummate the marriage. However, she suspected that I might be HIV positive on the basis that I worked for the HIV/AIDS Alliance. Instead of telling her whether or not I am positive, I taught her safer sex. She was not satisfied and I lost contact with her thereafter. My "father" once paid a special night visit where we discussed S/M in detail. The discussion we had has yet to turn into action. I meet the wedding guests now and then. Many of them are now enthusiastic gay/bi activists running their own organizations. One night stands are no longer so controversial in their view, but married gay men still stay silent. As for me, I became a wedding addict. I got married one more time after the wedding in Beijing and still wonder who I will marry next. I now work in Delhi for The South and Southeast Asia Resource Centre on Sexuality, where I continue my mission to challenge marriage normativity.

III

Representations

7

Porn Power: Sexual and Gender Politics in Li Han-hsiang's *Fengyue* Films¹

Yau Ching

This chapter seeks to queer a part of Hong Kong cinema history considered to be most heteronormative through studying some of the most controversial works of one of the most prolific and influential Chinese filmmakers. Li Han-hsiang's (Li Hanxiang) (1926–96) achievement is best remembered for his big-budget, elaborate Chinese historical epics. Alongside his award-winning *huangmei diao* (romantic musicals) and *gongwei* (palace chamber) dramas, he has also directed and scripted a significant number of "smaller" and less discussed softcore pornographic films mostly set in the late Ming. These films constitute a genre of its own known as *fengyue pian*, a genre invented by Li, who was especially attracted to late Ming literature deemed obscene. In re-examining Li's film authorship of various genres in Hong Kong from the 1970s to 1990s intertextually, focusing on *fengyue* as a discursive site in foregrounding the contradictions produced by the meeting of early modern (late Ming) and contemporary (Hong Kong) Chinese desires, I seek to explore the various ways in which diverse and non-normative forms of sexual representations and spectatorships (could) have been constructed in Hong Kong cinema, including at moments when this cinema has been considered culturally traditional, as well as artistically and politically conservative. This chapter, in strategically reading between Li's genres and mapping their consistencies, traces the cultural assumptions and prejudices underlying the dismissal of *fengyue* as a genre, in contrast to Li's other genres, and the ways in which in retrospect, the invention of *fengyue* could be re-read as an interventionist response against (increasing) sexual conservatism in contemporary Hong Kong. In order to shed light on a much suppressed trajectory in Hong Kong cinema, this chapter reclaims Li as a radical classicist not only to further illuminate the political criticality of his authorship held in high regard by film history but also to highlight the ways in which this criticality was represented specifically and no less, through the representation of sexuality.

A Different Modern

In the process of working on this project, I found an overwhelming stereotype of the *fengyue* genre among Hong Kong intelligentsia. Audiences in Hong Kong somehow expect the genre to be mildly softcore, with very little or even entirely without any sexually explicit material. Once when I was cueing my clips (one of them being the action sequence of Pan Jinlian raping Wu Song in *The Amorous Lotus Pan*, discussed later in this chapter) before a paper presentation when most people had left the conference room for a tea break, a colleague responded with shock: "You're not for real, are you?". She just couldn't believe I was going to show *that* to a room full of square-faced middle-aged academics.

Li Han-hsiang has been lauded effusively by critics for inaugurating two genres of huangmei diao opera films and palace epics in Chinese cinema, but critics remain tight-lipped about the sizable body of softcore erotica known euphemistically as fengyue, literally meaning "wind and moon", that Li made upon his return to Shaw Studios in the 1970s. Should the subject ever crop up in a commentary, it was brushed off as in the following: "Run Run Shaw made him (make these films)",[2] "folding under the pressure of money" (Dou 1997: 410), "selling his soul to the lowbrow" (Dou 1997: 410), "bad taste" (Teo 1984: 96), "cynically forgoing his convictions, or obligations, as an artist" (Teo 1984: 96), losing his faith in film and sullying himself with the vulgar (Teo 1984: 93), etc.

A consummate multi-tasker, Li was shooting *Golden Lotus* (1974) while making plans for *The Empress Dowager* (1975) and *The Last Tempest* (1976), and between the little hiatus of *Empress* and *Tempest* he put out *That's Adultery!* (1975) and *Love Swindlers* (1976); when he was scouring Bangkok and Los Angeles for the elusive beast in *Tiger Killer* (1982), he set in motion the pre-production for *The Burning of the Imperial Palace* (1983) and *Reign Behind a Curtain* (1983), and timed *Palace*'s release before *Take Care, Your Majesty!* (1983) shot back to back. So what could possibly propel the critics to reach the antipodal verdict that Li has a Jekyll-and-Hyde character—the painstakingly thorough historian and meticulous filmmaker of his palace epics, and a revolting cynic who had effectively made his "statement of faithlessness" (Teo 1984: 98) with *fengyue* films? Is this assumption of artistic haves and have-nots useful in helping us understand Li's multi-tasking authorship with a vast and varied body of work? Or is it rather that steeped in our sexphobic tradition, Li's *fengyue* films are doomed to suppression, buried in oblivion, deprived of public discussion alongside their literary counterparts? Consider for example, *Forever Li Han-hsiang*, a 144-page publication (Yu 1997) that details twenty of his "*magnum opuses*", but contains a scanty one-page commentary each on *The Warlord* and *Tiger Killer* (1982), and even scantier and more ambiguous notes on his twenty odd *fengyue* films.[3]

Li Han-hsiang was the trailblazer of *fengyue* films, but the genre—one of the most important contributions he made to Hong Kong cinema history—has been shunned by film scholars and critics alike. Those few critics who did review the genre readily delineated a boundary between the "refined" (Li's "joyous but not indecent" *fengyue* films) and the "crude" (i.e. the "obscene" hardcore ones made by others), in manners similar to the dichotomy of the erotica/ pornography divide.[4] Such dichotomy is not only arbitrary (what strikes me as erotica might be porn to you, an oft-made point), it also entails a politics of deliberately desexualizing sexual imagery and representation, blatantly creating an imaginary space for cryptic referencing and inviting a sanctified reading of sexually explicit material to repress its affect of producing sexual arousal. Beneath this assumption is a hypocritical and biased moral swipe at sex as a biological, social and cultural need, and source of pleasure. Is the space of imagination created by the representation of pornographic (or erotic) materials necessarily at odds with sexual responses of the body? How likely are consumers of erotica/pornography going to attain a "sanctified" reading of the subject of sex minus the sexual responses? Is a "sublimated" reading of sex what viewers want or crave for, and if not, whom does it serve and against what standards is it measured?

"Pornography" as a category did not come into being in Europe until it had been "invented" during the process of modernization; the construction of the genre has been closely tied to the major moments in the emergence of Western modernity: the Renaissance, the Scientific Revolution, the Enlightenment, the French Revolution and the protection of class privileges of upper class males during the Victorian age (Hunt 1993; Kendrick 1987). Benefiting from the advances of printing and education, what used to be an exclusive domain of the elite could be accessed by the masses, which riled the privileged enough to turn to the legislation of pornography and to set up the dichotomy of art and pornography to protect their social advantages, regulating and keeping a curb on the circulation of sexual imagery. Urbanization, coupled with the emergence of the nuclear family, the petite bourgeoisie and the middle-class lifestyles justified a more complex regulation system which sought to limit and contain sexual expression within the private and domesticated bounds of the family.

In this chapter, I will discuss the ways in which Li's *fengyue* complicates the genre of pornography on three fronts. First, Li's body of *fengyue* work engages with film critics who struggle to unify, simplify and/or stereotype his work and the sexual hierarchies assumed in their characterization/categorization of art versus porn (versus erotica). Second, this body of work invents Chinese pornography through appropriating Chinese literary and sexual culture as a theorizing of modernity different than the one studied by Euro-American scholars, localizing and relocating a historicity of sexuality as a root to modern capitalist culture. As a migrant artist from modern China who had seen a much less evenly regulated sexuality than the one propagated in colonial Hong Kong, Li, in his writings and his films, celebrates obscene texts (*yinshu*) and obscene women (*yinfu*) as a critique of Hong Kong's desexualizing colonial modernity. Third, Li seduces his audience through a variety of cinematic styles and techniques not normative in Western porn, including the use of period drama and subtle dialogues, elaborate plots and *mise-en-scène*, shifting and multiple perspectives, centring women's subjectivity, deferral of, blocking and maintaining camera distance from sexual acts, variable self-referential rewrites of the same plot, and malleability of genders. In its endless titillating of its audience through and coupled with self-reflexive strategies, Li's *fengyue* challenges its audience to reflect on our (endless) want to be titillated as voyeurs and *only* as voyeurs, leaving us to be confronted with our *own* construction of pornography and with the fact of pornography *only* as representation.

Hong Kong Bound

Li grew up and studied western painting under Xu Beihong[5] in the turbulent days of the 1940s when the revolutionary and feudal monarchical forces collided, and his initiation into the world of modern art clashed with a wave of reorganizing sexual and gender roles that was sweeping the new China. The young Li Han-hsiang was caught up in the fervor and became a revolutionary and an exile of sorts: a stranger in the totalitarian modernizing China (of the north) and a dreamer with a yearning in both body and mind for the liberating and exuberant south in his imaginary, foundering on the shores of colonial Hong Kong.[6] These contradictory sensibilities collided and blended in Li's *fengyue* films where rare glimpses into representations of (Hong Kong and) Chinese sexual politics offer a vantage point from which to reflect on the social, political and ideological operations of his times.

The rapid urbanization and the emergence of the middle class in the 1970s and 1980s in Hong Kong coincided with Li's creative summit in the *fengyue* genre in the wake of an increasingly tight institutional control over sexual identities and behaviours. The principle of monogamy was affirmed by the law enforced in Hong Kong in 1971, stipulating that no man can lawfully take concubines or child brides as in Chinese custom, which saw non-heterosexual, polygynist and other sexual relationships outside the institution of marriage increasingly marginalized. In 1988, a three-tier film rating system came into effect, and films rated Category III became limited for exhibition to adults over the age of eighteen only. This censorship system on the one hand makes more sexually explicit representations previously banned from viewing possible, thus providing a short-term stimulus to the porn film industry in the early 1990s. On the other hand, it institutionalized the regulation of consuming sexual expression according to arbitrary age categories. Most of Li's works, produced in the 1970s and 1980s, have been available for all ages during the times of their theatrical release. But in the spring of 2007, just before the Li Han-hsiang retrospective was held at the Hong Kong Film Archive, many of these previously uncensored works found themselves classified as IIb (not recommended for teenagers and children) and III (18 or above only), leaving much of the publicity materials to be corrected last minute. In one of the symposiums held concurrently with the retrospective, Li Han-hsiang's daughter, Margaret Li, alluded to this historical irony by retelling the story of how her father enjoyed bringing his children to watch his *fengyue* films, and would not shy away from encouraging her to browse freely in daddy's collection of magazines like *Playboy* so that she could learn "aesthetics" from them. Apparently Li saw porn as a venue for the "education of desire", not unlike Richard Dyer's affinity with gay porn: "Gay porn seems to make that [education of desire] all the clearer, because there is greater equality between the participants (performers, filmmakers, audiences) which permits a fuller exploration of the education of desire that is going on. Porn involves us bodily in that education ..." (1992 [1982]: 484).

It is important to remember that locally made porn films—mainly softcore but with some hardcore too by today's standard—constituted one of the most dominant genres of the 1970s and was considered *the* most innovative genre at the time. "Explicit depiction of sex and nudity was an important feature of Hong Kong cinema in the seventies. Though the number of sex films was not as great as that of comedies and action films, it was nonetheless substantial— and besides, a good number of films incorporated all three genres. While comedies and action films reworked existing formulae, sex and nudity were 'new' inventions and 'breakthroughs'—not only in Hong Kong cinema, but in Chinese cinema as a whole" (Sek 1984: 82). "In 1973, Lung Kong's *The Call Girls* was the third top grosser, Li Han-hsiang's *Illicit Desire* and *Facets of Love* were the 5th and the 6th respective ... Among the 40 top blockbusters, 13 of them were erotic films" (Chen 2000: 50). This 1970s trend of popularizing porn films subsided in the 1980s, and except with a small comeback in the early 1990s due to the stimulus of the three-tier classification system, came all the way downhill to a Hong Kong today when almost all porn films are imported and porn is seen as an "underground" genre.

It is within a historical trajectory of contradictions in which Hong Kong has witnessed a mainstreaming of sexually explicit materials since the 1970s alongside the increasing regulation of sexuality—especially non-normative ones—in the name of modernity that Li's groundbreaking and prolonged engaging with the erotic discourse developed in late Ming fiction could be mapped as a politicizing move. Most of the novels rewritten in films by Li had emerged towards the end of the sixteenth century and flourished in the first half of the seventeenth. These novels were later categorized and policed by the Qing state as *yinshu* /"obscene books". Can the (re)making of erotica full of references to historic Chinese sexual imagery be seen as a filmmaker's response to a more disciplined space for (non-normative) sexual expression and the systemic domestication of sexual imagery in 1970s Hong Kong be a self-reflexive response to the construction of (Hong Kong) Chinese modernity? When we re-situate these films within the historical contexts wherein they were made and consumed, perhaps we could begin to discern the dissident spirit of Li's work in refusing to obey the strictures of procreative heterosexuality, not unlike the anecdotes of his newspaper column:

> There was this famed courtesan in Shanghai called Wang Wenlan who went by the nickname Supremo.[7] As the story goes, Wang threw an all-celebrity dinner party for her 14 guests, 13 men and a woman, who were big names either of the screen or stage, and who all shared one common bond—each of the fourteen of them had had an intimate episode with the hostess which therefore made her everyone's 'Babe'. Arriving in Hong Kong after the war, Wang resumed her 'old trade' and stayed true to her indiscriminatory nature ... Coming home at midnight, Wang had an encounter with an exhibitionist who was inching his way towards her while in the process of disrobing and exposing his genitalia. It was only a matter of seconds before Wang regained her composure and gave the exhibited body part a generous once-over and offered her sympathetic annotation, in her native Shanghainese: 'Jeez, innit a bit small?' As she turned away, she couldn't help but render a more refined Cantonese translation of her remark to the man's baffling 'Pardon?'...
>   A famous actor who was on his way home after a friend's wedding had a real urge to answer the call of nature. Finding a shady spot by the roadside, he unbuttoned his fly and was about to relieve himself when a cop's howl of 'Pissing in the street, Fella?' fell upon him like a thunderbolt. But an actor is an actor and he answered nonchalantly, 'Me pissing? I was just checking on John Thomas.' And lowering his head, with a deep sigh he said: 'Still the same good old John as fifty years ago.' (Li 1997b: 34–35)

These are two of the numerous sex jokes/juicy sexual narratives extracted from the column "Heaven on Earth" that Li Han-hsiang penned for the *Oriental Daily News* in the 1990s. Trading his camera for a pen as a sideline, Li was equally unequivocal in his penchant for licentious/lustful women (*yinfu*), a social type notoriously stigmatized for their expertise in breaking up (heteronormative) families or pathologized for not being able to play the virtuous feminine roles in such families themselves. Under Li's pen, the seen-it-all and had-it-all woman of the world Supremo needs no sympathy or congeniality during her second tenure down south. She easily weasels her way out of the role of a "victim" of a man who exposes himself with her sharp mind and even sharper banter. The "pissing in the Street" joke was also a parody of legislative hubris to keep private matters to homes and off the street, and to anybody who has lived in Hong Kong during the 1980s and 1990s, an obvious taunting of the pre-1997 political discourse of Sino–Hong Kong relations (China promised: "Hong Kong will remain unchanged for 50 years after 1997"). With vividly crafted language Li told two jokes, of two exhibitionist and licentious characters from both genders, both without shame in their sexuality and in fighting intimidation, both prompting their readers to ponder on sexual politics and representation, issues pertinent to understanding Li's work.

Power Relations in History

In constructing a site that seduces the erotic imagination, Li's pornographic imagery turns seemingly harmless tangible elements into a hair-raising and nerve-racking rollercoaster of sensual delights, and manifests meanings that range from the allegorical to the workings of social and political signification. Unlike most pornography made in the West, Li's *fengyue* consistently takes pleasure in classical narratives, busy with characterization, plots and camera movements, elaborate sets and costumes, understated expressions and lyrical dialogues. It is often Li's meticulous *mise-en-scène*—rather than naked bodies or the sexual acts themselves—that takes centre stage, foregrounding the power of "settings" and "narratives" in providing prohibitions, deferrals and digressions which all serve to sexualize human relationships. The cinematic quality of Li's work constantly reminds its audience that pornography as a language of sexual representation extracts its voice and potency from prohibitive contexts where sexuality is surveillanced and regulated all around. The meanings and significance of Li's pornography is derived from the power of the moral institutions, social situations/scenes and political narratives in which it has been embedded and subjugated.

Anti-porn discourses have argued that pornography universally perpetuates unequal power relations between the sexes, is demeaning to women, reinforces gender stereotypes, degrades the quality of sexual relationships and justifies sexual violence such as rape. It has also been concerned with the way the porn industry has been prejudiced against women and how its consumption is shaped by a chauvinistic view of sexuality and sexual desire (Dworkin 1981; Griffin 1979, 1981; Marcus 1981; Steinem 1978; Hong Kong Film Critics' Association

2000). Critics of *fengyue* followed a similar track: "The women of Li's *fengyue* films exploited their sexuality and functioned as sexual objects of male desires ... The worst of the *fengyue* films assume that sex is vulgar, a form of human behaviour in the same register as spitting and farting" (Teo 1997: 83–84). Li's films, however, illuminate the female protagonists' sexual subjectivity in his *fengyue* films *as much as* the women's political subjectivity in the palace epics and *huangmei diao* films: *Diau Charn* (1958), *The Kingdom and the Beauty* (1959), *Yang Kwei Fei, the Magnificent Concubine* (1962), *Empress Wu Tse-tien* (1963), *Beyond the Great Wall* (1964), *Hsi Shih: The Beauty of Beauties* (1966), and the mini Cixi series kicked off by *The Empress Dowager* (1975–83), representing a historical who's who of women with a beady eye in bed as much as on the throne. Women who have been blamed for the downfall of men (too much sex) and men's kingdoms (women with too much power) get their grievances and agencies redressed side by side in these narratives. Li's making *fengyue* films alongside epics and musicals could thus be re-read as a political intertextual strategy in commenting on women's social positioning in Chinese history, rather than as merely a financial necessity or as moral degeneration. It is through reading between Li's various genres that one might begin to see how in Chinese history, women have always been subjugated to the territory of the pornographic—were they having sex or not is besides the point—thus redressing the power of porn becomes a useful and in fact essential strategy to redress the power of women.

Rather than functioning as sexual objects of male desires and deprived of agency, women in Li's films are endowed with sharp-sightedness, courage to both love and hate, a strong sense of self-determination, and a feisty can-do-it-all spirit; they are shrews, sluts, dreamers and fighters all at once.[8] In Li's films, women are marked and admired for their boldness and agency, especially in their relation to their sex. It is in the representation of women's sexuality that the vacillating dynamics of power and resistance are most foregrounded. Inevitably imbecilic and muddle-minded, (male) emperors and/or the literati scholars who are both guarantors and victims of the feudal system pale in comparison. The released DVD of *The Amorous Lotus Pan* (1994) comes with this official synopsis: "Helmed by the aesthetic Li Han-hsiang, *The Amorous Lotus Pan* features former Blue Jeans band member Shan Li-wen [Shan Liwen/Sinn Lap-man] in a dual role as Wu Sung [Wu Song] and Hsimen Ching [Ximen Qing]. The reverse narrative tells the story of Wu Sung [Wu Song], who was pardoned from prison and seeks the libidinous Pan Chin-lien [Pan Jinlian] (Huang Mei-tsing) to avenge his brother's death. The remorseful Pan recounted her pathetic life, which began when she was traded to the rich Changs as a maid. But she was raped by her master and flirted with Hsimen Ching [Ximen Qing] and other gentleman callers ..." The film itself, however, establishes a narrative revealed through Pan Jinlian's literally gazing (back) into *her* past, with close-ups of her face and point-of-view shots, as she unfolds for the audience from the gendered vantage point her life story. While the novel *Jin Ping Mei* (Lan Ling Xiao Xiao Sheng) tends to be read as organized toward the male protagonist's point-of-view, luring the readers to identify with him as the privileged subject of the narration,[9] Li's last filmic adaptation of the novel is, from the outset, paced through a "woman's time". This is not to say that this structural device necessarily avoids all the potential violence exuded by Pan's permissive to-be-looked-at-ness, but rather carves out a spectatorial space for viewers of all genders to identify with the self-reflexive female subject looking at her own objecthood, and the negotiations in-between. In the scene in which Pan Jinlian rapes Wu Song after drugging him,[10] a moment most radically departing from the novel but one that obviously parallels Wu Song with Ximen Qing and Wu Dalang, the camera stays in a series of long shots with deep focus near the bedroom door, far from and moving along and around the bed, with veils, curtains and pieces of furniture blocking most of the shots, creating simultaneously a possible sense of critical distance from the sex act, as well as seducing the audience even more into the tabooed outburst of incestuous intimacy. While the meticulous attention to design details emphasizes the materiality of desire and power (a ploy which Li uses constantly in his palace films), the scene further perfects its art of titillation through weaving between the eyes of the (bystanding, spatially confined and not omnipresent) voyeur and the all-powerful seducer (in this case a woman), thus slowly luring its viewer-participants into a vertigo of delayed, anticipatory pleasures and the erotics of transgression. In contrast to commonplace arguments of sexual imagery seen from third-person perspectives as necessarily ineffective,[11] Li demonstrates how a choreographed shifting of diverse perspectives, produced by a combination of *mise-en-scène*, camera movements, spatial and material details could be employed to accentuate the pornographic affect.

In genres other than the historical epics, *huangmei diao* and *fengyue*, such as the romance melodrama which Li has also tried his hands at, female subjectivity also takes up a central place. *The Winter* (1967), made during Li's Grand Motion Pictures tenure, is a contemporary social realist tale of Old Wu's forbidden love for Jin which he silently buries beneath the dividing walls of class and age, the disapproving gaze of the onlookers (his brother warns him that he has "a reputation to uphold", and that "love between a man and woman shouldn't be taken frivolously"), and her marriage to another man. Jin finally returns, a divorced mother of a son, to seek solace with the man she yearns for as well as the answer to a riddle haunting both of them for decades. "You really don't seem to like me much, do you?" Jin says as she browbeats Wu into a confession long overdue in the deep of the night. Li's ambitions in subverting conventional gender stereotypes and relations, and in representing non-normative sexual relations could be traced consistently beyond his *fengyue* films, though they are most explicitly realized in his *fengyue* films. In other words, Li's films could be seen as "pornifying" cinema in order to comment on the ways in which women have long been "pornified". "First, pornification provides spaces for media performances subverting the generic conventions of porn and facilitates novel representational spaces, ideas, and agencies. Second, and perhaps more paradoxically, pornification also implies reiteration and recycling of representation conventions that are telling of the generic rigidity of porn. In this sense pornification has implications for pornography different from those for mainstream media" (Nikunen and Paasonen 2007: 30). Not only does Li's work blur the boundaries between porn and other genres, his films also push the conventional expectations of porn (and cinema) in order to foreground and challenge the ways women have been *seen as* disempowered in order to reduce the threat of women's sexuality. Through remaking porn as one of the (many) genres capable to be turned around for and about women, Li re-examines the locus of sexuality as a locus *of* women's power, and not as always already *at the expense of* women.

Rereading Lust

Among Li's *fengyue* films, the most famous are his various adaptations of *Jin Ping Mei*, five in all. The earliest is one of the episodes in *Illicit Desire* (1973) which quotes from Jin Ping Mei under the title "Tianxia Qishu" ("Wonder Book of the World"), made to test the waters for *Golden Lotus* slated for release the following year. The latter had become the benchmark of the genre and made Hu Chin (who played Pan Jinlian, translated as Lotus Pan in the English titles and subtitles in Li's films) and Tanny Tien (who played Li Ping'er) sex goddess archetypes of two appeals. Li took a leaf out of the romantic arc between Wu Song and Pan Jinlian in the novel *The Water Margin* (Shi) and concocted *Tiger Killer*, and by shifting the narrative voice to Li Ping'er put together *The Golden Lotus: Love and Desire* (1991), and finally reconstructed Pan's life from childhood on in *The Amorous Lotus Pan*. The sex scenes get more explicit with each of these renditions, true to a maverick who defied the rules of the game that *fengyue* necessarily equals "non-gamy, non-fishy",[12] "savourous", hinting towards titillating (but not graphic), contributing to the stereotype of the genre. Li helped himself to an infinitely rewritable text in offering annotations and footnotes to the "same" vernacular literary text over and again, trespassing his old selves in every step.[13] In doing so, he found creative ways to register his own limitations in each adaptation and engage with these limitations.

Branded a licentious woman (*yinfu*) in *The Water Margin*, Pan Jinlian has an illicit affair with Ximen Qing and when found out, kills her own husband. Wu Song, the victim's brother, is on the hunt for the murderer: in front of the spirit tablet of Wu Dalang, Wu Song "rips open her [Pan's] bodice. In just a fraction of a second he draws his whetted blade and stabs her in the chest. Blade between lips, he reaches for her butchered torso and guts it, sprawling its content out on the tablet as tribute. With great speed and ferociousness, he hacks off the head, and blood is spilling all over the place" (Shi 1970: 314). Song wraps the head up with a bed sheet before setting off to take on Ximen Qing. "To be devoid of love [romantic love], desire [sexual desire], and women [especially pretty ones]" (Wei 1997: 2) is the number one doctrine of the 108 heroes of *The Water Margin*, in which the biggest enemy of a hero is not ill fate, treacherous officials, or death but the temptation of a woman. Wu Song senses a threat in Pan's allure and flirtation and possibly incestuous affection for the sister-in-law he cannot fight. Writers and scholars have attempted to reverse the verdict for Pan Jinlian since *The Water Margin*. Zhou Zuoren described Shi Nai'an's depiction of Pan's death as "overtly detailed and gruesome", to the extent of "gratuitous self-lauding" as if the writer derives from it sadistic pleasure (Zhou). Wei Chongxin identifies four male archetypes: "The lewd and filthy Old Man Zhang" who rapes the teenage Jinlian, "The diminutive and sterile Wu Dalang", "The dauntless Wu Song capable of killing a tiger but incapable to love", "The sly womanizer Ximen Qing"; in total, it charted the journey of Pan's broken life, floating from one man to another: doled out by the landlord Zhang to Wu Dalang, and driven by Wu Song's rejection to the arms of Ximen Qing. "She is a plaything, a victim in the patriarchal world, a sacrifice offered by a male-dominated society, the offering on the altar of moral rectitude" (Wei 1997: 27). Pan is either touted as a rebellious woman who sees no fault in pursuing free love, or condoled for her degradation and ill-fated sacrifice in petitions written by those who have attempted to right her wrongs. Pan Jinlian in *Jin Ping Mei*, however, has been commonly read as a bad seed rotten to the core (her yielding to Zhang without putting up a fight), and step by step profiles a malicious and venomous killer (responsible for the death of Dalang and woes inflicted on Song Huilian, Laiwang, Li Ping'er, Guan'ge and Ximen Qing, the ultimate prey of her sexual aggression) thus evoking more spite than pathos for her. In the wake of this onslaught, her petitioner-scholars have sought to "rescue" this woman with a humble origin and a "fragile heart" by attributing her "tragic fate" to her "degenerated" body and soul (Zeng et al. 2000: 39–49). "Pan isn't a yinfu!", "Pan is a victim of [Ximen Qing's] lust!" have been the two main arguments made in Pan's favour, both of which embody a puritanical zealotry that echoes a Confucius condemnation of "lust as the primary evil".

In retrieving the Pan case from the closed shelves time and again, Li Han-hsiang rewrites the file of a condemned woman through, first and foremost, acknowledging her lust and her "badness". In the 35-page introduction to his script of "The Golden Lotus Trilogy", Li quotes tirelessly from passages in *Jin Ping Mei* which illustrates Pan Jilian's "licentious character" as "alive and kicking", to come to his conclusion that "C'mon, keep trying to reverse her file if you want! Pan Jinlian is too alive/strong to be reversed" (Li 1985: 40–42).

Equal Opportunity

The evolution and complexity of Li's interpretations can be further appreciated if Li's various "rewrites" of *Jin Ping Mei* are put side by side and read as provocatively and intricately woven (inter-)texts ("alive and kicking"). To reduce Pan Jinlian to a jealous but nevertheless devoted wife of the philandering Ximen Qing in *Golden Lotus* might be the biggest flaw of Li's earliest adaptation, especially in comparison with his later renditions. Li made *Golden Lotus* with the premise that there is genuine consent and mutual attraction by opening the film with the meeting of Pan and Ximen in lieu of a Wu Song-centered narrative. Suspecting an affair between his wife and the young zither player, Ximen gives the young man the boot and yanks out a whip and begins to lash Pan, who assures indignantly: "Let me tell you this. I did have a fling once. With Ximen Qing!" (This is a scene redone by Li in the later adaptations with very different overtones.) It sings of Pan's unrequited love for Ximen, aching for his care and attention which he generously parcels out amongst his women (Pan, Li Ping'er and Chunmei, among others). Under Li's camera, Pan fights tenaciously for the freedom of love and struggles to serve dutifully as a wife. Corralling the same cast as *Golden Lotus, Illicit Desire*, in contrast, features a very different and elaborate bedroom sequence that involves Ximen Qing and Song Huilian in bed and Pan outside the bedroom door. As Ximen lights the scented incense on Huilian's nipples and gives her oral sex, the camera moves onto Huilian's face and her groaning and moaning, and on Pan and her lustful gaze. The scenes are intercut, suggesting the currents of desire and passion flowing through and among them. Has the swooning woman leaning against the door just telepathed her blessing to Huilian and Ximen or invited herself to a threesome in an arena of sexual power play? Dispelling her indignation and teeth-clenching outbursts, her jealous rage finds new expression in the voyeuristic gaze which catalyzes her first foray into self-gratification and the zone of desire. Li further takes Pan to another level of proactiveness with her flirting with son-in-law Chen Jingji in the code of a cat meowing in the backyard, and affords the film a broader space for the art of titillating. Sexual imagery grows bolder and more diverse after

Golden Lotus (where Pan takes little pleasure and demonstrates much pain in masochism), manifested in Ximen's obsession with Huilian's dinky bound feet (Pan's three-inch lotus feet pale in comparison) admitting to the unbounded pleasures of foot fetishism (which the entire narrative of *Jin Ping Mei* could be said to rest on, with the first character of the novel "Jin" referring to Jinlian's name—which refers to her bound feet), and his engaging of various women in an array of experimental BDSM games, shown to be enjoyed by all parties involved. In these renditions towards a polygynist utopia playing out many subjects' desires, the binary of public vs. private (domain), upper vs. lower (order), male vs. female (gender roles), pain vs. pleasure are powerfully blurred and transgressed.

In *The Golden Lotus: Love and Desire* the sites/sights of desire become more polygamous and diverse than ever. The one-on-one sex acts in *Golden Lotus* have escalated into games of three or four (that involve Li Ping'er, Ximen Qing and two bondmaids, or Ximen Qing, Pan and Chunmei). Pan's voyeuristic gaze in *Illicit Desire* has erupted into diverse voyeuristic possibilities: Li Ping'er and Pan Jinlian are seen masturbating to pornographic books (and hence disputes the assumption by anti-porn discourse of men being exclusive users and consumers of pornography), and then educate Ximen in anal sex and perform it as illustrated. Women, young and old, find joy in voyeurism: Old Ma Feng, Li Ping'er's wet nurse, is shown blown away catching Li and Ximen in the act, thus breaking the deeply embedded taboo of elderly (women's) sex. Pan is no longer confined to the masochistic, passive roles of being flirted with, and made love to, in the marital chamber in *The Golden Lotus: Love and Desire*. She actively seduces the zither boy (which she is wrongly accused of doing in Li's earlier *Golden Lotus*), strips the clothes off the maid and whips her naked (a treatment she has been subjected to), and lords over Ximen in the bedroom. Although in bondage, she bellows commands at Ximen like a drill sergeant—"Don't you stop! Keep going!" These scenes know no boundaries of age (the players range from sixteen to sixties), sex, the direction of the sexual gaze and sexual act traffic, parading a dazzling variety of sex in its many manifestations and in doing so, making the seeking of sexual pleasure by both men and women (and not only Pan) in (and outside) the filmic text seem like an everyday event.

Reconfiguring Gender

Li Han-hsiang's strategies in facilitating his audience's identification with female subjectivity could be witnessed through his renditions of male characters as venues for critique and parody. Wu Song, the hero in *Tiger Killer*, announces self-righteously: "I want to see (if you have) your heart!" holding a knife about to plunge in Pan, whereas Pan protests: "My heart is made of flesh, unlike yours— of stone!" *Tiger Killer* the film is largely faithful to *The Water Margin* the novel but Pan's seduction of Ximen is portrayed as her dire effort to fill the emotional void left by Wu Song's rejection. The moral lesson: "venomous is a woman's heart" (as the source of all evil) in *The Water Margin* is unlearned as "stone-hard is a man's heart" takes its place.

The Amorous Lotus Pan is not only Li's last annotation and conclusion to the serial adaptation but could also be seen as his response to Clara Law's *The Reincarnation of Golden Lotus* (1989) released a few years back, in which Joey Wang plays the contemporary reincarnation of Pan Jinlian. In Law's adaptation, her doomed encounter with Wu Song begins in the Mainland during the Cultural Revolution. Their reunion comes too late for Pan who has already married his brother, the cake shop owner Wu Dalang in Yuen Long (a suburban town located in the New Territories of Hong Kong mostly seen to be populated by new immigrants and the working class). Reclaiming her right to pursue happiness as a modern woman, Jinlian, when called a slut by Wu Song, rebukes him with: "You said you love me so why didn't you leave with me? You're a jealous coward faking as a martyr and I have nothing but contempt for you! So leave your brother alone and be done with me!" Wu Song's last-ditch effort to "start all over again" (a favourite trope with Hong Kong films, as if the ways things go are always wrong) is thwarted by his fatal car accident. This romanticized tale of star-crossed lovers seeks to clear Pan's name by transferring the stigma away from Pan to the country bumpkin cum nouveau riche Wu Dalang who stands for "banality", Ximen Qing for "lust" ("sexual promiscuity"), and "adultery" repudiated by Hong Kong's apparently modern legal system and moral dogma that (re)define the bounds of sexual expression. While re-appropriated as a feminist symbol of a woman's right to "free" love, the late 1980s Pan Jinlian in *The Reincarnation of Golden Lotus* conforms and contributes to a homogenized Hong Kong modernity partly constructed through the ideologies of romantic equalitarian coupledom, monogamous marriage and middle class superiority.

However, Li revisiting Pan Jinlian in the early 1990s gives her yet another new reading. As in *The Reincarnation of Golden Lotus*, Wu Song receives his share of backlash from Pan in *The Amorous Lotus Pan*: "You have the daring to kill a tiger but not to touch a woman ... Ximen Qing does all the women in the world but why can't I? ... You're such a chicken that you wouldn't dare run away with me. I did you but a loser like you only think[s] and never act[s]. So save your acts of fake generosity and moral superiority and kill me if you must. Grab your knife and plunge it in right here!" Pan then goes on to rip her clothes to bare her chest, as if to throw down a challenge to her executioner, who dissolves in painful wails while avoiding meeting the eyes of his "victim". Her death is portrayed as less an "honour killing" by the righteous brother-in-law than foul play on a subject/object of affection at whom the sexually inhibited man directs his fear and frustration to love and be loved. When Pan said she "did him", she did so after spiking his drink and forcing herself on him. The scene marks the climax of the film, in which Wu Song revels in the warmth of Pan in his drug-induced stupor and outburst of sexual repression. Sobering up, Wu races to the garden, throws himself down on his knees, and pours out his confession of sin in the rain: "I'm sorry for what I did to you, Brother!" This is a flare-up of a man who has unwittingly unlocked the moral shackles of desire, foreshadowing Pan's death under his blade.

Gender becomes malleable in the pornographic imagination and contingent upon the context in which it is expressed, as demonstrated by Pan Jinlian in *The Golden Lotus* and *The Golden Lotus: Love and Desire*, who slips from the role effortlessly as the worn-out lover, panting and pleading "please spare me" with great tenderness to another where she effects the shrew who dopes and ravages Wu Song and Ximen Qing.[14] " [P]ornography's fantasy is also of gender malleability, although one in which it's women who should be the malleable ones. Whereas feminism's (and romance fiction's) paradigm of gender malleability is mostly that men should change. It's possible that the women who are most adversely affected by pornography are those most invested in the idea of femininity as something static and stable, as something inborn that inheres within us" (Kipnis 1999: 200). It is noteworthy that while Kipnis registers that the feminine gender is much more malleable than the masculine in (Western, heterosexual-biased) pornography, creating "a fantastical world composed of two sexes but one gender", scholars of Chinese literary and cultural studies (Vitiello 1996, 2000; Sommer 2000; Song 2004) have charted a vibrant trajectory of (largely unlexicalized) gender- and sexual-variant subjectivities. These subjectivities developed during late Ming towards the material experience of the body, and clarifies the intellectual contingencies of the emergence of pornography (and its convergence with philosophy) and the discourses on sex and gender articulated therein. Vitiello (1996) argues persuasively that the gender fluidity characterized by (male) heroes who wears both "cap and hairpins" epitomizes in fact a *moral* negotiation between the masculine and the feminine—hybrid "exemplary sodomites" whose romantic originality and perfection is produced by setting the female virtues in an equally virtuous male body, resulting in a movement towards more holistic life forms (of desire) as well as towards a greater sense of integrity and spiritual cultivation (also seen as a form of desire). In these pornographic literary texts, malleability of the masculine gender is the norm; desire leads to salvation *and vice versa*.

Li draws from the resourceful and voluptuous tradition of Chinese erotic/ pornographic literature to talk back to the gender and sexual norms of Hong Kong in the 1990s. Filling the shoes of the tiger-killing hero of *The Water Margin* and *Jin Ping Mei* in both Law's *The Reincarnation of Golden Lotus* and Li's *The Amorous Lotus Pan* is Pal Sinn Lap-man, who doesn't look like or even try to act the part. Using the same lead from *The Reincarnation of Golden Lotus* (where he played Wu Song) to play both Wu Song and Ximen Qing in *The Amorous Lotus Pan*, Li's film helps the audience to rethink how the conventions of masculinity, as historical constructs, have evolved from the macho guerrilla-fighting world of *The Water Margin* to "civilized" Hong Kong in the 1980s, foregrounding Sinn as a fine specimen of the moaning, self-pitying and self-loathing sap that frequented Hong Kong cinema in the 1980s and 90s (how unlike Wu Song), and sexually and emotionally inhibited (how like Wu Song). Through establishing Ximen Qing as the "double/stand-in" for Wu Song (and not as the counterpart), this double casting builds in an internal critique of the interchangeable male (Wu Song and Ximen Qing), rendering Pan Jinlian's desires and tragedy in unprecedentedly sympathetic lights, and further highlights the gender malleability of men, both in late Ming and in contemporary Hong Kong, perhaps for different reasons but no less malleable and doubled.

Seeing/Wanting/Making More

Li's pornographic texts expresses our primary longing for plenitude (Pan Jinlian to Ximen Qing: "Don't you stop!"), and foreground the ways in which such desires have been "endlessly activated to keep us tied to the treadmill of the production-consumption cycle" (Kipnis 1999: 202). As a director of more than fifty films, including five rewrites of *Jin Ping Mei*, situated in the historical contexts of a Hong Kong of the 1970s to the 1990s increasingly driven by the capitalist work ethic, Li could be seen as a producer working in and for an economy of desire in which there is always not enough as much as there is always too much. His tireless authorship preempts/seduces/produces an equally tireless spectatorship which, through his films, bears witness to Pan Jinlian's insatiable drive for more sex.

Pan Jinlian's life (where work and sex have always been metonymic with each other) becomes his work becomes our desire. From *The Golden Lotus: Love and Desire* to *The Amorous Lotus Pan*, the audience is led to increasingly reflect on Pan Jinlian's position as a worker (motivated and gifted no doubt) on this turf of sexuality—a turf which Pan, like almost all women in *Jin Ping Mei*, has been designated to occupy and one she has perfected her skills to capitalize on. Told in retrospect, *The Amorous Lotus Pan* unfolds Pan's life stories of her childhood experience, deadly encounters with Wu Da, equally deadly encounters with Wu Song and marriage with Ximen Qing, as they are framed through her present status of a *thing* up for retail sitting in Wang Po's chamber. "So ill-fated all my life I know not happiness. I work and pray for a better day but something, somewhere always turns out wrong". The film has Pang bemoaning her fate, defending her unrelenting quest for lust as a form of resistance against such fate ("I *work* and pray for a better day"), while Wang Po gets to speak on behalf of sex workers and their *mamasans* (brothel madams): "Yours [wives'] are wholesale, and I do retail". At this stage Wang Po not only acts explicitly as Pan's agent and retail broker but Pan, in the interim between jobs (mediated through Wang Po), also does what she does best in taking the initiation to seduce Wang Po's adolescent (uninitiated/virgin) son, thus again turning the tables on herself as a product being sold to becoming the driver of the ebb and flow of her young owner's desires. "... [B]ondmaids-concubines are punished for familial maneuvering and sexual opportunism, via precisely the sex that constitutes their sole resource and recourse to power in the intimate politics of polygamous everyday life" (Ding 2002: 165).

Porn Power and Salvation

In both the episode "The Child Groom" in *Legends of Lust* (1972) and the similarly plotted "Lady of the Hans" in *Madame Bamboo* (1994), a twenty-something girl is coerced into marrying a child heir of a rich family. In protest against the forced marriage of convenience, the (lower class) lover of the (upper class) bride storms into the nuptial chamber and makes love to her the whole night, right next to the (upper class) child groom tied to a chair, with the child's father, his high class acquaintances and police officers pounding helplessly outside. In the last episode of *Legends of Lust* "The Cuckold", the wife, in order to have adulterous sex with the steward, choreographs a scene where a tree in their garden becomes a "licentious tree" (*yinshu*), and one who climbs on it would see everybody down below naked and/or performing sexual acts. Lured into testing its magical powers himself, the landlord husband gets to see the shocking sights of not only his wife having sex with his servant in the garden in broad daylight, but also the bondmaids in line bringing desserts and tea into the garden stark naked—a sight that drives him mad according to the wife's proud recall. These episodes strike as a powerful force to strip naked and destabilize established power structures, political, class, gender and moralistic regulatory forces (you fantasize what you fear; you see what you fantasize). Pornography (what you see under the spell of *yinshu*) is literally represented here as a crucial political space for civil disobedience: an invitation to explore, enjoy and express sexuality and sexual imagery sanctioned and exiled by the statist male (husband's/father's/police) gaze and the public sphere, denounced as obscene, indecent, immoral, unfaithful, or simply mad. It is also foregrounded as a *necessarily* self-willed fantastical space simultaneously constituted by regulation and one which allows (temporary) exemption from personal liability, class, gender, moral and legal constraints, where one may experience (dangerous) possibilities for redistributing bodily and social resources with previously unregistered scenarios.

Looking at *Fengyue* Looking at You

Li's pornography is, for me, an irresistible invitation to contemplate the pornographic nature of visual images, which perhaps brings me closer to some of the anti-porn arguments than they might have originally intended. "It (pornography) ends with a root meaning 'writing about' or 'description of' which puts still more distance between subject and object, and replaces a spontaneous yearning for closeness with objectification and a voyeur" (Steinem). Whether it is peeping through the camera viewfinder at the activities inside the bedroom across the street in *That's Adultery!*, or peeping through a telescope at Lee Pang-fei sneaking stolen glances at "The Carnal Prayer Mat" in *Take Care, Your Majesty!*, or blatantly gleaning details of what's going on behind the closed doors by backyard voyeurs, we as viewers find ourselves feasting on the sights arising from an innate need for voyeurism which gives birth first to pornography, and then to cinema. The pear tree in *Legends of Lust* becomes an erotically charged symbol during a game played most energetically by the hoaxer and the hoaxed, turning actuality into erotic virtuality, and vice versa. And loitering between the two realms, Hu Chin in *That's Adultery* flashes a bewitching, self-reflexive glance into the camera, teasing her husband who caught her in the act as well as those on the other end of the camera with a mesmerizing smile: "Everything that (you just saw) happen was a misunderstanding. It's all been a misunderstanding!", followed by the Shaw trademark on the freeze frame of her smile (Figure 7.1). It is a delectable joke made directly in the face of the "fourth look" (Willemen 1992), which catches the audience in an act of cinematic voyeurism and causes shame, reminding the audience that they have been conflating materiality with reality, taking the fantastical for the real; it is also a contemplative gaze at this film language at once familiar and defamiliarized, spellbinding, passionate, truly obscene and unapologetic, hence political and pornographic.

Figure 7.1   Freeze frame at the ending of *That's Adultery!* (frame capture)

Conclusion

In rewriting some of the possible meanings of some of Li Han-hsiang's key *fengyue* films, this essay seeks not to uncover the "truths" of sex or of porn, but rather to explore the various subject positions enabled by these texts and their authorship. Linda Williams (2008: 326) has confessed in her study of porn, "the very act of screening has become an intimate part of our sexuality". This small study—rather unprecedented in Hong Kong as well as Chinese cinema studies— aims to explore and take seriously the ways in which Li's work has contributed not only to our cinema history but also to the construction of our sexuality, while such an intimate relationship has been historically denied. Finally, I would add that this history of self-denial is perhaps also an intimate (and invisible) part of our sexuality in contemporary Hong Kong.

8

Queering Body and Sexuality: Leslie Cheung's Gender Representation in Hong Kong Popular Culture[1]

Natalia Sui-hung Chan

> "It's more appropriate to say I'm bisexual," [Leslie] Cheung notes. "I love the film *Gone With the Wind*. And I like Leslie Howard. The name can be a man's or woman's, it's very unisex, so I like it."
>
> (Corliss 2001: 46)

Top Canto-pop star and Hong Kong actor Leslie Cheung proclaimed his bisexuality in an interview in 2001 after finishing his last concert tour, the *Passion Tour*, during which he wore six Jean Paul Gaultier outfits, from a white tux with angel wings to a naughty skirt and long black wig. His bisexuality is not only revealed by the English name he adopted in the early 1970s when he attended high school in England but also by his androgynous appeal on stage and cross-dressing in films in the 1990s.

Born in 1956, Leslie Cheung Kwok-wing was the youngest son of a Hong Kong tailor who made suits for William Holden and Alfred Hitchcock (Corliss 2001: 46). Cheung was brought up by his grandmother and did not have a happy childhood but rather one marked by quarrels, fights and family conflicts. After a year studying textile management at the University of Leeds, he returned to Hong Kong and later won first runner-up in ATV's Asian Music Contest in 1976. He began his career as a TV actor from 1978 to 1985 on local television programmes where he was typically cast as a rebellious youth or an aristocrat because of his angular features, delicate beauty and noble gestures. He released his album *Restless Breeze* in 1983, which launched his career as one of the most popular singers in Hong Kong. He released over 50 albums, including *Summer Romance* (1987), *Virgin Snow* (1988), *Side Face* (1988), *Salute* (1989), *Final Encounter of the Legend* (1990), *Red* (1996), *Big Heat* (2000) and *Crossover* (2002), in Hong Kong, Taiwan, Japan and Korea beginning in the mid-1980s, and won numerous music awards including the golden prize of best male singer as well as accomplished performer in both Hong Kong and Asian music festivals. Although Cheung started his film career in the late 1970s, he did not receive much public attention until 1987 when he starred in John Woo's *A Better Tomorrow* and Stanley Kwan's *Rouge*. He was awarded best actor at the Golden Film Festival in Hong Kong for his brilliant performance in Wong Kar-wai's art film *Days of Being Wild* in 1991. He gained international recognition later when Chen Kaige's gay opera film *Farewell My Concubine* was awarded Best Foreign Picture at the Golden Globe Awards in France in 1993.

As a Canto-pop singer, Cheung distinguished his stage performance by his seductive image of a dandy in the 1980s and his crossover style in the 1990s. As an actor, he presented his charm, tenderness and elegance in such films as *Rouge* (1987) and *A Chinese Ghost Story* (1987) and his gay femininity in *Farewell My Concubine* (1993), *He's a Woman, She's a Man* (1994) and *Happy Together* (1997). He put an end to his glamorous life at the age of forty-six when he leapt to his death from the twentieth-fourth floor of the Mandarin Oriental Hotel on 1 April 2003. Cheung's suicide became the top story in Hong Kong as well as other Asian cities, for he represents a queer figure of gender-crossing unprecedented in the history of Hong Kong popular culture.[2] My chapter discusses the cross-gender identity of Cheung. What I interrogate includes Cheung's crossover style and intersexuality in music videos, his androgynous dressing and make-up in concerts and the multiple images of his male/gay femininity in films. My purpose is to investigate the body politics, the sexual identity and the gender performativity of Leslie Cheung as a queer subject of position.

Theorizing Cheung's Bisexuality and Androgyny

> My mind is bisexual. It's easy for me to love a woman. It's also easy for me to love a man, too. (Law 2003: 19; all translations between Chinese and English mine)

> I believe that a good actor should be androgynous, and ever changing. (Lam 2002: 55)

Cheung made the above personal statements in two interviews in 1992 and 2002, respectively. The former declares his own sexuality while the latter presents one of his central ideas about film acting. Cheung's proclamations interestingly echo Virginia Woolf's notion of androgyny. Woolf believed that there are two sexes in the mind corresponding to the two sexes in the body. In *A Room of One's Own*, Woolf proposed the idea of androgyny as the normal and comfortable state of being. She wrote:

> ... in each of us two powers presides, one male, one female ... a great mind is androgynous. It is when this fusion takes place that the mind

is fully fertilized and uses all its faculties ... It is fatal to be a man or woman pure and simple; one must be woman-manly or man-womanly. (88–94)

Woolf believed that androgyny is the unity of mind that helps to fully develop one's sex-consciousness, human creativity and vitality. Being woman-manly or man-womanly means that the female side and the male side of the mind collaborate in order to accomplish the art of creation. Such collaboration helps the whole of the mind lie wide open so that writers can communicate their experiences with perfect fullness. On the other hand, it is dangerous and incomplete to use only one side of the mind because it makes artists protest against the equality of the other sex by asserting the superiority of their own. As an accomplished actor and stage performer, Cheung's ideas of androgyny and bisexuality show the multiplicity and complexity of his gender concerns. To be androgynous and ever-changing means that an actor should possess a certain kind of capability and capacity which helps him to play different characters with various types of sexes, temperaments, qualities, and gender identities. Being androgynous serves as a way to act and role-play fully, that is, to play a man within a woman or a woman within a man. Being man-womanly, for example, can refer to Cheung's feminine, passive and elegant image in *Rouge*, and his campy and gay femininity in *Farewell My Concubine* and *Happy Together*. It can also refer to his drag queen performances in concerts and music videos.

In *Farewell My Concubine*, Cheung plays the Peking opera cross-dresser Chen Dieyi, who passionately falls in love with his heterosexual male partner Duan Xiaolou. It is a story about the love affairs and struggle for survival of two male operatic singers during a period of political turmoil in early modern Chinese history. Dieyi and Xiaolou grow up together in a Peking opera troupe, and train to be the most popular performers from the 1930s to the 1960s in Beijing. With his elegant mannerisms and feminine voice, Dieyi plays the male-to-female transvestite in such classical dramas as *Farewell My Concubine*, *Peony Pavilion* and *The Drunken Concubine*. He devotes himself and all his efforts to the art of Peking opera while at the same time being affectionately attached to Xiaolou, on whom Dieyi deeply depends in everyday life and with whom he is very much in love. However, Dieyi's homosexuality is suppressed and condemned by the social mass. Xiaolou refuses Dieyi and finally marries a prostitute. In the final scene, it is the end of the Cultural Revolution in China where Dieyi and Xiaolou are offered to perform the drama of "Farewell My Concubine" again onstage. Dieyi cross-dresses as the Concubine Yu, the sole woman who stays with the King in wartime. In the last dancing sequence, in order to be faithful to the King and to preserve his everlasting love for Xiaolou, Concubine Yu in the play and

Dieyi in real life commit suicide by cutting her/his throat with a sword. Dieyi dies in his/her most glorious moment of life during which he/she buries his forbidden love and homosexual desire.

There is a certain kind of *doubleness* of Cheung's acting in *Farewell My Concubine*. S/he is the woman who sacrifices her/himself for the King onstage, and at the same time, he is also the man who adores Xiaolou off the stage. Acting a man within a woman or a woman within a man, Cheung is both Dieyi and the concubine in the androgynous sense. His queerness in the film is explicated in terms of his gay femininity in which he not only doubles his image, woman-manly or man-womanly, on and off the stage but also accomplishes his fullness both in acting and sex-consciousness. In an interview, Cheung explained that Dieyi is an egocentric person like him. Dieyi is a tragic figure because he was abandoned by his mother in his early childhood and has never had a happy life except when he performs and acts on stage. Cheung further pointed out that he did not want to be Dieyi but felt proud to perform such a brilliant and tragic character.[3] On the one hand, it is Cheung's male femininity that enables him to achieve Dieyi's artistic image in the movie, and on the other hand, it is also Dieyi's tragic sense of being that fulfills Cheung's fantastic role-playing in gender-crossing. Cheung's androgyny not only collapses the gender line between man and woman but also creates an alternative space for gender performance in a bisexual sense.

In her "The Laugh of Medusa", the French feminist critic Helene Cixous explains that bisexuality is each one's location in self of both sexes, nonexclusive either of the difference or of one sex. It is the multiplication of the effects of the inscription of desire and body (1996: 341). Although Cixous's discourse mainly concerns female sexuality,[4] we can broaden her concept and extend her discussion to gender-crossing. Bisexuality, in Cixous's terms, is the multiplicity of gender in relation to sex and body. It is the self-consciousness of both sexes inscribed in the body that evokes a multiple and changing sexuality. It transgresses the binary opposition of the two-sex system on the one hand, and on the other, goes beyond the boundary of masculinity and femininity. "My mind is bisexual" and "a good actor should be androgynous": What Leslie Cheung proclaims is his body politics and intersexuality of gender representation. Bisexuality, here, should be understood in metaphorical sense. It refers not only to Leslie's sexual orientation,[5] but also to his tactic of intervention in acting skill. However, Kristeva states in her "Manic Eros, Sublime Eros: On Male Sexuality" that "androgyny is not bisexuality". This is because bisexual implies that each sex is not without some characteristics of the other and would lead to a nonsymmetrical doubling on both sides of sexualization. As to the androgyny, "he is unisexual: he is two of himself, conversant onanist, bounded totality, heaven and earth jammed together" (1987: 70). That means that bisexuality is the component parts of one's sexuality in which we can distinguish the unique expression of male femininity or female masculinity. Androgyny, on the other hand, is the faultless and perfect selves that merged together. Under these theoretical considerations, Cheung's proclamation contains a certain kind of contradiction. How can an actor be bisexual and androgynous at the same time? Perhaps we have to rethink Cheung's notion from his original language or linguistic expression. *Bisexual*, which is *shuangxing* in Chinese, and *androgyny*, or *cixiongtongti*, carry a similar connotation in Cheung's interpretation and linguistic usage. They both refer to the doubling of one's sex. Cheung used them to describe his acting skill in film and on stage, which is the impersonation, performativity as well as the ability of putting oneself in and changing oneself from one gender to another. In other words, both masculinity and femininity can be interchanged under his mode of remaking. It was a state of flux and an act of flowing that he always emphasized as "intersexuality" from time to time in his performance. His sex-consciousness was doubled or multiplied by his embodiment of androgyny from which a new kind of male femininity or female masculinity was created. In other words, it was his male body that embodied femininity, and at the same time, surpassed the physical marks of gender and sexuality. Figure 8.1 from his drag performance in *Leslie Cheung Live in Concert 97* displays Cheung's androgynous body and his bisexuality on stage. The make-up, the accessories, and the pink high heels he wears juxtapose with the physical marks of his male body like the short haircut, the flat chest, his male voice and his Adam's apple. In her discourse on unisex and fashion style, Rebecca Arnold points out that "androgyny seeks to unite male and female, masculine and feminine in one body" (2001: 122). It is the

androgynous body that masquerades, fuses and confuses one's own outer appearance and inner sexuality. The rhetoric of cross-dressing in his concerts, as Cheung explained, is meant to express a femininity that he had within. He destabilized the conventional gender distinctions and reconstructed the erotic fantasy by acting out a man crossover in woman's clothes.

Figure 8.1 Leslie Cheung's drag on stage, 1997 (courtesy of Daffy Tong)

Cross-dressing and Camp Sensibility: Intersexuality and Intertextuality

Leslie Cheung's drag performance in Figure 8.1 can be defined as "working with pieces" on stage (Garber 1997: 152). It is a mixed and self-contradictory style of cross-dressing in which the artifactuality of the "feminine" or the "feminine pieces" is acknowledged by the juxtaposition with the masculine body and clothing. Cheung's drag performance is androgynous in the sense that sex and clothes are both interchangeable. In *Orlando*, Woolf announced that sex can be taken on and off like clothing since "there is much to support the view that it is clothes that wear us and not wear them; ... they mould our hearts, our brains, our tongues to their liking" (Weil 1992: 157). The politics of drag, in other words, is to subvert gender categories and identities, complicate the interplay of sexualities, and double or multiply the possibilities of gender effects in cultural representation. In *Leslie Cheung Live in Concert 97*, Cheung's drag queen image stylizes his gay male femininity in three aspects. First, his androgynous figure embodies a certain kind of intertextuality and intersexuality of masculinity and femininity. It offers a double reading and expression of body politics. If clothing is a social metaphor of gender, then Cheung's transvestism not only denaturalizes the signification of sex and sexuality but also interplays the boundary-crossing of gender construction. What he visualizes onstage is the artifactuality and performativity of gender. He mounts a new production of self by breaking the rule of the social metaphor of clothing within the binary system of sex. Second, Cheung's "working with pieces" is formulized by camera movements and angles.

The music video of the concert we now have contains many close-ups of Cheung's body parts and his accessories. The shots are quick and short. Both Cheung's body and his clothing are cut into pieces. We have his hands and the ring, his face and the make-up, the high heels and the dancing steps—piece by piece on screen without any coherence or connection. The audience can reorganize and reconstruct the whole and complete image of the singer by using free association and imagination. The video creates a seductive plane of fantasy in which Cheung represents himself as a queer object of desire. Besides, the "working with pieces" of the camera also blurs the gender line of Cheung's sexuality. The pieces of his body parts and the close-ups of his clothing depict an incomplete picture of the subject in which gender identity is unrecognizable. We may be seeing a woman's hand wearing a diamond ring or we may be seeing a lady's legs with a pair of pink heels dancing on the screen. The images signify the illusion of appearance and the playfulness of gender. Third, Cheung's gay identity is pronounced in his drag performance when he makes close body contact with the handsome and sexy male dancer Chu Wing-lung. Their body gestures, facial expressions and eye contact are seductive and erotic. The dance, the song and the music compose a drama in which Cheung acts as a gay lover of fatal attraction who is self-willed, sensitive and flirtatious. He makes himself an object to be gazed upon by presenting a bewitching smile, an effeminate manner, and rhythmic body movements and dance steps. His queer subjectivity, consequently, was constructed through his body politics of drag and gay consciousness. The male dancer Chu recalled in an interview in 2004 that Cheung was a talented and brilliant dancer. It was the film *Happy Together* that inspired Cheung to design the dance step sequences for *Red*. He not only breaks the traditional rule of heterosexual couples in dancing form but also artistically creates an ambiguous image beyond the gender line onstage, which is neither male nor female but a combination of the two (Chu 2004: 34–35). With the heavy beat of the music acting like a heartbeat and the flashes of lighting projecting the erotic sense of imagination, Cheung's androgynous body and phantasmal image construct a new dimension of male femininity, which is sensual, mysterious and elegant.

There are a lot of dancing scenes of the two male protagonists in *Happy Together*, which symbolize homoeroticism as well as the exoticism of the film. Two gay lovers, Bo-wing (Leslie Cheung) and Yiu-fai (Tony Leung), start their journey from Hong Kong to Argentina in 1997 before the handover of the colonial city. Theirs is not only a physical journey from a hometown to a foreign country but also a cultural search of (queer) sexuality and identity.[6] One day, Yiu-fai buys a souvenir lamp in Buenos Aires and both of them are attracted by the lampshade of the Iguazu Fall. They decide to go to the waterfall together but they lose the way in the middle of their journey. At the same time, Bo-wing is tired of staying with Yiu-fai, then the two lovers separate. Yiu-fai works at nights for a living at a gay tango bar and encounters a series of conflicts in his love-hate relationship with Bo-wing. In *Happy Together*, Cheung plays an erotic gay lover who is self-indulgent, willful and dissolute. He betrays Yiu-fai from time to time and goes around with different lovers every night. William Cheung, the art director of the film, commented that Cheung perfectly embodied the loneliness as well as the turbulent state of emotion of the character. He was so well prepared for the role and performed it so well that some people misunderstand Cheung to be the same kind of person he portrayed.[7] In fact, Cheung was self-controlled, tidy and serious in real life rather than wicked and selfish. He had spent a lot of time and effort fathoming and learning the personality of Bo-wing (Cheung 2004: 44). In these regards, Cheung's acting skill was based on his personal understanding and exuberant imagination of the character. He was particularly competent in acting the sullen and recalcitrant youth who possesses both good and evil sides to his character.[8] It is also interesting to note that the gay image of

Happy Together, to a certain extent, was designed by the director Wong Kar-wai in a feminine way. It is Yiu-fai's gentleness, virtuousness and patience played by Tony Leung and Bo-wing's tenderness and reliance by Leslie Cheung that explicates the feminine side of men. Such gender role playing is symbolically put in the dancing sequences of the two protagonists. The dancing scenes in *Happy Together*, performed within a stylistic setting of lotus-flower wallpaper pattern and colourful interior design, present the intimacy, the romantic love and the ecstasy of the two gay lovers. The director tactically adapts the melancholy, decadent, and erotic music of Argentinean musician Astor Piazzolla. The musical pieces that Wong chooses include "Milonga for Three" and the prologue and the finale of "Tango Apasionado", which are full of melodic and rhythmic complexity.[9] Combining the sensuality of the music and the body gestures of Cheung and Leung, the dancing sequences in *Happy Together* powerfully convey homoerotic feelings of love and lust, pain and passion. Cheung, with his sexy mannerisms, body movements, facial expressions and dancing steps, incarnates all the campy qualities of a gay lover.

In her "Notes on Camp", Susan Sontag explained that "camp" is a sensibility of artifice and stylization, a quality discoverable in objects and the behavior of persons; and "androgyny" is one of the great images of camp sensibility, for the most refined form of sexual attractiveness and sexual pleasure consists in going against the grain of one's sex: "What is most beautiful in virile men is something feminine; what is most beautiful in feminine women is something masculine" (Sontag 1983: 106–108). According to Sontag, a camp image embodies the form of androgyny in terms of travesty, impersonation and theatrical role-playing. It is the convertibility of man and woman. Although Sontag did not mention the concept of "drag", her ideas about "camp" and "campy taste" do imply the meanings of transvestism and performativity later developed by Marjorie Garber and Judith Butler respectively. In addition, although Sontag's discourse concerns the new art that emerged from the eighteenth to the early twentieth century, it can also be applied to Cheung's gender-crossing in films and popular music in an Asian queer context. Not only can we refer Cheung's early image in the 1980s to the "modern dandyism" discussed by Sontag, but we can also examine Cheung's gay femininity, bisexuality and androgyny in stage performance since the 1990s with reference to camp sensibility. To Sontag, camp is a cultural product of the age of mass culture. It is formulated by the psychopathology of affluence in society. "Camp is the modern dandyism" means that the dandy is a mass-produced object in an age of mass culture and affluence (Sontag 1983: 116–117). Camp represents a new personal taste and a modern style of living, which receives social appreciation, admiration, or even replication.

The 1980s was Hong Kong's heyday in terms of political stability, economic growth and social prosperity. It was also the golden age of the development of Hong Kong popular culture and consumerism in which the production of music, film and TV programmes reached its highest standard of international recognition, and products were promoted widely in overseas markets like Taiwan, Japan, Korea, Singapore and Malaysia. As for Cheung, he grew up in a wealthy family where his father had three wives and owned a lot of land and property in Hong Kong. Cheung announced his campy taste and dandyism in his youth by wearing suits by Jean Paul Gaultier, YSL and Giorgio Armani (Figure 8.2). His dandyism was characterized by his aristocratic manners in everyday life and the image of Prince Charming or the unconventional lover he conveyed in popular songs. As mentioned before, Cheung broke through his popular image in the 1990s by introducing his androgyny and gender-crossing both in musical performance and film acting. He even announced his gay relationship with the banker Daffy Tong in a concert in 1997. His homosexual coming-out earned him a higher prestige in gay communities in Hong Kong, Taiwan, Japan and overseas Chinese communities. He continued wearing the fashion of YSL, Jean Paul Gaultier, Alfred Dunhill and Dior Homme but in a different form of embodiment. Unlike his heterosexual figure in the 1980s, he blurred the gender line between masculine and feminine. As Andrey Yue points out, Cheung "lured with lovelorn lyrics, teased with androgyny and re-defined norms. He was a crossdresser. He was everybody's favourite Gor Gor. Teenage girls and boys, lesbian, gay and straight" (2003: 39). His homosexual aestheticism, in terms of effeminacy, camp and dandyism, not only presented his personal trademark in everyday life as well as mass culture but also turned him into a popular icon in Hong Kong and Asia. To conclude, Cheung's flamboyant mannerisms, homoerotic appeal, his spirit of extravagance, the anguish as well as the cruelty of the character in such films as *Farewell My Concubine, Days of Being Wild, Happy Together, He's A Woman, She's a Man* in the 1990s produced a new kind of camp sensibility that is unprecedented in the history of Hong Kong cinema. On the other hand, his epicene style, artificiality,

Figure 8.2 Leslie Cheung's dandy look in the 1980s (courtesy of Daffy Tong)

theatricality and playfulness in gender-crossing on stage and in music videos subverted the heterosexual hegemony of Hong Kong society and contributed a new image of male/gay singer in Hong Kong popular culture.

Cheung's music video *Grieving Man* is another example that shows his campy taste and the interaction between the displacement of cross-dressing and sexual identity. The video tells the story of how a group of male cross-dressers who work as professionals in the daytime transform themselves into drag queens at night. These male transvestites include a policeman, a sales manager, a lawyer and an electrician. They wear their uniforms when they have to play their career roles in the workplace, but they cross over at nightclubs by putting on shining jackets, fur coats, skirts, wigs, lipstick, earrings and eye-shadow when off duty. The song and video present the interchangeability of clothing and sexuality, and how clothes change male bodies. Most of the sequences of scene focus on the exhibition of male body parts and the process of cross-dressing. One's gender identity and sexuality are constructed as well as displaced by what one wears. In other words, gender construction is always a flowing process of negotiation, regulation and operation. In addition, the interior setting and the clothing of the cross-dressers that are shown in the music video are so exaggerated and vulgar that they produce the sense of kitsch. As Sontag pointed out, clothes, furniture and all the elements of visual decor made up a large part of camp. Camp art is often decorative, emphasizing texture and style in extravagant content and rich form. Successful camp reveals self-parody, self-love, and kitsch (1983: 107–109). In *Grieving Man*, the red, silver, gold and neon colours of the clothes, as well as the powerful make-up of the cross-dressers, are so seductive, gorgeous and dazzling that they enact a new image of the "femme fatale" by men, or the so-called "homme fatal" who exaggerates his sexual characteristics and personality mannerisms in kitschy ways. With his smoky eyes and alluring smile, Cheung's charming appeal in the music video manifests that men need love and pretty clothes. It breaks the conventional rule and the social taboo of masculinity in which men have been forced to concern themselves only with their minds, careers and social responsibilities rather than their bodies, sexualities and sentiments. "Men need love and pretty clothes" means that men should enjoy their right and pleasure to explore their bodies and sexuality in terms of the crossover style in gender construction. In her "Imitation and Gender Insubordination", Judith Butler declares that gender is *drag*, and it is an imitation and a performance that produces the illusion of an inner sex or psychic gender core. Gender and sexuality, in Butler's term, are "performative". They are a production of "self" structured and motivated by various kinds of sociopolitical, cultural, racial and historical forces (Butler 1993: 317). In her *Gender Trouble*, Butler elaborates:

I would suggest as well that drag fully subverts the distinction between inner and outer psychic space and effectively mocks both the expressive model of gender and the notion of a true gender identity ... The performance of drag plays upon the distinction between the anatomy of the performer and the gender that is being performed. But we are actually in the presence of three contingent dimensions of significant corporeality: anatomical sex, gender identity, and gender performance. If the anatomy of the performer is already distinct from the gender of the performer, and both of those are distinct from the gender of the performance, then the performance suggests a dissonance not only between sex and performance, but sex and gender, and gender and performance. (1990: 137)

What Butler suggests here is the fluidity of identities and the constructedness of gender. According to Butler's queer approach, gender is a repetitious imitation of social practice without origin. It is regulated by compulsory heterosexuality.[10] To queer one's sexuality is to open up all the possibilities of gender performance in which one may be a heterosexual, a homosexual, a bisexual, a transsexual or any combination and transgression of these categories. There is no coherence between sex, gender and performance, for they are always in the process of transformation and have all kinds of combinations. That gender is performative means, on the one hand, that it is socially and culturally constructed, and on the other, that it is ready for any kinds of disruption, interruption and intervention. That gender is drag means that it is transient, creative and symbolic. It can be signified by various kinds of dressing and make-up. It also can be taken on and off according to one's sex-consciousness and personal taste.

Drag and Gender Performativity

In Butler's discourse, "drag" is a metaphor describing the construction of gender and sexuality. The notions that "gender is drag" and that it is "a kind of imitation for which there is no original" (313) imply that gender and sexuality are recurring practices of the established norms of masculinity and femininity as well as compulsory heterosexuality. According to Butler, gender and sexuality are therefore not naturally given but articulated and cultivated by such networks of power as law, education, medical discourse, government policy, social custom, culture and history. On the other hand, Butler's statement also suggests that gender is a performative act in which one can create and initiate a new face of the inner self each time one pronounces or performs one's sexual identities. In this regard, gender and sexuality are not only always in the process of invention and intervention but also destabilized and multi-faceted. To review Cheung's drag queen show with reference to Butler's idea of gender performativity is productive, for it helps to open a new critical vision of Cheung's subversive act in gender representation, and at the same time, to examine the social bias and the media reception of a generally homophobic city toward Cheung's sexuality.

In 2000 and 2001, Cheung held his last concert tour, the *Passion Tour,* in Hong Kong and overseas. He invited the world-famous Jean Paul Gaultier to be his stage costume designer. Gaultier presented his fashion message "From Angel to Devil" by creating six outfits for Cheung—the Angel in white suit with fairy wings, the Pretty Boy in skirt ornamented with shells, pearls and beads, the Latin Lover in golden jacket, the Devil in black tights and red opera coat. The concert denotes a mixed style of impersonation as well as a cross-cultural drag performance, which visualizes Cheung's androgynous body and bisexuality. Cheung erotically puts on his long black wig, the haute couture with feminine colour and cutting on the one hand, and on the other, exposes his moustache, his masculine facial features and body shape. As Farid Chenoune points out, Gaultier brings out the tension between masculine and feminine genres in his fashion design. He has projected onto fashion and found design equivalents of the continuing reverberations of two particular cultural trends with their roots in the 1970s: the feminist movement, and, perhaps even more significantly, homosexual coming-out (Chenoune 1998: 10–11). What characterizes Gaultier's fashion design is a mix-and-match style between the two sexes, such as a man in a skirt or a woman in a man's dark suit. His collections for men in the 1990s, like "homme fatal", "pretty boy", "couture man" and "androgyny"[11] implied a transgression of traditional sexual dimorphism in Western society. These collections present a new kind of male/gay femininity in the postmodern age, for they not only create pastiches in the fashion genres between the past and the present, hybridizing the styles of garment-making from various traditions and racial groups, but also cross the gender lines in terms of colour, fabric, cutting and decoration. As for Cheung's *Passion Tour,* what Gaultier presents is a story of initiation. The changing stage costumes tell how a pretty boy turns to be an evil lover. At the beginning, Gaultier dressed Cheung as the White Angel fallen from heaven (Figure 8.3). Cheung dresses in white and sings the song "Intoxicated Life and Dream" behind a white curtain. It represents the image of purity. Then, the angel transforms into a Pretty Boy wearing a transparent sailor top with silver sequins in an Egyptian style and a skirt seamed with shells in a Greek style (Figures 8.4 and 8.5). It is a new kind of male elegance, which is unisex and romantic. In the middle part of the story, Cheung becomes the erotic Latin Lover in golden jacket and black tights, a sexy object of desire and spectatorship (Figure 8.6). Finally, the Latin Lover turns into the Devil in black and red (Figure 8.7). At that time, Cheung acts like a phantasmal figure—mysterious, alluring and self-indulgent. In fact, the *Passion Tour* concert illuminates Gaultier's gay philosophy of fashion and Cheung's body symbolism. Cheung is the "homme fatal", the "pretty boy", and the "couture man" whose body gives ambivalent codes of gender and dressing in presenting Gaultier's theme on androgyny. As a queer subject of position, the ambivalence of Cheung's body image imprints a novel manner of effeminacy and a new vogue for male/gay femininity. His visual pleasure and gender visibility are enacted by his energetic body gestures. Both sex and gender are destabilized and denaturalized by means of his queer performance. The stage, in its splendid design and theatrical sense, acts as an imaginary space or a dreamland where the performer achieves the fluidity of his sexual identities beyond the critical eyes of the heterosexual and homophobic society.

Figure 8.3 Leslie Cheung: "White Angel" (courtesy of Daffy Tong)

Figure 8.4 Leslie Cheung: "Pretty Boy" (courtesy of Daffy Tong)

Figure 8.5 Leslie Cheung: "Man in Skirt" (courtesy of Daffy Tong)

Figure 8.6 Leslie Cheung: "Latin Lover" (courtesy of Daffy Tong)

Figure 8.7 Leslie in "Opera Coat" (courtesy of Daffy Tong)

Although the *Passion Tour* contributed to a breakthrough in stage performance and gender representation in Hong Kong popular culture, local media disapproved of it. Most of the local newspapers and magazines were of a conservative bias against Cheung's crossover style and gay identity.[12] They condemned Cheung's cross-dressing, arguing that a man should not downgrade his own masculinity by wearing a skirt and long black wig. They even attacked Gaultier's stage costumes by saying that the six outfits he designed for Cheung were outdated and old-fashioned. For example, a local psychotherapist, Bo-neng Lee, commented that what Cheung presented onstage is a kind of mental and behavioural disorder. Bo-neng Lee claimed that Cheung cross-dressed because he hated his own body and was eager to change into a woman. Moreover, Lee also concluded that the act of self-stroking by Cheung in the dancing sequence showed the weakness of Cheung's character as well as his shame for his male body (Lee: 2000).[13] Both Cheung and Gaultier were frustrated by these comments and prejudices. Gaultier was so disappointed and angry that he sent an e-mail to Cheung to protest against the mistreatment and misunderstanding by the Hong Kong media. He even proclaimed that he would never design stage costumes for any Hong Kong artists in the future. All these negative comments about Cheung's cross-dressing and gender-crossing by the local media, however, explicate the social prejudice towards homosexuality, gay identity and the body politics of drag. Such social mistreatment also shows how a gay/bisexual performer suffers from moral judgment, social pressure and constraint.[14] In her "Homophobia: Why Bring It Up?" Barbara Smith points out that people are generally threatened about issues of sexuality, for the existence of homosexuals calls their sexuality/heterosexuality into question. Therefore, one way to protect one's heterosexual credentials and privilege is to put down lesbians and gay men at every turn (Smith 1993: 100).

It is obvious that the criticism of Cheung's cross-dressing by the Hong Kong media represents the stigmatization of gay images by the heterocentric and homophobic elements of the dominant culture. In Chinese culture, "sexuality" is viewed as a personal affair that should be kept in the private realm. Public discussion of it is prohibited, especially discussion of sexual deviance. Cheung's queer performance onstage, in its publicly subversive form, reaffirmed the effeminate side of men on the one hand, and on the other, challenged manhood as a social norm as well as the patriarchal order of social culture. To question masculinity within a strictly patriarchal society threatens the existing balance of power (Arnold 2000: 111). In terms of homosexual panic, people in a heterocentric society always internalize the straight culture's homophobic attitudes towards those who fail to comply with the right gender. Cheung's effeminacy and androgyny, as a result, were attacked by the public media. Not only was his song and music video about two gay lovers banned by local television, but also his sexual orientation was questioned and his endeavour in drag performance was neglected by the heterosexual critics in newspapers and magazines. In 2001, Cheung made his music video *Bewildered* with the help of art director William Chang, whom Cheung had collaborated with in Wong Kai-wai's film production. It is a music video about the intimacy of two men. Cheung featured a Japanese male ballet dancer Nishijima Kazuhiro as his gay lover in the music video, and they displayed their half-naked bodies in an erotic sense. However, the music video was banned by TVB, the local top channel in Hong Kong. They condemned the music video for being immoral, for it advocated homosexual relationships. They requested that Cheung censor all scenes of homoeroticism before screening the video. Cheung refused to re-edit the scenes and the music video was finally banned.

In contrast, the *Passion Tour* concert was highly appreciated by overseas media. Cheung's drag performance and Gaultier's costume design were supported and admired by various newspapers and magazines from Japan, Korea and Canada. Cheung was honored as the most successful and prestigious drag performer from Hong Kong, whose style was among the most distinguished in the history of Hong Kong popular culture. The Japanese newspaper, *The Asahi Shimbun*, proclaimed that the *Passion Tour* was an extraordinary show and Cheung was the most highly gifted performer ever seen in Hong Kong. The well-known Japanese musical critic Ogura Eiji even defended Cheung against the accusations and suppression by the Hong Kong media. He wrote that what Cheung performed onstage was a remarkable image of a mature man with lots of glamour and dignity. All the negative comments about Cheung were clearly based on heterosexist presumptions, the homophobic point of view, and the moral judgment of Hong Kong society against gender-crossing. They not only held biases against Cheung's sexual identity and queer position but also ignored the contribution of his creativity in musical arrangement, dancing and vocal performance, stage and costume design.[15] The polarity between the local response and the overseas reception of Cheung's cross-dressing in the *Passion Tour* interestingly explicated the conservative side of the city.

As a Chinese community, Hong Kong still holds traditional values regarding sexuality in education, culture, and social custom in spite of its historical process of colonization and Westernization since 1842. The mass media are always ignorant of and discriminate against homosexual coming-out and transgenderism in favour of heterosexualism. Images of gay people are distorted in media events and such cultural productions as film and television.[16] If Cheung were not a gay artist, he would not have been attacked by the media. He was not the only one who cross-dressed on stage. Such supposedly straight actors and singers as Andy Lau and Aaron Kwok are highly appreciated for their cross-dressing in films and popular music. Andy Lau was even awarded the best actor in 2000 for his portrayal of a male-to-female transvestite in the gangster movie *Running out of Time*. As for Cheung, his sexual orientation as well as gay identity were the focal points of the local media attacks, rather than his art and performance, although he only cross-dressed onstage and not in everyday life. In other words, it was his "queerness" that caused the trouble, the rumours, the stigmatization, the social discrimination, and even contributed to his suicide.

Conclusion

On 1 April 2003, when the city was preoccupied by the SARS virus, Cheung killed himself by leaping from the 24th floor of the Mandarin Oriental Hotel in Central. His body was later found on the pavement of Connaught Road. The day after his death, Cheung's suicide note was made public. He wrote:

> Depression. Thank you to all my friends. Thank you Professor Felice Lieh Mak. This year has been tough. I can't stand it anymore. Thank you Mr. Tong. Thank you to my family. Thank you to Fat Sister. I have not done one single bad thing in my life, why is it like that? Leslie.

Daffy Tong, Cheung's gay lover, told the newspapers that Cheung had attempted to kill himself with sleeping pills in November 2002, as he had seriously suffered from depression. Professor Felice Lieh Mak, who is mentioned by Cheung in his suicide note, was actually a famous therapist in Hong Kong who had taken care of Cheung's depression for almost a year. In spite of the rumours of love affairs spread by local newspapers as well as the Internet, there is no doubt that Cheung's suicide was caused by his depression and health problems. However, the local media in Hong Kong made Cheung's tragic story into a negative example that linked being gay to being depressed and suicidal. Newspapers and magazines published a series of special columns discussing how to prevent suicide, cure depression and correct sexual disorientation. Psychologists, educators, social workers and sociologists worried that Cheung's suicide would have a tremendous impact on young people. As a popular icon, his death would be mourned, and at the same time, deified by the young generation who might follow him as an example and imitate his behavior. The chief inspector of the Hong Kong Police Force even claimed that Cheung's suicide might set a social trend and provoke depressed people to take the same action when faced with difficulties and pressure. The worst of it was that some people declared that homosexuality, like the SARS virus, was a kind of infectious illness which could easily infect young people with dangerous ideologies and a disordered life. They identified homosexuality with the violent act of suicide and the mental illness of depression. They warned that gay identity led to a miserable life of depression and self-destruction, for homosexuality, depression and suicide were interrelated. People argued that Cheung's case should be used as a social lesson to discourage youth from homosexuality and suicide. The social response to Cheung's death by the Hong Kong media, again, showed discrimination against homosexuals as well as suicides. It is unfair to magnify the tragic end of Cheung's life and his impact in terms of social morality and responsibility. If we have to blame a gay artist for killing himself, how about the heterosexuals who also suffer from depression and commit suicide? Indeed, among gay people, depressives and suicides are a social minority, who are always marginalized by the heterosexual hegemony and stigmatized as social deviants by the mass media. As a gay artist in a society intolerant of gays, Cheung's life and death doubles his sufferings, marginalization and stigmatization because he was a public figure. His acts and speech were always supervised and inspected by the watchful eyes of the media and society. Although some of the newspaper reports after his death focused on his artistic achievement in films and popular music, his gay/bisexual identity was the main topic of argument in public discussion. Before his death, Cheung mentioned several times that he was so depressed by the negative comments about his *Passion Tour* concert that he would never perform it again. He even planned to retire from stage performance under the pressure, the anxiety and the severe strain of being a gay artist in Hong Kong. *Passion Tour* was Cheung's last concert, and it is also the most unique piece of art in gender-crossing in Hong Kong and Asian popular culture. As Winnie Chung stated at the time, "Cheung [was] one of the original Hong Kong male divas— from long before Hong Kong had its four Canto-pop kings, Andy Lau, Leon Lai, Jacky Cheung and Aaron Kwok". Cheung's proclamation, "I am more myself as Leslie instead of selling an image", in an interview in the *South China Morning Post* in 2002 (Chung) showed his self-identification of the onstage image with his everyday life practice. As a controversial figure, Cheung challenged the traditional image of men, breaking the boundary as well as bridging the gap between masculinity and femininity. His bisexuality and androgynous body politics onstage signified an openness to gender reconfiguration. In spite of his suicide and death, his charisma, his beautiful face and voice onscreen preserves his everlasting image, fame, life and glory.

9

Performing Gender, Performing Documentary in Post-socialist China[1]

Shi-Yan Chao

In the 1980s and early 1990s the People's Republic of China saw the fluorescence of independent documentary filmmaking. Wu Wenguang, Duan Jinchuan, Zhang Yuan and Jiang Yue launched a wave of documentary filmmaking commonly referred to as the Chinese New Documentary Movement. The movement's filmmakers generally reject the official tradition of newsreels and *zhuanti pian* (literally, special topic films), which are characterized by images compiled in accordance with pre-written scripts, and by directly addressing the audience from a grand, top-down angle (Berry 2007: 115–134). Rather, they highlight a sense of immediacy and an "unscripted spontaneity" (Berry 2007: 122), showing a deep concern for "civilian life" from a "personal standpoint" (Lu 2003: 14–15, 335). Distancing themselves from official discourses, they choose to document the lives of ordinary people, especially those on the margins of society, such as peasants, migrant workers, the homeless, the elderly, the homosexual, etc.

Whereas lesbianism has been the focus of several films in the past few years,[2] female impersonation, transvestism, and transgendering are also salient queer subjects in this wave of independent documentary filmmaking. This chapter examines two recent documentaries, *Tang Tang* (Zhang Hanzi 2004) and *Mei Mei* (Gao Tian 2005).[3] Although each documentary centres around a female impersonator, they approach their subjects in distinct ways. Whilst *Mei Mei* portrays its subject with nuance and profuse emotional investment, *Tang Tang* lays special emphasis on formal experimentation. In the first of four sections in this paper, I employ the vantage points offered by the realist aesthetic of *xianchang* (literally, on the scene) and the device of reflexivity to examine the ways in which *Tang Tang* blends fiction into documentary. Positioning *Tang Tang* at the intersection of what I call the film's "performing documentary" and the subject's "performing gender", I argue in the second section that the reflexivity permeating *Tang Tang* foregrounds the openness of the queer subjectivities it portrays.

While technologies of representation comprise the first focus of this chapter, my investigation looks beyond the textual. It aims at understanding each film's subjects as human beings materialized in and through a matrix of social, political and economic conditions marked by spatial and temporal parameters. With such a matrix forming its second focus, this chapter, then, turns to *Mei Mei*. Casting the practice of cross-dressing in terms of geopolitics, the third section explores the multilayered significance of female impersonation as contingent upon the contexts of its expression. In the final section, I locate the cross-dressing subjects of both films at a time of social transition in order to highlight the ways in which gender-crossing performers negotiate their subjectivity in post-socialist China.

Because of its dual focus, this chapter takes an interdisciplinary approach, tentatively weaving film studies into performance studies, sociology, economics and anthropology. A panoramic view on the films' subjects hopefully comes through this. As for the naming of Tangtang's and Meimei's performances, "*fanchuan*" is the term preferred by the performers. Literally meaning "gender-role reversal" performance, *fanchuan* originally refers to the theatrical practice of female/male impersonation in Chinese opera. Even though their performances do not belong to the operatic stage, Tangtang and Meimei favour this terminology primarily due to its artistic connotation, while they strongly oppose the label "*renyao*" (literally "human prodigy") for its pejorative denotation. If they likewise reject the English translation "drag", I assume it has something to do with the term's susceptibility to the stigma associated with *renyao*, and the implication that their performances are of less quality (as lip-synching is often the case in drag, but not in *fanchuan*, professionally). In the following I use cross-dressing, female impersonation and gender-crossing performance interchangeably to refer to the subjects' *fanchuan* performances. A discussion of *fanchuan vis-à-vis* human agency also follows.

Performing Documentary: "Xianchang" Aesthetic and Reflexivity

Several elements of fiction are blended into *Tang Tang*. Revealed over the course of the film, they result in a curious parallel between the film's "performing documentary" and the subject's "performing gender". The story of *Tang Tang* itself unfolds around its title character, a Beijing-based female impersonator. In nightclubs and large family-style restaurants across the city, Tangtang performs songs and dances in modern female attire (Figure 9.1). During the filming of this documentary, Tangtang meets a lesbian couple, Xun and Lily, who are mesmerized by his performance, and a friendship follows. At the same time, a romantic relationship develops between Tangtang and Xiaohui, a young man. Eventually, Xiaohui leaves Tangtang without explanation, and Xun and Lily's

Figure 9.1 Still from *Tang Tang* (courtesy of Zhang Hanzi)

relationship turns sour. Xun drops her plan to go abroad with Lily, while Lily leaves for New Zealand. In their loneliness, Tangtang and Xun bond and even come to identify themselves as a "couple".

It is noteworthy that Lily and Xiaohui are both played by actors. That is, the sequences involving the two are reenactments based, according to the director, "on true events" (Zhang Hanzi 40). Below, I elucidate how Zhang Hanzi foregrounds the performative nature of *Tang Tang* as a documentary. In particular, I focus on the reenacted sequences associated with Lily, as well as the beginning and ending of the film. Whereas performing documentary in *Tang Tang* presupposes the filmmaker's view of documentary as a genre fashioned in counterpoint to fiction, I argue that his blending of fiction into documentary expresses his reflections on the ontology of the genre. That is, the filmmaker directs our attention away from treating *Tang Tang* as a piece of evidence from the historical world to considering the status of documentary itself. While the "truthfulness" of the film is the primary concern when taking documentary as evidence, I emphasize a major effect concomitant with treating documentary as a genre: the *reflexivity* of the work, which in *Tang Tang* is enhanced by the film's persistent revelation of its own constructed nature. In shifting the emphasis from "truthfulness" to reflexivity, I do not mean that authenticity becomes insignificant to *Tang Tang*. Rather, the film's exploration of these matters raises such questions as: how does reflexivity respond to the issue "truthfulness" as a foundational characteristic of documentary film? In what sense is the combination of reflexivity and documentary in *Tang Tang* pertinent to the representation of the subject as queer? What roles do performance and performativity play in this operation? Ultimately, what kind of queer subjectivity is portrayed in *Tang Tang*?

Lily (as a character) is shown in four reenacted segments that problematize assumptions about authenticity in documentary filmmaking. Lily is last seen in a sequence where she and Xun sit close to each other, enjoying a moment of shared intimacy at a park. Along the margins of this heartwarming imagery, however, runs a subtitle informing the viewers that Xun is stranded in Beijing, while Lily has left for New Zealand alone, anticipating that Xun will join her there. This sequence, which contains no dialogue, is accompanied by a non-diegetic soundtrack of simple yet lyrical piano-playing. In other words, this reenacted segment is a "montage sequence" that, rather than depicting a specific past event, conveys a general idea or impression. It attempts to portray what it *felt like* between the couple during their best days, inflecting the scene with a sense of sentiment and nostalgia. In contrast, the first three reenacted segments associated with Lily exhibit the qualities of more conventional documentary filmmaking, apparently "documenting" specific events. The first sequence occurs when Xun and Lily come backstage to meet Tangtang after one of his performances, marking the first encounter among the lesbian couple, Tangtang and the film crew. During the second reenactment, the director wants to invite the lesbian couple to be in the documentary, and he incidentally interrupts an intimate moment between them. When the director explains his intent to Xun and Lily, their conversation is suddenly brought to an end by Xiaohui's entrance. In the third reenactment, Xun remarks to the director on her relationship with Lily. She also expresses curiosity about the sound recorder and is encouraged to try on the headphones (Figure 9.2). Finally, Lily arrives and suggests the three continue the conversation elsewhere.

Figure 9.2 Still from *Tang Tang* (courtesy of Zhang Hanzi)

These three reenactments deliberately imitate a sense of on-the-spot realism to render certain qualities associated with documentary filmmaking. These qualities are played out in three interrelated ways. First, they intentionally highlight the *un*intended nature and spontaneity of the events documented. For instance, Xun and Lily join in only after the project has started; Tangtang is surprised by Xun's unexpected request to allow her to kiss him; and Xiaohui comes upon the videotaping process, accidentally interrupting the conversation between the director and the lesbian couple. Second, the acting and the spoken lines incorporate a misleading sense of improvisation and non-professionalism. For example, Lily (as an actor) acts out a sense of uneasiness in front of the camera; parts of Tangtang's remarks appear extemporaneous; and the director himself sometimes stutters. Third, all three sequences underline their production process, for example by allowing the audience to spot, through the reflection in a mirror, the filming equipment, director, and sound technician; or directly to witness the soundman with his recording equipment. The subjects (or characters) also show their awareness of the camera's presence. More importantly, all three sequences capture the continuous interactions occurring in front of and behind the camera, such as the conversations between the director and the lesbian couple, or when Xun tries to stop uninvited shooting with her hand (Figure 9.3). In other words, by highlighting the spontaneous nature of the events as well as the extemporaneous quality of the interactions among participants, *Tang Tang* presents certain events *as if* they were happening unplanned. Meanwhile, by exposing the filming process itself, *Tang Tang* intends to have the audience witness the filmmaking *as if* it were really unfolding. Taken together, the film wants the audience not only to see the reenacted events themselves, it wants us to see those *pre*arranged events with a heightened sense of *un*mediated immediacy.

Figure 9.3 Still from *Tang Tang* (courtesy of Zhang Hanzi)

Such an intrinsic paradox even becomes provocative if we take into account the beginning and the ending of the film. Though separated diagetically, these two parts develop around the same event. In the film's prelude, we find Tangtang applying makeup in preparation for an interview with the director, who supposedly has been intermittently documenting Tangtang for a long time and is right now videotaping. Once Tangtang and the filmmaker are ready for the interview, however, Tangtang unexpectedly fetches a pistol from his handbag. Following a verbal exchange, he proceeds to shoot himself in the mouth. The scene erupts into chaos, followed by the film's title: *Tang Tang*. This incident is taken up again toward the end of the film, where Tangtang's performance on Valentine's Day 2004 is marked as the director's "last" available footage of the subject's performance. Tangtang's singing is a bridge into the next sequence, which begins in slow motion with Tangtang shooting himself (as seen in the prelude) and falling to the ground. With the imagery gradually becoming stabilized and the speed normalized, the director announces, "Cut! Very good!" The film crew then swarms over Tangtang, helping him get up. Simply put, the subject's suicide is fabricated, and is revealed as such in the finale.

On the one hand, the form (or "look") of this suicide sequence resembles the reenactments involving Lily. For example, during the prelude, Tangtang's suicide is portrayed as an unanticipated event beyond the director's control. The verbal exchange between Tangtang and the director immediately before the shooting also simulates the unrefined feel of improvisation (e.g., the director informs Tangtang, "I am shooting. I have been ... I never turned off the camera"). Furthermore, a sense of immediacy, particularly a sense of being both temporally "at-present" and spatially "on-the-spot", is invoked through the constant interaction between Zhang and Tangtang (e.g., the latter asks for a cigarette from the former), as well as by the director unveiling his filming process (setting up the camera, adjusting the focus, etc.) simultaneous with the event's unfolding. To a certain degree, the aesthetic in question resonates with the concept of "*xianchang*" central to contemporary Chinese independent filmmaking. According to renowned documentarist Wu Wenguang, "*xianchang*" can be described as "of the 'present tense' and 'being on the scene'" (Wu 2000: 174–175). It is a filmic approach to temporality and spatiality. In film scholar Zhang Zhen's interpretation, the essence of "*xianchang*" also lies "in the sensitivity toward the relationship between subject and object, and in a conscious reflection on the aesthetic treatment of that relationship" (Zhang 2002: 116). As for the aforementioned sequences associated with Lily and with Tangtang's suicide, they do succeed—on the surface—in simulating the quality of "being at present" and "being on the spot", thanks to the narrative and filming both rendered as *being* in process. Meanwhile, a deep concern for the relationship between subject and object is discernable through the filmmaker presenting his engagement with the events unfolding.

On the other hand, we must not neglect the paradox at the core of these sequences. The semblance of documentary (*jishi*) is, in fact, deliberately planned out and executed. These sequences constitute, in brief, *performed documentary*. With the incongruous overlaying of a *xianchang* style onto fictitious content, Tangtang's suicide sequence foregrounds *xianchang* as subject to appropriation. Stated differently, if *xianchang* represents "a cinematic practice and theory about space and temporality, which is charged with a sense of urgency and social responsibility" (Zhang Zhen 2002: 116), it is first and foremost a means by which contemporary Chinese independent filmmakers negotiate and express their concern for social reality. In *Tang Tang*, such a creative concept and practice is nonetheless appropriated and emptied out through pastiche; that is, through a "knowing imitation" (Dyer) of the style of *xianchang*, an "effect of *xianchang*" (*xianchang gan*) is thereby produced and rendered duplicable. However, what is the significance of pastiche, and pastiching *xianchang* in particular, in *Tang Tang*?

Three observations and inferences follow here. First, a comparison between Tangtang's suicide segment and the first three reenactments involving Lily reveals that their similar renditions of the "effect of *xianchang*" reference different formulations of reality/fiction: pure fiction vs. events "based on real events". This difference reflects the undeterminacy of the signifying process of the "effect of *xianchang*". Conversely, it points to the ostensible expressiveness or performativity of *xianchang*. The performativity of *xianchang* along with the fact that *xianchang* itself may be appropriated, underscores the parodic relationship between *xianchang* and the "effect of *xianchang*", destabilizing the assumed correspondence of *xianchang* with reality. Second, the performativity of *xianchang* also calls into question the assumed meaning of reenactment. If, as is usually the case, the audience cannot judge or verify the extent to which a reenactment is true to the original events, the kernel of a reenactment is, then, not so much the truthfulness of the reenacted events than whether the reenacted plots *look* real enough in the eyes of their beholders. That is, the audience may take for real a reenacted event due to its documentary style, but they may also downplay the fact that reenactment is itself a form of (re)presentation that may deviate from the original events. Third, *Tang Tang*'s destabilization of the assumed correspondence between *xianchang* and reality, and its reflection on the role of the audience's perception, illuminate the constructedness and opacity of the meaning of the text in question. This destabilization, coupled with the film's revelation of its own production, equips the film with a heightened sense of reflexivity.[4]

In other words, pastiche, in particular the pastiche of *xianchang* documentary aesthetic, is key to *Tang Tang*'s artistic reflexivity. What, then, is the significance of *Tang Tang*'s reflexivity? On what grounds is this reflexivity unusual to contemporary Chinese cinema? In what sense is it relevant to the "authenticity" of the film in general and the "queer subjectivity" of Tangtang in particular? Indeed, reflexivity is discernable in a number of works by China's Sixth-Generation filmmakers.[5] So far as those films exhibit an innovative film language that "comments on and critiques social reality instead of simply mirroring it" (Zhang Zhen 2007: 7), they are arguably endowed with a sense of reflexivity. Although the blending of documentary into fiction has become a reflexive device common to Sixth-Generation cinema, the core of such mixtures remains fiction. In contrast, *Tang Tang* is foremost a documentary. Further, *Tang Tang* demonstrates a mode of reflexivity with a self-deconstructive ramification uncommon to Sixth-Generation cinema. If one trend of Sixth-Generation cinema is marked by its critical relationship to social reality, *Tang Tang*, I argue, contemplates upon the very nature of reality and representation.

As noted, *Tang Tang*'s pastiching *xianchang* and the film's blending of fiction into documentary redefine the cultural practice of *xianchang*. It challenges the audience's expectation that assumes a correspondence between a documentary look and reality. Meanwhile, the prelude and ending of the film foreground and deconstruct (at least ostensibly) the film's authority purported by the director / camera: we witness the filmmaker losing control of his subject (i.e., Tangtang's suicide decision appears to have been a shock), and the subject negotiating with the filmmaker (i.e., before "killing" himself, Tangtang requests that the director delete all of the footage documented before). In so doing, Zhang Hanzi calls attention to the subject-object relationship between filmmakers and their subjects, implicitly posing such questions as: Do the "subjects" of documentary films have any claim to "authorship" of works about them? If the subject of a documentary retains autonomy during the filming, how much authorship then can the subject enjoy (as opposed to that claimed by the filmmaker)? Significantly, as *Tang Tang* time and again deliberately reveals its own filming process, it also makes its viewers aware of the artifice of the film, the constructedness of its meaning, and even their very viewing behaviour. As a sense of tension between the film and its main subject is (ostensibly) played out, so is the role of the *audience* stressed by this film: it appeals to the audience's attention to issues regarding film production and representation. According to Bill Nichols, relative to other modes of documentary film, reflexive documentary is especially characterized by its attention to "the processes of negotiation between filmmaker and viewer" (2001: 125). And "[i]n its most paradigmatic form the reflexive documentary prompts the viewer to a heightened consciousness of his or her relation to the text and of the text's problematic relationship to that which it represents" (1991: 60). That is, when watching a reflexive documentary, we are frequently drawn to "the filmmaker's engagement with *us*, speaking not only about the historical world but about the problems and issues of representing it as well" (2001: 125; emphasis added). Rather than *"seeing through* documentaries to the world beyond them", we are invited "to *see documentary* for what it is: a construct or representation" (2001: 125; emphasis original).

Performing Gender/Subjectivity through Reflexive Documentary

To a large extent, the integration of reflexivity into documentary filmmaking has shifted the focus of the latter from the represented to the representing process. In the West, the popularization of the discourse on reflexivity has much to do with the "poststructuralist critique of language systems" (Nichols 1991: 63) that interrogates the "transparency" of languages, concepts and representations. In poststructuralist theory, "concepts and representation ... are inevitably caught up in discourse, power, intertextuality, dissemination, and *differance*" (Stam 1992: xv), while language systems constitute and structurally condition individual subjects. In her essay, "The Totalizing Quest of Meaning", documentarist-scholar Trinh Minh-ha likewise adopts a poststructuralist (and postcolonialist) stance, dissecting the interconnections between knowledge/power regime and the myth of documentary verisimilitude. Proposing a non-fiction epistemology to challenge the nexus between filmic patterns and authority, Trinh maintains that, instead of replacing one source of unacknowledged authority with another, we must "challenge the very constitution of authority", "empt[ying] ... or decentraliz[ing]" any single source of authority (41–42). Although Trinh also endorses the notion of reflexivity, she cautions against having it "reduced to a question of technique and method", where the concept of reflexivity merely serves to perpetuate the knowledge/power regime. She rather underscores the importance of the "reflexive interval" between the textual and the extra-textual: "No going beyond ... seems possible if the reflection on oneself is not [simultaneously] the analysis of established forms of the social that define one's limit" (46–48). Significantly, if a documentary film "displays its own formal properties or its own constitution as work", and if the epistemic and power relations between Same and Other are being challenged, then the subject "points to him/her/itself as subject-in-process": the identity or subject takes the form in which "the self vacillates" and embodies a certain amount of elasticity (48).

In other words, not only does reflexive documentary emphasize the mechanism of representation, but the subject or identity constituted through the work is inclined to a sense of instability and resiliency—or, say, it is characterized by some *non-essentialism*. Therefore, to the maker and the subject of a reflexive documentary, the question of whether the represented is "true" to him/her/itself may not be the most pertinent issue, as such an inquiry is premised upon a different epistemology. A concern with the truth rests upon the belief that documentary film opens a window to the historical world, and through that window offers audiences access to truth or reality. Such a belief, however, may seem idealistic to practitioners and participants of reflexive documentary. On one hand, it implies a kind of teleological thinking that overemphasizes the singularity and absoluteness of meaning, while downplaying the multiplicity and relativity of meaning. On the other hand, such a belief or quest also presupposes a full trust in the completeness of human agency and subjective autonomy, while underestimating the opacity of meaning and the social and cultural influences on meaning making. If the subjects being documented are inscribed by salient cultural and identitarian differences, this quest for "truth" may as well be implicated with "essentializing" others who share those differences, as if the documented could represent the whole group, and the whole group possessed a homogenous and transcendental essence that could in turn be captured on camera.

As the subject of reflexive documentary is inclined to a sense of non-essentialism, the eminent quality of reflexivity portrayed in *Tang Tang*, I suggest, similarly endows the audience with a non-essentializing appreciation for the film subjects. Especially with the film's mixture of documentary and elements of fiction, we can hardly determine Tangtang's "authentic" subject, or point to a preexisting being behind his representation. If we consider questions regarding performance and performativity *vis-à-vis* the subject, an intriguing part of *Tang Tang* involves the relationship between Tangtang and Xun, particularly following their separations from Xiaohui and Lily, respectively. Indeed, a significant portion of the film depicts and "documents" that relationship. Tangtang ("originally" a gay man) and Xun ("originally" a lesbian) at first cohabitate as "good sisters" (*hao jiemei*), then, gradually come to identify themselves as a "couple". Although they deliver the face value of a "straight" couple, their partnership embodies a reversal of traditional gender roles, wherein Xun is more like the "husband" of a household, and Tangtang the "(house)wife". In regard to the development of their relationship, I do not question the possibility of such a happening in our worldly reality, but I suspect that an element of drama or performance is involved. I posit that Tangtang and Xun's desire and potential to perform are evoked and induced by the presence of the filmmaker/camera, so that under those gazes they partially imitate the filmmaker's highlighting of the fluidity of identity by interpreting and acting out their relationship with a degree of self-consciousness.

Nonetheless, I also want to propose that, even if the more recent development of Tangtang and Xun's relationship is inflected by some coefficient of performance, it does not automatically follow that their relationship is untrue, or even fake. The subjectivities of Tangtang and Xun are not necessarily "distorted" by the scenario that they are not just "being" themselves. According to Judith Butler, neither gender nor subjectivity is expressions of free will. Rather, it is through non-voluntaristic performative reiteration of heterosexualized gender norms that individuals "approximate" heterosexualized gender identities and socially assigned subject positions. Nonetheless, precisely because this process of phantasmatic imitation and approximation "is bound to fail, and yet endeavours to succeed", it propels itself into an endless repetition. Simultaneous with this "compulsive and compulsory repetition", the *effect* of the "naturalness" of gender and that of the "originality" of heterosexuality are produced (1991: 21). Therefore, drag is to gender, or gay is to straight, "not as copy is to original, but, rather, as copy is to copy" (1990: 31; 1991: 22); drag, in imitating gender, "implicitly reveals the imitative structure of gender itself" (1990: 137). Yet Butler's elucidation seems to better account for the situation of the social mainstream than that of sexual minorities. As Chris Straayer points out, Butler's model "seems more useful for understanding [the social mainstream's] attempts to live up to an ideal—that is, their complicity with the maintenance of sexual difference [and gender norms]—than for understanding feminist [and sexual minorities'] rejections of the ideal" (218). The gendering and regendering of some transgender individuals' bodies, for instance, cannot be explained simply as a failure to repeat gender norms. Therefore, Straayer differentiates between "a *failure* to repeat" and "a *refusal* to repeat" (218), so as to highlight the subject agency engaged in the latter.

To synthesize Butler's formulation of "gender performativity" (as opposed to voluntaristic performance) and Straayer's emphasis on queer agency, I suggest we approach Tangtang's subject status—both as a performer and in relation to his being represented—with "strategic essentialism". Strategic essentialism, in Gayatri Spivak's account, stresses "a *strategic* use of positivist essentialism in a scrupulously visible political interest" (1987: 205). Nodding to the fact that identity is inevitably essential, Spivak suggests we strategically view identity "not as descriptions of the way things are, but as something that one must adopt to produce a critique of anything" (1990: 51). Substituting an identitarian essence for the subjective experience contingent to that identity, strategic essentialism thus appeals to a non-essentialized subject position. Arguably, such a position foregrounds the subject agency, as emphasized by Straayer, but without downplaying the regulatory mechanism, as seen in gender performativity. From the perspective of strategic essentialism, queer subjects, then, straddle the line between voluntaristic performance and non-voluntaristic gender performativity; they are in constant struggle with "failures to repeat" and "refusals to repeat". Between gender performativity and voluntaristic performances also emerges the possibility of queer performativity: subversion animated through acts that challenge the heteronormative reiterative practices configuring gendered identities, and that in effect transform the signification of "shame" (Sedgwick 1993; 1998).

Tangtang's cross-dressing performances constitute first and foremost a kind of theatrical performance against gender performativity. From the perspective of Tangtang as a sexual dissident, we must recognize his willful resistance to regulatory gender norms. As queer performativity is willfully exerted through female impersonation, so is queer subject agency routinely vitalized in the performer. Meanwhile, cross-dressing performance can be considered a survival strategy for queer subjects like Tangtang. Other than the monetary reward, such performance offers its performer a way to negotiate his subjectivity in public. As the film shows, Tangtang regularly compares his performance to that of Mei Lan-fang (1894–1961), a legendary *fanchuan* male artist in Peking opera. During his performances, Tangtang's subject, then, "straddles a fine line—publicly announcing his sexuality but at the same time plausibly denying it by couching it in performance and artifice".[6] Strategically, Tangtang fashions his own subjectivity *against* heteronormative gender codes in public, while he himself retains a degree of ambivalence: after all, his performance is *by nature* an artistic citation of gender codes developed in the operatic system. Flirting with the curiosity and imagination of the public, his subject nevertheless situates itself between the gender norms of quotidian life and those of the theatrical arena, between a full expression of one's will and a semi-voluntaristic citation of artistic conventions. His performance, in short, is self-empowering yet not meant to translate the "essence" of his identity. In a sense, Tangtang's non-essentialist strategy of self-representation coincides with the device of reflexivity integral to the film, insofar as they both highlight the process of something: subject and filmmaking, respectively.

Moreover, Tangtang's faked suicide is more than a scripted act. Tangtang's performance mocks the contracted imagination of the social mainstream which assumes that social and sexual dissidents are prone to a tragic end. When general audiences see the prelude of *Tang Tang*, they may expect the rest of the film to be a candid portrayal of the deteriorating circumstances of Tangtang's life. However, not only does the film never explain why he chose to kill himself, but at the end it divulges his suicide to have been fabricated. Tangtang's performance of a pre-scripted act thus has the effect of queer performativity, for it taunts the public imaginary of tragedy about a social non-subject who routinely subverts the gender norms that performatively constitute social subjects.

If there is indeed some coefficient of performance in Tangtang and Xun's relationship, the making of this documentary, I contend, must have helped the subjects further engage with what Anthony Giddens terms the "everyday social experiments" (1992: 8) facilitated by wider social changes. Challenging the ways intimacy is traditionally pictured, the couple's relationship bears echoes of Giddens's meditation on the transformation of intimacy, particularly his conceptualization of the emerging "confluent love": a democratic form of relationship that cuts across the heterosexual-homosexual dichotomy, that highlights personal choices, and that needs not to be combined with sexual fidelity, marriage, or modelled on the heterosexual family (1992: 61–64).

Resonant with confluent love, Tangtang and Xun's union is simply sustained by a negotiated consensus. Even so, intimacy abounds the couple's lives: they tenderly take care of their feline "son"; they share the same bed and blanket; Xun affectionately kisses Tang on his cheeks, etc. Notably, their relationship also contests Giddens's conceptualization. While Giddens considers "reciprocal sexual pleasure" (1992: 62) key to confluent love, the role of sex in this couple's intimacy is never made clear. To be sure, the notion that sex is prerequisite to intimacy is itself questionable. As Lynn Jamieson rightly puts it, "it is quite possible to have intensely intimate relationships which are not sexual and sexual relationships which are devoid of intimacy" (1999: 478). Further, Tangtang and Xun's intimacy is interspersed with quarrels over issues ranging from money to house chores. As Giddens's formulation has been criticized by some for its over-optimism and insufficient empirical support (Jamieson 1998: 136–157; Bell et al. 2000: 126–127), so are these quarrels symptomatic of the tension, inequality and fragility potentially inherent in any couple's negotiating and sustaining their relationship. At once convergent with and divergent from confluent love, Tangtang and Xun's relationship registers an openness characteristic of their subjects-in-process. While the subjects challenge the gendered dynamic of traditional coupledom, they also embody the progressive meaning of queer performativity, fleshing out their queer subjectivity.

In sum, performing/pastiching documentary in *Tang Tang* functions as a means to reflexively approach its queer subjects, Tangtang and Xun. The emphasis on reflexivity in this film both directs our attention to the very process of representation, while incisively responding to the unfixed nature of the film's queer subjects. To a great measure, the film's stress on reflexivity recognizes in its subjects the self-fashioning technique of "strategic essentialism", through which Tangtang's agency emerges between voluntaristic performance and gender performativity, and through which Tangtang and Xun negotiate their queer subjectivity and explore the possibilities of alternative intimacy. *Tang Tang* thus represents not only the queer subjects of the film; it also exemplifies a particular means to approaching these queer subjects with the camera.

Mapping out Gender-crossing Performance across the Geopolitical Landscape

I now turn to the documentary film, *Mei Mei*, to analyze how it makes us rethink the ramifications of gender-crossing through the lens of a geopolitical specificity. The film follows Meimei's journeys mapped out on the plains of both geography and life trajectory, capturing the nuanced and multilayered significance of cross-dressing—particularly the ways in which cross-dressing in differing contexts registers varying cultural connotations and social valuations.

我有花一朵 种在我心中
I have a flower growing in my heart

Figure 9.4 Still from *Mei Mei* (courtesy of Gao Tian)

Like Tangtang, Meimei is a Beijing-based female impersonator (Figure 9.4). Originally from Northeastern China, Meimei has been performing in various nightclubs, pubs and gay bars in Beijing since 1998. About ten minutes into the film, we are informed that the main subject is preparing for his "farewell concert", for he is soon starting a new life in Shanghai with his partner, an insurance salesman. Prior to his relocation, Meimei also wants to pay another visit to his family in Dandong, a border city in Liaoning Province. In fact, the original conception of this documentary only consisted of the happenings surrounding Meimei's farewell concert in Beijing and subsequent trip to his hometown.[7] It was supposed to be a retrospective of Meimei's life and career before his married life in Shanghai. However, Meimei ends up leaving his husband and returning to Beijing after only a month in Shanghai. A sequel to the failed marriage plot follows. Having spent most of his savings, the subject tries to return to the spotlight but he can barely make ends meet. What's worse, he falls ill unexpectedly and—unable to afford the high medical and living expenses in Beijing—is taken home by his parents. Initially, Meimei hopes to be back on stage by the lucrative Christmas season. Nonetheless, five months after his departure from Beijing, he is still in Dandong when the film crew makes another visit. Even though Meimei appreciates his family's loving care, he eventually desires to leave for the outside world. The film ends without providing the audience with conclusive information regarding Meimei's next step in life.

On one level, the ways Meimei dresses himself in quotidian life (as opposed to onstage) have much to do with where he is, and a geopolitics is enacted along the axis of urban/rural difference. Meimei remarks at one point that when he is in Beijing, he sometimes chooses to wear skirts even when he is offstage, for passers-by are likely "only to comment that this woman is somewhat taller than other women". When he leaves for Dandong, however, he must wear trousers instead, so as to eschew the scrutiny and gossip of locals, who may ask, "Is that person a man or a woman?" Similarly, we can perceive that although Meimei occasionally wears makeup out on the streets in Beijing, he never does once he returns to his hometown. Clearly, Meimei enjoys more autonomy in regard to his looks in Beijing, a metropolis, than in his hometown, a remote small city.

Meimei's limited autonomy beyond the metropolis is poignantly depicted in the latter part of the film, when he sojourns in Dandong. The subject is first shown in a series of following shots through which we witness him leaving home, walking alone through the streets and alleys. Not only has he given up makeup, but he is now in plain attire obviously designed for men, and his long hair has been trimmed short. Apparently, Meimei has accommodated himself to the customs of the local community in the past few months. One particular shot is especially saddening. Capturing Meimei from behind, that static short take provides a lyrical glimpse into the subject. He seems to have lost weight due to his illness and at one point he has a coughing fit. The physical frailty of the subject seems incongruous with the slightly loose, somewhat awkward fit of his men's attire, which appears imposed on rather than tailored for him. This contrast between the weakened physique and seemingly forced attire entails a sense of helplessness involving the confrontation between the will of an individual and normalizing social institutions. Meanwhile, beneath Meimei's shortened hair we notice for the first time a thinning area on the back of his head. The relentless disclosure of this spot must be somewhat embarrassing to Meimei, for the subject, as his stage name vividly suggests, always wants to look "beautiful" in front of others ("Meimei" in Chinese means beautiful).

As a small-town sexual dissident whose personal desire contradicts public expectation, Meimei could have sought relative autonomy in metropolitan

Beijing. However, Meimei cannot help but concede to the more constricted regulatory institution of his hometown after losing his mobility to his poor health and economic inferiority. Gesturing toward the heteronormative oppression of society, the scenario depicted hence underlines how this oppression is differently played out on the one hand along the urban/rural dynamic, on one hand. On the other, it hints at what Caren Kaplan emphasizes as the "material conditions" of travel/displacement often dismissed in contemporary theory (110), highlighting the financial terms of the individuals involved. If, to queer subjects, rural-city migrations represent degrees of freedom and independence, such migrations must be at one and the same time materially conditioned.

Furthermore, Meimei's performances in Beijing mainly take place in nightclubs, discos and gay bars. The emergence and popularization of these venues has been facilitated in densely populated Chinese metropolises since the 1990s by myriad interrelated factors: urbanization, the expansion of commerce, the formation of consumer culture, etc. Dandong has neither a robust economy nor a vibrant consumer culture and so there is no prosperous nightlife scene. However, other opportunities for gender-crossing performance exist in Dandong. When Meimei is still recuperating, he begins learning and practicing Peking opera to cast away the tedium. At one point, wearing neither makeup nor a costume, Meimei performs in a "Peking Opera Concert" sponsored by the local branch of the Party and held at a local "community centre". It is noteworthy that Meimei's high-pitched operatic singing employs some falsetto, a vocal skill in which he already excels, yet which contemporary male pop singers have rejected as being "effeminate" and "unnatural". Although there is no overt gender ambiguity in Meimei's looks here, there is a gender-bending element in his voice. In a broader sense, we must take into account that in *jingju*, a matrix of "formulated" (*chengshi hua*) skills associated with various role-types (*hangdang*) together with an abstract signifying system of stage installation have been developed throughout the centuries. Not only are its vocal styles unbound to the falsetto/"natural" voice divide (itself a relatively modern concept), but the genders of various role-types do not have to match a performer's biological sex. The gender system in *jingju*, in other words, is not fully subject to the principles of "reality". The operatic cross-dressing (predominantly female impersonation) is able to divorce itself from the social stigmas associated with "gender inversion", precisely because it is justifiable as a form of "art" and even "national heritage" (*guocui*). The fact that Meimei practices *jingju* while stranded in Dandong can thus be understood as an expedient through which he can moderately channel his desire for female impersonation, yet simultaneously keep any negative imaginaries at bay. As discussed, Tangtang in Beijing negotiates his identity and performance by strategically referring to *fanchuan* in *jingju* and particularly its icon, Mei Lan-fang. Given the sense of voluntaristic agency and queer performativity in Tangtang's reference to Master Mei, Meimei's practice of *jingju* can be understood as a means for him to negotiate his queer subjectivity while *involuntarily* coming to terms with social pressure.

Interestingly enough, female impersonation is seen in still another type of public performance in Meimei's hometown. One night before he heads for Shanghai, Meimei visits an old friend, Mr. Lee, who also engages in stage performance. On this night Lee performs at a beer garden that presents a nightly variety show. It is a place where families and friends gather for meals and drinks while being entertained. Although Lee's cross-dressing here and Meimei's in Beijing both take the form of popular entertainment instead of the artsy operatic mode, differences mark their styles. Meimei, in his female impersonation in Beijing, endeavors to *pass* as a "real" woman in terms of *both* the visual and the vocal, whereas Lee's performance highlights the *incongruity* between the visual and the vocal. That is, Lee's female impersonation features a visual hyper-femininity—ranging from his makeup and costumes to his gestures—in sync with a voice that is not quite feminine in song, and that employs even less femininity in speech. Rather than pursuing the effect of passing as a woman, Lee strives for a comedic effect. This particular mode of cross-dressing, I suggest, also registers a tacit consensus between the performers and their audiences. This consensus is premised on the male performers' mimicry of "woman" in such an *im*perfect way that not only the "performative" quality of the imitation is foregrounded, but the subversive potential of cross-dressing gives way to some comic effect and public entertainment.[8]

Even though Lee's performance is not intended to achieve the effect of passing and, with its emphasis on the comedic, is not meant to be taken seriously by the audience, a sense of tension is nonetheless perceivable between the impersonator and some of the audience. A curious episode immediately after the show is symptomatic of this tension. Most of the customers have left the beer garden, but a small group lingers near the shabby backstage where Lee is changing his clothes. These local residents apparently have a voyeuristic curiosity about the performer: they hope to see "something" from behind the curtain. Lee appears before long, putting on his pants. With some of his makeup unremoved, his masculine torso is nonetheless bare (Figure 9.5). I read this as the audience's implicit wish to affirm the female impersonator's "real" gender identity. I suggest, further, that this moment embodies the surveillant mentality and gaze of the public, who want to ensure that cross-dressing is solely for entertainment purposes and that gender ambiguity is "properly" limited to the stage.

Figure 9.5 Still from *Mei Mei* (courtesy of Gao Tian)

Situating Gender-crossing Perfomance in Post-socialist China

In the previous section I explored the geopolitical specifics of gender-crossing in *Mei Mei*. In this final section I situate the gender-crossing performances in both *Mei Mei* and *Tang Tang* within the socio-economic milieu of post-socialist China. Since the late 1970s China has seen the reintroduction of Western culture and the redevelopment of the market economy. In China's pre-reform era, labour— without a functioning labour market—was allocated to various work units (*danwei*). Neither the individual nor the work unit was free to choose. Although full employment was attained through the government's administrative measures, it happened at the expense of labour productivity and economic efficiency. In the reform era, labour flexibility has been emphasized along with labour reforms in three primary areas: the reduction of state regulation of the labour force; the diversification of channels of labour allocation; and the establishment of a labour contract system (Lee 2001: 16–21). The resulting changes have attested to the "ideological acceptance of labour as a commodity" and the "marketization of labour" in post-socialist China (34). On the supply side of the labour market, workers now face considerable freedom and competition over their choices of employment, whereas employers, on the demand side, adopt various market- and profit-driven policies.

Competition in the labour market in particular has proven obsolete a pre-reform public mentality associated with the "iron rice bowl" (*tie fanwan*): "the protective embrace of a paternalistic state" that centred on one's job assignment, enveloped by "a range of welfare services including housing, health, education and pension rights" (Flynn et al. 2001: 3). Concomitant with a secure job and a relatively valorized (low) pay, the "iron rice bowl" mentality was mirrored in people's low incentive to work and their poor productivity. Not surprisingly, people in post-Mao China have commonly accused previous regimes and their social policies of teaching the workers to "eat out of one big pot" (*chi daguo fan*): no matter how much or how little workers produced, they all ate the same "food", that is, they received the same wages (Rofel 1999: 108). However, as Lisa Rofel points out, by "essentializ[ing] ... a disposition in workers [of previous times] toward laziness, disorderliness, and transient material desires", those workers were conceived a hindrance to "China's effort to realize modernity" (107–108). Such a conception, on one hand, breaks with previous power/ knowledge schemes that hinged upon *labour*, through which socialist subjects came into being. On the other hand, by stereotyping the workers of the previous era as a hindrance to modernity, "new modes of discipline" are simultaneously installed (Rofel 1999: 108). Now a multitude of capitalist tenets (the emphases on self-interests, monetary gains, consumption, time and efficiency, among others) have come to play a significant part, competing with other ideas or ideologies in constituting human subjects in post-socialist China. Simply put, if "labour" under socialism served as "the principal cultural site for the production of identities", the "market" has emerged as a new arena for the cultural production of modern subjects (Rofel 1999: 122–123).

At the macro-economic level, post-Mao China has seen the emergence of a labour market along with the development of both the commodity and capital markets. At a micro level, we may consider our film subjects, Meimei and Tangtang, as independent workers/production units. Technically speaking, because they provide their talent to the performance arts circle in metropolitan Beijing, they directly sell their labour/commodities on that market. So far as their jobs are not officially registered, they also engage in "underground" economic activities. Inevitably, such unofficial economic activities are facilitated by the development of a market economy in a macro sense and the acceptance of capitalist logic in the larger society, where *money* has become a crucial mediator between forms of demand and forms of supply. To some degree, the introduction of a market economy into this socialist nation has destabilized its socio-political structure, allowing Meimei and Tangtang the room to publicly act out their queer desires in some metropolitan areas. Even though their desires and performances are not acknowledged by the "official", Meimei and Tangtang still can earn a living through gender-crossing performances *as* "unofficial" economic activities. As long as the audiences or customers like them, their labour/commodities are valuable on that market.

In terms of competition, the performance arts circle/market in Beijing is no exception. As mentioned in the film, Meimei's wish to retire is partly due to the "competition" exacerbated by newcomers who have lowered their prices to compete with other performers. Meanwhile, as is usually the case in other modes of performing arts, age, too, is a major concern in China's gender-crossing performance circles. Among the numerous cross-dressing performers in Beijing, Meimei belongs to the "elder" generation, while youth is to the advantage of newcomers, who, by reducing their prices, become even more competitive.

The issue of age also has a wider resonance in China's post-socialist climate. As noted above, labour reforms in the 1980s were accompanied by the introduction of new wage systems. Replacing the seniority system that had defined labour valuation in socialist China, new wage systems are predicated on a new cultural valuation of tasks, where youth—in the name of "productivity"— has become a preferred criterion of labourers (Rofel 1999: 115–117). The new wage systems at once reflect and reify the changing cultural interpretations of age correlated with the changing socio-political paradigms. Furthermore, the issue of age, and the stress on youth in particular, strike a cord with a neologism, "rice bowl of youth" (*qingchun fan*). A figure of speech that has gained wide currency since the early 1990s, "rice bowl of youth" originally referred to "the urban trend in which a range of new, highly paid positions have opened almost exclusively to young women" (Zhang Zhen 2000: 94). With youth and beauty being the foremost prerequisites for their jobs, those "professional" women, though, often function as "advertising fixtures with sex appeal" (94). In a broader sense, if the figure "iron rice bowl" has, in retrospect, become a trope for a socialist economy characterized by inefficiency and inertia, the figure "rice bowl of youth" symbolizes the exuberant labour force of those who, in order to enjoy the consumer culture, are eager to cash in on their youth in the market economy by taking up highly lucrative, if often unstable and sometimes risky, jobs. Building upon its cultural "appreciation" since the 1980s, youth is the most important economic capital of those individuals, and they must make the most of it before it depreciates. As Meimei advises his young friend, female impersonators like them, who eat out of the "rice bowl of youth", must better manage their incomes precisely because of their relatively short-lived careers.

By highlighting the market mechanism and capitalist tenets operating in post-socialist China, I do not mean that the market has totally replaced socialist thinking to monopolize the production of modern Chinese identities. To say the least, the government never gave full rein to the market; the regime tethers economic reform to its political authority through what it calls "socialism with Chinese characteristics". Not only is the rhetoric of "socialism" imperative to the regime's political legitimacy, it is by consistent intervention into the relations between market mechanisms and socialist concerns that the party-state persistently affirms its legitimacy to citizens. Market forces and "traditional socialism" thus remain in tension. According to Arif Dirlik and Zhang Xudong,

Chinese post-socialism is characterized precisely by the *coexistence* of capitalist and socialist economic, political and social relations. This coexistence represents "a departure from ... a Chinese modernity, embodied above all in the socialist revolutionary project" (Dirlik et al. 1997: 3). That is, the "post-" in China's post-socialism must be grasped in relation to (the failure of) the state project of "modernity as revolution and socialism" (Dirlik et al. 1997: 8). Chinese post-socialism, then—as Chris Berry puts it—is "China's specific experience of postmodernity", where "Maoist socialism would be the particular grand narrative of modernity that has lost its credibility with the Cultural Revolution, and yet which *continues* to condition all that has developed since the end of that event and Mao's death in 1976" (emphasis added).[9] It is therefore no surprise that the socialist conceptualization of "labour" still informs certain aspects of human behavior and reasoning. In particular, socialist discourse on labour joins a range of capitalist tenets in configuring subjects in post-socialist China.

In *Mei Mei* the stigma associated with gender inversion and, in particular, the subject's gender-crossing performance, is recast in terms of *both* the socialist reverence of labour and the capitalist emphasis on wealth. When discussing his family's attitude toward his career, Meimei says that his father has been supportive and justifies it by referring to an old Chinese proverb, *xiao pin bu xiao chang*. Literally meaning that "people deride the poor but not prostitutes", the proverb generally expresses the idea that some societies judge a person in terms of how much wealth one possesses, rather than how exactly (read: "immorally") one acquires it. In a post-socialist context, this saying points to China's continuing yet uneasy transition toward a capitalist consumer society, during which money has ascended to a status atop a range of social values and traditional morals. While this phenomenon is troubling to some, to others like Meimei and his father, it is enabling and liberating. Meimei and his father further justify the son's gender-crossing performance by arguing that what the son does is "in no way against the law", and that "he earns a living by his own labour". Whereas the abovementioned proverb resorts to a capitalist valuation of social status in terms of one's wealth accumulation, the other two arguments appeal to the socialist tradition that values one's labour and hard work. The statement that "somebody makes a living by his own labour" interestingly blends a capitalist rationale (of making money) into a socialist reasoning.[10]

The capitalistic turn of the larger society also influences forms of intimacy. In *Tang Tang*, for instance, Tangtang and Xun develop a kind of alternative intimacy, with Tangtang and Xun taking up gender roles opposite those traditionally assigned to heterosexual couples. According to Tangtang and Xun, one reason for their gender reversal within the family has to do with their incomes. Partly because Xun contributes a bigger and relatively stable monetary share to the family, she is the "husband" of the two; Tangtang is considered the "wife", and compensates for his lesser financial contribution by doing more household chores. Money affects the relationship between Meimei and his "husband" even more deeply. In an interview conducted after their breakup, the husband tells the filmmaker, "My salary and other aspects are pretty satisfactory." "[Since] Meimei didn't ask for much", he adds, "I could satisfy him." He attributes the failure of their relationship to social pressure and Meimei's unreadiness to give up the spotlight. However, according to Meimei, the husband never rented the apartment he promised, but instead made him stay at a friend's abode. Even though Meimei had little money, he gave the husband RMB 600 yuan on his arrival to Shanghai, for the husband somehow had only one hundred at hand. Meimei was also pressured to meet his friends so that the husband could sell them insurance. When Meimei finally leaves, "the only thing [the husband does is take] out a 100-yuan bill to buy me a McDonald burger and [leave] me with the change." In other words, by Meimei's own account, the most decisive reason for leaving his husband is neither social pressure nor his desire for the spotlight. It is rather about their relationship, which, though, is always imbricated in and foreshadowed by money. If we accept Meimei's account as more credible, the husband's dismissal of the monetary influence on their relationship may be taken as a disavowal that precisely attests to the significance of what it denies. In this sense, the film—by juxtaposing these somewhat contradictory views—also brings to the fore the monetary factors integral to modern intimacies against the backdrop of China's post-socialism.

Another aspect constitutive of the modern subjects in post-socialist China is "the increasing cosmopolitanism of the homeland" (Yang 1997: 289). In tandem with China's reopening of its doors to the world and its integration into the global economy, cosmopolitan experiences and imaginaries have gained a footing in certain coastal cities and the metropolitan areas through the transnational flows of capital, people, media, ideas/ideologies and technology.[11] Whilst in post-socialist China "the modernist imaginary of the nation-sate" competes with its capitalist counterpart by emphasizing "essentialism, territoriality, and fixity" in Chinese citizenship (Ong 1997: 173), cosmopolitan experiences and imaginaries demonstrate what Anthony Giddens coins as the "disembedding" effect (namely the "lifting out" of social relations from the local contexts of interaction) (Giddens 1990: 21–29). As *Tang Tang* reveals, a cosmopolitan outlook is at once liberating and otherwise. At one point, Tangtang mentions to Zhang that he has been interviewed by some European journalists, whom he claims regard his performance as artistic and even "avant-garde". Through this comment, he contrasts the praise of his performance by some Westerners with his public harassment by some Chinese male patrons, whom he considers tasteless and of low "quality". To be sure, Tangtang's reasoning presupposes an unthinking Eurocentrism that rests on a conflation of the West with progress and greater civility. Privileging the valuation of Europeans, Tang's rationale unwittingly echoes a colonialist power/knowledge scheme and is, indeed, not unproblematic. Yet it must be stressed that such a rationale also represents the means by which a social subaltern like Tangtang legitimizes his performance and lifestyle. We should not ignore the agency involved in Tangtang's negotiating his subjectivity.

When discussing cosmopolitanism in present-day China, we must also pay attention to cultural influences on a regional scale and the role of the mass media. According to Mayfair Yang, the mass media in present-day China "harbours potentials for liberation from hegemonic nationalism and statism". Combined with the forces of overseas capital, they have become significant "vehicles for imagining ... the larger space beyond the national borders", enabling "the transnationalization of Chinese identity out of the confines of the state" (1997: 288; 296). However, Yang argues against critical theories that identify "capitalism only as a Western force". In many cases, she maintains, the cultural "Other" that post-Mao China encounters is facilitated not by Western capitalism *but* by "the regional or transnational ethnic capitalism of overseas Chinese in Hong Kong, Taiwan, and South Asia". Importantly, what many Mainland Chinese identify with are not so much the subjects of the West *than* those associated with "the modernized and commercialized Chinese societies of Taiwan, Hong Kong, and overseas Chinese" (1997: 300–304).

Interestingly, if Maoist socialism once manipulated the concepts of women's liberation (*funü jiefang*) and gender equality to channel the energy of *both* men and women into the state project of nation-building, post-Mao China has witnessed a *regendering* or "sexing" of society (Sang 2003: 168). From a post-socialist vantage point, Maoism has been understood as having "deferred China's embrace of modernity by impeding Chinese people's ability to express their essential humanity". Similarly, the state feminism has been reinterpreted as "a transgression of innate femininity that repressed gendered human nature" (Rofel 1999: 31). The "sexing" of post-Mao society thus presupposes and imposes an essentialized view of gender, comprising a central motif of what Rofel calls "the post-socialist allegory of modernity" (217). Such an effort to "naturalize" gender also finds its expression in the transnational Chinese imaginary through the mass media. As Yang points out, Mainland Chinese consumers of the mass media from Hong Kong and Taiwan are able to imagine "a different way to be Chinese, where state identity diminishes in importance and female and male genders become salient categories" (Yang 1997: 301–302). Rejecting the Maoist subjectivity that sought, for example, in the Maoist loyalty dance, to merge the self with the body of the state, audiences now embrace "a Chinese cultural Other of Taiwan or Hong Kong who has a gender" (301–302).

In the same vein, the main subjects of *Mei Mei* and *Tang Tang* choose pop songs from Greater China for their gender-crossing performances. Tangtang's favourite is "How Many Dear Sisters on Earth Do You Have?" (*Ni jiujing you jige hao meimei*) from Taiwan; Meimei opts for "Woman as Flower" (*Nüren hua*) from Hong Kong.[12] Performed in Mandarin Chinese, both of these songs adopt and simulate women's perspectives. Whereas "How Many Dear Sisters" portrays the mood of a girl in love with a ladies' man, the performer of "Woman as Flower" figuratively compares herself or himself to a blossoming flower that needs love and tendering (presumably) from men. As is typical of mass cultural products, gender plays a crucial part in the processes of identification and desire of those who perform or consume these songs. Through performance and consumption, individuals learn to varying degrees to desire and to identify with gendered social positions, thus becoming gendered subjects performatively and phantasmatically. As discussed, in post-socialist China gender is a key component of transnational Chinese imaginary and marks ways of being Chinese that are not only distinct from Maoist socialist subjectivity, but are related to the subject experiences associated with other Chinese societies deemed as more modern and affluent.

To the general public, such processes at once inform and are informed by the efforts to naturalize gender in the larger society. To female impersonators like Tangtang and Meimei, however, they engage with the transgression of the gender norms sanctioned and naturalized in the mainstream media. Neither Tangtang nor Meimei comes from economic privilege, and their sumptuous costumes indicate that their performances intersect with the imaginary of an economically more privileged class. Arguably, to Chinese female impersonators like Tangtang and Meimei, the performance and consumption of pop music from Hong Kong and Taiwan not only manifest their engagement with a gendered trans-local Chinese imaginary, but to a certain degree, gender itself, to borrow Butler's formulation, forms the very "vehicle for the phantasmatic transformation of ... class" (1993: 130). Cross-dressing performance animates the fantasy of becoming a woman—a "real" woman—in order to find an imaginary man who represents the promise of permanent shelter from homophobia and poverty. For some Chinese female impersonators, accordingly, the consumption of transnational mass media involves the negotiation of a trans-local imaginary mediated by gender, where gender is always embedded in class and inseparable from sexual orientation. It is through the transgression of gender norms that a trans-local imagination free from poverty and homophobia is simultaneously activated. Such processes, I argue, configure another crucial dimension integral to the subject-formation of numerous male-to-female gender-crossing practitioners in post-socialist China.

In this chapter I have examined a number of salient points associated with cross-dressing performances by male artists in post-socialist China. The first half of this essay punctuates the specificity of documentary as a form of expression. Through the themes of *"xianchang"* realist aesthetic and generic reflexivity, it investigates the relationship in *Tang Tang* between the performance of documentary and the performance of gender. I argue that the work's appeal to reflexivity and its stress on non-essentialism reverberate with the film's queer subjects who are always in process and straddle the boundary between performance and performativity. Implicitly, through its reflection on *xianchang*— an artistic concept and practice rooted in China's post-socialist soil—*Tang Tang* also writes Chinese postsociality into its experiment with form. Meanwhile, *Mei Mei* sheds light on other aspects of cross-dressing by drawing our attention to formal variations of cross-dressing that are beyond the experience of metropolitan Beijing and are socio-geographically ingrained. In the last section I pay special attention to the ways in which female impersonators like Meimei and Tangtang negotiate the significance of their performances and their queer identities in the context of post-socialist China. In particular, I situate the life experiences of the two subjects among a range of issues, including the state's redevelopment of a market economy, the changing valuations of "labour" in the larger society, the monetary impact on forms of intimacy, the deepening influence of cosmopolitan experiences and imaginaries on human subjectivities and the consumption of the mass media in relation to subject-formations. Importantly, all these processes, at once post-socialist and trans-local, constitute the everyday experiences of those individuals who perform and transgress gender norms on a daily basis.

Notes

Introduction

1. Although the Hong Kong Special Administrative Region has been part of China since 1997, Hong Kong has been culturally and politically developed under the British rule for some 150 years before the handover. This book therefore primarily addresses China and Hong Kong as two different but closely related entities.

2. Literally translated as "comrade" or "people with the same ambitions/aspirations", *tongzhi* used to be a common term to denote a Chinese Communist Party member. It has been appropriated as a self-identification by LBGTIQ peoples in Hong Kong and Taiwan since the early 1990s. It is now commonly used to refer to non-heterosexuals in Chinese-speaking communities.

3. In response to the leftist discourse of "moral panic", the Christian Right in Hong Kong has coined the alleged liberal critique/"fear" of morality as "freedom panic" in order to preempt and rationalize its own fears and moralistic stances. "At this moment, we really need not produce 'freedom panic' and should not seek to demoralize Hong Kong society. Rather, we should reaffirm the significant role of morality in our free society, and continue to work hard to find a balance between the two poles" (Hong Kong Sex Culture Society 1).

4. Currently in Hong Kong, most intellectual work done on sexuality is from the Christian front, who have the resources to coordinate activist and theorist work in such a way that the production of cultural discourse and social movement work seamlessly together, which they disguise as moral education and "charity" services. To name just one example, Kwan Kai Man, an associate professor at the Department of Philosophy and Religious Studies of the Hong Kong Baptist University, has authored and co-authored, edited and co-edited more than fifteen books including *Reflection on Human Rights and Homosexuality* (Hong Kong: China Alliance Press, 2000), *In Search of Authentic Sexuality* ("Intellectual" Series 1) (Hong Kong: Fellowship of Evangelical Students, 2003), *Equal Rights? Hegemony? Examining the Homosexual Issue* (Hong Kong: Cosmos, 2005), *Stem the Tide—The Affection of Sexual Liberation Movement* (Hong Kong: China Alliance Press, 2007), and numerous articles philosophizing his anti-sexual rights and anti-gay stances. He is also a key figure in some of the most activist faith-based organizations, including being the founding member and coordinator of the Alliance of Christian Groups for Decency, the founding member of Hong Kong Alliance for Family, the founding member of Pro-life Family Network, the founding member and Board member of the Society for Truth and Light, and Chairman of the Hong Kong Sex Culture Society.

5. "... the open mesh of possibilities, gaps, overlaps, dissonances and resonances, lapses and excesses of meaning when the constituent elements of anyone's gender, of anyone's sexuality aren't made (or can't be made) to signify monolithically" (Sedgwick 1993: 8).

6. "Queer" has been translated into Chinese by literary, cultural circles in Taiwan as "酷兒", "酷異" (*qu'er/qu'i*). Partly due to these translations' close associations with the English word, these translations have not been able to travel very far beyond the gender studies classroom in Hong Kong and China. While *tongzhi* carries politicized connotations, the term "攣" (*lun*), literally meaning "bent", is often used in Cantonese popular culture to denote queerness.

7. Fang Gang, *A Qualitative Research of the Construction of Masculinity of Male Sex Workers*, an unpublished PhD dissertation in Chinese on male sex workers who serve women, is a rare example. Its description and some of its chapters are available online and has been openly seeking a publisher since August 2007.

8. In Hong Kong gender-variant subjects would include but are not limited to cross-dressers, transsexuals and *TBs*—a local expression which would "dub" the Euro-American *tomboys*, analogous to *Ts* in Taiwan and China, *Toms* in Thailand, *Tombois* in Indonesian, etc.

9. This reading strategy could also be seen as a response to Love's critique of the "continuing denigration and dismissal of queer existence": "One may enter the mainstream on the condition that one breaks ties with all those who cannot make it—the nonwhite and the non-monogamous, the poor and the underdeviant, the fat, the disabled, the unemployed, the infected, and a host of unmentionable others. Social negativity clings not only to these figures but also to those who lived before the common era of gay liberation—the abject multitude against whose experience we define our own liberation" (2007b: 10). Chapter 7 has been written in the spirit partly to resist this "temptation to forget".

10. "In the era of gay normalization, gays and lesbians not only have to be like everybody else (get married, raise kids, mow the grass, etc.), they have to look and feel good doing it. Such demands are the effect, in part, of the general American premium on cheerfulness: being a 'gay American,' like being any kind of American, means being a cheerful American. Because homosexuality is traditionally so closely associated with disappointment and depression, being happy signifies participation in the coming era of gay possibility" (Love 2007a: 54). Perhaps mowing the grass is not that normative in China and in Hong Kong, for different reasons.

Chapter 1

1. I would like to thank my previous institute, the Department of Applied Social Sciences, the Hong Kong Polytechnic University, for funding this project. I would also like to thank UNAIDS, which funded the NGO involved to conduct an HIV prevention programme on male sex workers in China for which I was invited to be the research consultant and thus gained access to this population. Special thanks go to the involved NGO, Mr. Chung To, Mr Rager Shen and Mr. Steven Gu, and the two anonymous reviewers for their positive and constructive comments on the earlier draft.

2. Li (2006) argues that administrative penalties and Party discriminatory sanctions, though they have no solid legal foundation, posit a real threat to homosexuals in China. These practices are used arbitrarily to control activities of those "who are deemed to have committed offences against the social order, but whose criminal liability is not viewed as sufficient to bring them before the courts or to warrant a criminal record" (p. 82). Subject to individual attitude towards homosexuality, the Chinese police can apprehend or interrogate certain homosexuals who are brought to their attention and they can report to these

homosexuals' work units (*danwei*) or families, which will bring substantial consequences for their futures, such as their chances of job promotion, housing allocation and so on. The situation apparently has improved recently (Kong 2010; Rofel 2007).

3. In China, male sex workers who serve men are most commonly called "money boys" by the workers themselves, as well as in the sex industry and the gay community. Other frequent terms are "duck" (*yazi*), "child" (*haizi* or *xiaohai*), or being simply referred to as "for sale" (*maide*). Male sex workers who serve women are usually called "ducks" (*yazi*) or "young masters" (*shaoye*). Although some of my samples serve both genders, their dominant clients are men. In this chapter, I use "money boys" and "male sex workers" interchangeably.

4. The bracket indicates the interviewee's pseudonym, his age, self-identified sexual orientation ("gay", "straight" or "ambivalent about his sexuality"), work type ("full-time brothel worker", "full-time independent", "part time worker/freelancer" or "kept by a man") and the length of his engagement in sex work.

5. See also my discussion of how Chinese male sex workers in the Hong Kong sex industry deal with the stigma of prostitution in relation to their masculinity (Kong 2009b).

6. In China, every individual is assigned a specific identification based on his/her locality and family background under a unique household registration system (*hukou*). Originated in 1958, *hukou* was used for resource allocation and is believed to be an effective means to control mobility in China, as an individual's *hukou* cannot be easily changed. Although the opening-up policy since 1978 has encouraged rural-to-urban migration, a lot of migrant workers in cities cannot enjoy various social and medical benefits because they have rural, rather than urban, *hukou* (Li et al. 2007; Zhu 2007; Amnesty International 2007).

Chapter 2

1. The writing of this chapter was partially supported by the Research Programme Consortium on Women's Empowerment in Muslim Contexts, led by City University of Hong Kong, with funding from the UK Department for International Development (DFID) for the benefit of developing countries. The views expressed are not necessarily those of DFID. Some of the themes from this chapter were first discussed in the article, "The Sexual Economy of Desire: Girlfriends, Boyfriends and Babies Among Indonesian Women Migrants in Hong Kong", in *Sexualities* (forthcoming).

2. Source: Hong Kong Immigration Department, personal correspondence, 17 August 2009.

3. It is not clear why these particular Indonesian terms are used. Literally, *sentul* means a "tall tree, bearing yellow fruit similar to the mangosteen but sour" (Echols and Shadily 503), while *kantil* is a Javanese word meaning "magnolia" (Echols and Shadily 259).

4. Cook quoted in Rupp (1990: 398).

5. According to Wieringa ("Jakarta Butches"), masculinized women, or butches, in Jakarta believe that they are "transgendered" at birth and they do not see themselves as women or men. While they conform to men's gender behaviour, they do not see themselves as men, embodying an ambiguous relationship to their bodies. While none of the respondents in my study wanted to be men or saw themselves as men, there were several who thought that they were "born this way" and like Wieringa's respondents, they did not see themselves as women.

6. By Western discourses, I refer to the development of lesbian feminist theory in Western Europe and North America during the 1970s, where feminism was identified as the theoretical basis on which lesbianism existed as both the practice and solution (Johnston 1973; A. Echols 1989: 238). Political lesbianism was strongly advocated as revolutionary action, e.g. Radicalesbians (240) proclaimed that "a lesbian is the rage of all women

condensed to the point of explosion", advocating lesbianism as a significant form of resistance to patriarchy and identifying lesbians as, first and foremost, feminist.

7. Women migrants in Indonesia: see, for example, Elmhirst 2000; Williams 2003. For Nepal, Thailand and Vietnam: Puri et al. 2004; Hettiarachchy et al. 2001; Belanger et al. 1998.

8. Exceptions are Constable (2000), Hawwa and Sim (2004b).

9. Constable (1997a, 1997b, 2000); Groves and Chang 1999; Lan 2006.

10. "Indonesia aiming to send one million workers overseas each year."

11. "70 percent of job-seekers underpaid, overqualified."

12. "Indonesian migrant workers send home US$2.9 BLN in 2005."

13. A term used to describe the government in Indonesia from 1965 to 1998 under President Suharto.

14. The Guidelines for State Policy (Garis Besar Haluan Negara, or GBHN) are set out by the government once every five years.

15. Transmitting national ideology through the educational system in Indonesia is one very successful means documented by Leigh.

16. "Government urged to improve protection of migrant workers."

17. Hong Kong Immigration Department's statistics, May 2006.

18. The ages of Indonesian women migrant workers are commonly adjusted to match market demands. According to AMC et al. "Baseline Research", most Indonesian women workers in Hong Kong are 21 years old, which agrees with the profile of respondents interviewed in this study. The youngest was fifteen when she first arrived in Hong Kong. See also, Loveband, 2003; Hugo "International Labour"; Robinson.

19. 99.6 % are women, Asian Meta Centre et al. 2001; Wee et al. 2003; Sim 2003.

20. "Satu Lagi, Pernikahan Sejenis di Tai Po."

21. United Nations Commission on Human Rights.

22. Eko Indriyani. Personal interview. 20 May 2003.

Chapter 3

1. It is important to note the various degrees in density among urban and rural areas in Hong Kong. If both urban and rural areas are included in the calculation of density, then Hong Kong's 2005 figure remains at 6,291 persons per square kilometre.

2. I am fully aware of the fact that my sample of interview subjects cannot fully represent the diverse lesbian communities in Hong Kong.

3. An oral history project organized by the Women's Coalition of Hong Kong SAR, Rainbow Action and F'Union has published a booklet collecting women's stories on their same-sex relations and desires. The booklet provides a map of existing and closed down bars and cafes. The booklet is available online at www.wchk.org.

4. Tung Lo Wan is located on the northern shore of Hong Kong Island including parts of Wanchai and Eastern districts. Tung Lo Wan used to be a fishing village with most of its land sitting on silt. Land reclamation has pushed the area's boundaries further into Victoria Harbour and has seen shopping areas and hotels sprang up in the area. For this chapter, I am mostly referring to streets popular with lesbian spaces such as Gloucester Road, Jaffe Road, Lockhart Road, Tung Lung Street, Yiu Wa Street and Yee Wo Street.

5. The industry report from Cushman & Wakefield is widely regarded as a definitive ranking of shopping locations and their leasing rates by the real estate industries worldwide. The October 25, 2006 press release was accessed on 29 August 2008 for this paper at http: // www.cushwake.com / cwglobal / jsp / newsDetail.jsp?repId=c7800055p&LanId=EN&LocId =GLOBAL

6. The emergence and social significance of lesbian bars has been documented in ethnographic studies and oral history scholarship on lesbian lives in U.S. cities including Detroit, Colorado, Boston, Buffalo, Massachusetts, Montreal, New York, San Francisco and Indiana.
7. The term "les" is commonly used by informants to describe their sexual identities as well as a term commonly seen in news media to denote lesbians.
8. TB vests are sports bra vests that function to flatten one's chest or bosom. Commonly used among tomboys or butch women in Hong Kong and Taiwan, these vests cost from HK$300 to 500.
9. The popularity of upstairs cafés have also seen chain operated cafés moving upstairs; most noticeably, the chain known as Paris cafés.

Chapter 4

1. The suicide of two transgendered women, Louise Chan and Sasha Moon, hit the headline news at the end of 2004. Cf. "Suicide of transsexual triggers activists' plea for better support"and "Suicide leap", *South China Morning Post*, 22 September 2004 and 24 September 2004 respectively.
2. In North America and many Western countries, the word "transgender" is used as "an umbrella term used to refer to all individuals who live outside of normative sex/gender relations—that is, individuals whose gendered self-presentation (evidenced through dress, mannerisms, and even physiology) does not correspond to the behaviours habitually associated with the members of their biological sex" (Namaste 2). I shall use this definition of transgender throughout this chapter, and use the term "transsexual", a term often used by the medical professions, to refer to those "who believe that their physiological bodies do not represent their true sex. Although most transsexuals desire sex reassignment surgery, transsexual people may be preoperative, postoperative, or nonoperative (i.e., choosing to not have surgical modification)" (Lev 400).
3. Cf. "Gender bender stole brother's ID card to get job at Wing On", *The Standard*, 4 August 2007.
4. Zung Kai-leon was charged for loitering and trespassing while wearing various kinds of female uniforms.
5. Cf. "Sexual Orientation Disorder man re-offended by barging into a female toilet and frightened a dentist during his suspension of sentence", *Apple Daily*, 19 August 2007; "Transvestite barged into the female toilet during his suspension of sentence", *Oriental Daily*, 19 August 2007.
6. Cf. "Feathers fly as residents' woes dog transvestite cabaret", *South China Morning Post*, 6 January 2006.
7. Cf. a brief chronicle in the website, 5 October 2005: http://www.sexuality.org/l/incoming/trbasic.html.
8. Not to mention the ethical issue of such attempts akin to administering reparative therapy to homosexuals which is a practice that is being condemned by the American Psychiatric Association.
9. Chapter IX without page numbers. Accessed online.
10. "Queen Mary suddenly removed its exclusive sex-change counseling clinic", *Ming Pao Daily News*, 8 March 2005.
11. Homosexuality as a mental disorder was deleted from DSM-II in 19731. The suicide of two transgendered women, Louise Chan and Sasha Moon, hit the headline news at the end of 2004. Cf. "Suicide of transsexual triggers activists' plea for better support"and "Suicide leap", *South China Morning Post*, 22 September 2004 and 24 September 2004 respectively.

Chapter 5

1. *Lala* is adapted from the Taiwanese localization of "lesbian". It first appeared as *lazi* in Taiwan, as the transliteration of "les" from "lesbian". When it was borrowed and further localized in China, *lala* has become the most widely used term. It is a community identity for women who have same-sex desires in China. It is used concurrently with *tongzhi*, an older and Hong Kong-derived identity, in its full or gender specific versions such as *nütong* (female *tongzhi*) and *nantong* (male *tongzhi*); and *les*, an abbreviation and a more informal term for "lesbian". There is contextual difference between the various identity terms. *Lala* and *les* are always used in informal or everyday and lesbian-specific contexts, while *tongzhi* is used in more formal and political occasions where community solidarity is emphasized. All identities are generally recognized and adopted in local communities across the country.
2. In comparison with other Chinese societies, the percentage of the unmarried population aged 15 or over in Hong Kong was 31.5% in 1996 and 31.9% in 2001 (Census and Statistics Department, Hong Kong Special Administrative Region 2005) while it was 34.1% in Taiwan in 2004 (National Statistics 2005a).
3. There is a park in downtown Shanghai where there is a Saturday matchmaking event once a month. It attracts many parents to look for suitable mates for their adult children. Regular participants of the event will hold a piece of cardboard on which is written the information of the person who is looking for a partner. Parents usually carry the cardboard which lists their child's personal information and also the kind of partner they expect for their children. Parents will exchange contact numbers if they are interested, and both sides will proceed to arrange meetings for their children if they are interested in seeing each other.
4. For example, the divorced population of people aged 15 or over in China in 2004 was only 1.07% (China Statistics Press 2005), while it was 5.2% in Taiwan in 2004 (National Statistics 2005b) and 2.7% in Hong Kong in 2001 (Census and Statistics Department).

Chapter 6

1. Monosexual means being attracted to only one sex. For example, heterosexuals and homosexuals are monosexual. Bisexuals are not.

Chapter 7

1. This research has benefited from financial support from the Research and Postgraduates Studies Programme in Arts of Lingnan University, Hong Kong. I would also like to express my gratitude to Wong Ain-ling for providing research support, Hong Kong Film Archive for publishing an earlier draft (Yau 2007), and to Agnes Lam for translating the first draft.
2. "'Me making *fengyue* films? Mr. Shaw, how could you make me? ...' A sudden flare of rage swelled up within Li. He took the script of *Illicit Desire* from Shaw, tossed it on the table without taking a look and ran for the door." This melodramatic scene from Dou Yingtai's (fictional) biography *Da Daoyan Li Hanxiang* (*Master Director Li Han-hsiang*) (1997: 391) tries so hard to maintain the portrayal of Li Han-hsiang as a "Master Director" to comic lights.
3. In the article "Li Hanxiang De Fushi Rensheng Yu Dianying" ("Li Han-hsiang's Floating Life and Film"), Yu (1997: 126–139) chronicles in detail the filmmaking career of Li but includes only a short paragraph on his *fengyue* films, ten of which had been made during the two years of 1973 and 74. The author registers the titles and the cast of these ten films without putting in a single line of description or commentary.

4. The dichotomy between pornography and erotica has been upheld and debated by numerous Euro-American critics and scholars. Soble (1986: 175–182) provides a concise summary. A similar divide is also implied in most of the Chinese criticism discussing Li's *fengyue* films, as noted above.

5. Xu Beihong (1895–1953) was primarily known for his lively depiction of horses in *shuimohua* (ink paintings). Having studied fine arts in Japan, oil painting and drawing in Paris at the École Nationale Supérieure des Beaux-Arts, he was considered to be one of the first Chinese artists who "modernized" Chinese art in his mastery of Western methods of composition and perspective as well as traditional Chinese media and techniques. Many of his paintings in the 1930s and 1940s were considered to have nationalistic and anti-oppression overtones. With his commitment to realism, he has openly denounced "modern art" and its tendencies of abstraction. http://en.wikipedia. org/wiki/Xu_Beihong; http://zh.wikipedia.org/wiki/徐悲鸿; http://www.lingnanart. com/chineseMaster/Master_XuBaihong_ch.htm. Accessed 10 January 2009.

6. Born in Liaoning in Northeast China in 1926, Li was a student leader of the National Central Academy of Fine Arts in Beijing who staged a rally in 1946 following the rape of a female student of Peking University Preparatory School by US servicemen. In 1948 he participated in the "Two Downs Three Strikes" student movement, advocating "Down with Civil War and Hunger; Labor Strike, Student Strike, Market Strike". In July 1948, Peking Garrison Headquarters openly suppressed the movement, killing eight and wounding thrity-six. Li was subsequently expelled by the academy. With a recommendation letter in hand, he fled south and enrolled in the newly inaugurated Shanghai Drama School. Legend has it that it was at the Cathay Cinema in Shanghai that he first saw Hong Kong films and made up his mind to leave Shanghai for Hong Kong for good (Yu 1997; Dou 1997).

7. Supremo (Zhizun Bao) was also the protagonist and title of a film directed by Zhu Mu and written by Li Han-hsiang under the pseudonym Sima Ke in 1974.

8. A similar argument about the licentious women (*yinfu*) and the bad/evil women (*è nü*) as potentially comrades and mutually constitutive has been made in Yau Ching, *Filming Margins: Tang Shu Shuen, a Forgotten Hong Kong Woman Director*, Hong Kong University Press, 2004. See also Ding Naifei (2002: 143–164): "Seduction: Tiger and Yinfu."

9. "*Jin Ping Mei* is a work that women should never be permitted to see ... How many women are there who are capable of responding appropriately to what they read? What would be the consequences if they were to imitate, however slightly, the things they read about? Its literary style is not such as could or should be studied by women." David Roy quoting Zhang Zhupo in "Chang Chu-po's Commentary on the *Chin P'ing Mei*" (1977: 236).

10. In the novel, Pan tries to seduce Wu Song her brother-in-law through drinking when Wu Dalang, Wu Song's elder brother and Pan's husband, a street-seller, is out working. However, she is rejected and scolded by Wu Song instead. While Pan is normally read as wanting Wu Song, and Wu Song sometimes read as also having repressed desire for Pan, their relationship is never consummated. What is consummated instead is the affair between Pan and Ximen Qing, a rich landowner in the region already with multiple wives. Pan later in the novel, with the help of Ximen Qing, forces Wu Dalang into drinking poison and kills him.

11. "Since sex is intended to be seen from a first-person perspective, viewing the act from the third-person causes it to lose its power and inherent connection. Sex was designed to be performed rather than observed which is why the most capable artist is unable to overcome the natural limits of perspective. By combining these two concepts (visual iconography and perspective) we can begin to understand why sexual imagery is inherently ineffective in film." http://www.evangelicaloutpost.com/archives/003465.html, accessed on 4 March 2007.

12. "... meticulously crafted images and painstakingly researched details make this *fengyue* film non-gamy, non-fishy and savour[y]", excerpted from Edwin W. Chen, "Profile: Li Han-hsiang".

13. As an amateur jinologist, Li has painstakingly collected ten complete versions of *Jin Ping Mei*, starting when he was twelve or thirteen years old. In his introduction to a collection of three of his *Jin Ping Mei* scripts *Jin Ping Mei Sanbuqu (The Golden Lotus Trilogy)*, he recollected how he and his wife were detained and questioned by Taiwan Police Headquarters for forty-eight hours due to his pursuits (1985: 7–42).

14. Keith McMahon (1995) has contended that (female) shrews, who attempt to punish the (male) superego and remake it in her own image, are in fact structurally constituted by (male) polygamists and misers, while all three creature types populated widely in vernacular literature of Ming and Qing China.

Chapter 8

1. I would like to dedicate this chapter to Leslie Cheung for his kindness and generosity in providing me with his colour photos when I published my Chinese book *City on the Edge of Time: Gender, Technology, and the 1997 Politics of Hong Kong Cinema* in 2002. Although his death is a great loss and grieves me, it motivated me to collect and reorganize all his materials, and finish this chapter.

2. It should be noted that Leslie Cheung is not the first singer or actor to cross-dress onstage in Hong Kong. Roman Tam and Anthony Wong are two other talented artists who created gay femininity in their performances of the 1970s and the 1990s respectively. Hong Kong cinema has also had a long tradition and history of cross-dressing since the 1950s. For further analysis, see my two Chinese books, *Decadent City: Hong Kong Popular Culture*, and *City on the Edge of Time: Gender, Technology, and the 1997 Politics in Hong Kong Cinema*.

3. For Cheung's interview on his art of acting in *Farewell My Concubine*, see the video recorded by the filmmaker and collected in the DVD of the film reprinted after Cheung's death in 2003.

4. Cixous writes, "In a certain way, 'woman is bisexual'; man—it's a secret to no one—being poised to keep glorious phallic monosexuality in view" (341).

5. It has been widely reported that Teresa Mo was Leslie's first girlfriend. They met each other in the late 1970s when they worked at local TV stations. Leslie often mentioned their good old days in front of the reporters. He even claimed that his life would have changed vastly had Mo not refused his proposal in their youth. Although there has been much gossip about his love affairs and many rumours persist, Leslie openly admitted that Teresa Mo and Daffy Tong were the only two lovers in his life.

6. Rey Chow's "Nostalgia of the New Wave: Structure in Wong Kar-wai's *Happy Together*" gives a critical analysis of the issues of cultural identity and queer sexuality of the film. Chow particularly focuses on the political significance and the diaspora of the film's two protagonists in relation to the 1997 hand-over of Hong Kong. Here, I focus merely on the artistic aspect of Cheung's acting.

7. For example, Audrey Yue's "What's So Queer about *Happy Together*?" holds the view that the character of Bo-wing in *Happy Together* shares a certain kind of similarity with Cheung's real personality.

8. Clare Stewart gives a detailed and thorough investigation of Cheung's acting skills in her article "About Face: Wong Kar-wai's Leslie Trilogy". The article is well written with passion and critical point of view in which Stewart examines Cheung's screen persona in *Days of Being Wild*, *Ashes of Time*, and *Happy Together*.

9. Wong Kar-wai published the soundtrack of *Happy Together* in 1998, which collects the tango music of Astor Piazzolla that he adapted in the film. The audio CD, *The Rough Dancer and the Cyclical Night (Tango Apasionado)*, contains the complete versions of Piazzolla's compositions, written and played by the musician himself. I would like to thank Mark Chan for introducing me to his professional knowledge of Piazzolla's musical world.

10. In her "Imitation and Gender Insubordination", Butler writes, "Drag constitutes the mundane way in which genders are appropriated, theatricalized, worn, and done; it implies that all gendering is a kind of impersonation and approximation. If this is true, it seems, there is no original or primary gender that drag imitates, but *gender is a kind of imitation for which there is no original*; in fact, it is a kind of imitation that produces the very notion of the original as an effect and consequence of the imitation itself" (313).

11. For colour photos of Gaultier's collections for men, see Farid Chenoune's *Jean Paul Gaultier*, 16–79.

12. Here the local newspapers and magazines include such tabloids as *Apple Daily, Oriental Daily, The Sun, Suddenly Weekly* and *Next Biweekly*, which characterize in vulgarity, sensationalism and degeneracy. Besides, the sources also include some traditional and customary publishing media like *Ming Pao, Singtao Daily*, and *The International Chinese Newsweekly*.

13. For the negative comments on Gaultier's costume design and Cheung's cross-dressing, see reports by the local Chinese newspapers in *Apple Daily, Sing Tao Daily, Oriental Daily* and *The Sun* on 2 August 2000.

14. The Canadian Chinese scholar Helen Leung in her book chapter "In Queer Memory: Leslie Cheung (1956–2003)" disagrees with my criticism of Hong Kong media. She argues that Cheung was also praised for his sexual courage by local media, and that my account has given too much power to the media while eliding the ways in which Cheung negotiated with the media through the arena of gossip and the form of queer agency (88–89). However, Leung's argument and refutation are invalid and incomplete, for she only makes reference to the newspaper reports and the comments about Cheung's sexuality and suicide from internet sources. The original copies of local newspapers and magazines had projected a fuller picture of the gossip arising from Cheung's gay identity in the past twenty years. In addition, the web sources that Leung cited are either the more "traditional" newspapers such as *Ming Pao, Hong Kong Economic Journal* and *Economic Times*, or the ones that are supported, approved and censored by the Mainland publishers in terms of moral standard and political correctness, like *Wen Hui Bao* and *Da Gong Bao*. Her argument did not refer to the two or three popular tabloids in Hong Kong, namely *Apple Daily, Oriental Daily* and *The Sun*. They are not only the bestsellers in Hong Kong but also have great impact on the everyday lives of the people as well as influencing social judgement and public opinion towards sexual minorities. They are the primary sources of materials for understanding the media culture of the city. For example, the columnist Lap-yan Leung uses the metaphor of "dog's buttocks" in *The Sun* to stigmatize and attack the sexual relationship between Cheung and his lover Daffy Tong even two years after Cheung's death. A more detailed critical analysis of the media discourse on Cheung can be found in my recently released Chinese book, *Butterfly of Forbidden Colours: The Artistic Image of Leslie Cheung*, which studies the queer representation, body politics, eroticism, narcissistic image as well as death instinct of Cheung in films, television and popular music. It also includes a discussion of the media discourse, fan culture and social reception of Cheung from 1978 to 2008.

15. For the comments on Cheung's *Passion Tour* concert by the Japanese media, refer to the Chinese translation of the articles collected in Cheung's *The One and Only: Leslie Cheung*, 53–55.

16. The social discrimination of homosexuality, indeed, is an imperative issue for discussion. Most of the television productions, media reports and commercial films on gay people made in Hong Kong give a conservative bias against and/or a stigmatized image of sexual minorities. For further discussion, one possible source is a local Chinese report, *Tongzhi and the Mass Media*, published in 2000 by Chi Heng Foundation.

Chapter 9

1. Special thanks to the two anonymous readers, as well as Yau Ching, Zhang Zhen, Angela Zito, Chris Berry, Charles Leary, Chen Xiangyang, Cui Zi'en, Shi Tou, Zhang Hanzi, Gao Tian and Bennett Marcus.

2. Please see my article, "Coming out of *The Box*, Marching as Dykes", in *The New Chinese Documentary Film Movement: For the Public Record*. Eds. Chris Berry, Lisa Rofel and Lu Xinyu. Forthcoming.

3. Zhang Hanzi is a graduate of the Central Academy of Fine Arts in Beijing. Before filming *Tang Tang*, Zhang directed and edited for television, commercials and music videos. Gao Tian, a young graduate from the directing programme at Beijing Film Academy, made his film debut with *Mei Mei*, which won the Jury Prize at Korea's Gwangju International Film Festival in 2005.

4. Borrowed from philosophy and psychology, the idea and technique of reflexivity in the arts refers to "the process by which texts foreground their own production, their authorship, their intertextual influences, their textual processes, or their reception" (Stam et al. 1992: 200).

5. I thank the reader who reminded me of this.

6. See the catalogue of the 2006 New Festival (The 18th New York Lesbian, Gay, Bisexual and Transgender Film Festival), 74.

7. An interview with Gao Tian by Liu Bin. "Di san jie jilupian jiaoliuzhou yingpian: Mei Mei" (A film in the third 'week for documentary film communication': *Mei Mei*), September 2006, http://www.fanhall.com/show.aspx?id=11688&cid=40.

8. Symptomatic of this dynamic is a shot where in the background Meimei's friend is performing onstage, and in the foreground Meimei, like most of the other customers on the scene, is eating, drinking, and not paying much attention to the show. All of a sudden, we notice that a middle-aged man joins Lee, dancing in the empty space between the stage and the audience. In front of all the other customers, that man in part imitates Lee's effeminate movements onstage and in part improvises his own acts to accompany Lee's singing. I think this intriguing episode more or less reflects how this mode of female impersonation is received by the audience. To the audience, the song-and-dance onstage is by no means serious performance and this kind of unserious mimicry of "woman" can be *further* mimicked, or casually duplicated with fun by any member of the audience. In so doing the sense of parody and amusement shared by the cross-dressing performer and audience is simultaneously amplified.

9. Chris Berry, "Watching Time Go By: Narrative Distention, Realism, and Post-socialism in Jia Zhangke's *Xiao Wu*", *South Atlantic Quarterly*. Forthcoming.

10. This sort of reasoning is similarly alluded to in *Beautiful Men* (Du Haibin 2006) another documentary film from China that features three cross-dressing performers in Chengdu, the most populated city in Southwestern China. When talking about his experience of becoming a cross-dressing performer, Tao Lisha, now in his late forties, confesses to the filmmaker that he used to be a burglar back in the early 1980s. Caught stealing, he ended in

a "labour camp" (*laogai ying*) for three years. By comparing his current performing career with his criminal record and having turned his life around through enforced labour (in a socialist system), he stresses that what he does now is by no means illegal, but simply a mode of supporting himself through his own labour. Like Meimei, Tao Lisha thus integrates a socialist rationale into a capitalist one, showing the specific means by which he negotiates his queer identity in relation to a post-socialist imaginary mediated by both a capitalist logic and a socialist rationale.

11. Arjun Appadurai outlines five "landscapes" as a framework for understanding the heterogenization and disjuncture in the processes of the culture on a global scale. See Appadurai, "Disjuncture and Difference in the Global Cultural Economy", *Public Culture* 2.2 (Spring 1990): 1–24.

12. "How Many Dear Sisters on Earth Do You Have?" was sung by Taiwanese female vocalist Meng Ting-wei from the early 1990s. "Woman as Flower" is originally performed by the late Hong Kong pop star, Anita Mui (a.k.a. Mei Yan-fung), also a lesbian/gay icon in Chinese societies.

Glossary

The Hanyu Pinyin system of romanization is used for all Chinese names and terms from Mainland China, followed by the Chinese characters. For Hong Kong-specific and Taiwan-specific names and terms, their locally used transliterations are noted here first, followed by their pinyin equivalents in brackets. Names and titles which are rendered differently in English are also provided here. Book, song, play and film titles are noted here in italics.

Pinyin or local transliteration (Pinyin)	Chinese	Names and titles in English where applicable	Chapter
A fei zhengzhuan	阿飛正傳	*Days of Being Wild*	8
An'zhan	暗戰	*Running out of Time*	8
Bawang bie ji	霸王別姬	*Farewell My Concubine*	8
Bei di yanzhi	北地胭脂	*Facets of Love, or, Northern Ladies of China*	7
beiyangde	被養的		1
biaoziwuqing	婊子無情		1
Buji de feng	不羈的風	*Restless Breeze*	8
Ying Zhao Nü Lang	應召女郎	*The Call Girls*	7
Ce mian	側面	*Side Face*	8
chai mui (cai mei)	猜枚	"Guess the little thing" game	3
Chang Suk Ping (Zhang Shuping)	張叔平	a.k.a. William Chang	8
Cheng Dieyi	程蝶衣		8
Chen Jingji	陳敬濟		7
Chengdu	成都		1
Chengshi hua	程式化		9
Cheung Kwok-wing (Zhang Guorong)	張國榮	a.k.a. Leslie Cheung	8
chi daguo fan	吃大鍋飯		1
chutai	出台		1
Chu Wing-lung (Zhu Yonglong)	朱永龍		8

Pinyin or local transliteration (Pinyin)	Chinese	Names and titles in English where applicable	Chapter
Chui lian ting zheng	垂簾聽政	*Reign Behind a Curtain*	7
Chunmei	春梅		7
Chunguang zha xie	春光乍洩	*Happy Together*	8
Cixi	慈禧		7
cixiongtongti	雌雄同體		8
dagongzai	打工仔		1
Da junfa	大軍閥	*The Warlord*	7
daling qingnian	大齡青年		5
Da re	大熱	*Big Heat*	8
Dandong	丹東		9
danwei	單位		5
Deng Xiaoping	鄧小平		1
Diau Charn (Diao Chan)	貂蟬		7
Dong nuan	冬暖	*The Winter*	7
Du Haibin	杜海濱		9
Duan Jinchuan	段錦川		9
Duan Xiaolou	段小樓		8
è nü	惡女		7
fanchuan	反串		9
Fengliu yunshi	風流韻事	*Illicit Desire*	7
fengyue pian	風月片		7
Fengyue qi tan	風月奇譚	*Legends of Lust*	7
Feng mama	馮媽媽		7
funü jiefang	婦女解放		9
Gao Tian	高天		8
Gin Gin (Jing Jing Shudian)	晶晶書店	Gin Gin's Bookshop	3
Gor Gor (gege)	哥哥		8
Gongwei	宮闈		7
Guan'ge	官哥		7
Guifei zui jiu	貴妃醉酒	*The Drunken Concubine*	8
Guo Fucheng	郭富城	a.k.a. Aaron Kwok	8
guocui	國粹		8
haizi/xiaohai	孩子／小孩		1
Hanjia xiaojie	韓家小姐	*Lady of the Hans*	7
hangdang	行當		9
hao jiemei	好姊妹		9
Hong	紅	*Red*	8
Hu Chin (Hu Jin)	胡錦		7
hukou	戶口		1

Pinyin or local transliteration (Pinyin)	Chinese	Names and titles in English where applicable	Chapter
Huangdi baozhong	皇帝保重	*Take Care, Your Majesty!*	7
huangmei diao	黃梅調		7
Huo shao yuanmingyuan	火燒圓明園	*The Burning of the Imperial Palace*	7
Jiang Yue	蔣樾		8
Ji hun ji	畸婚記	*The Child Groom*	7
jishi	紀實		9
Jiangshan meiren	江山美人	*The Kingdom and the Beauty*	7
jingju	京劇	Beijing Plays a.k.a. Peking Opera	9
Jin Ping Fengyue	金瓶風月	*The Golden Lotus: Love and Desire*	7
Jin Ping Mei	金瓶梅	(film or book title)	7
Jin ping shuang yan	金瓶雙艷	*Golden Lotus*	7
Jin zhi yu ye	金枝玉葉	*He's a Woman, She's a Man*	8
kaifang	開放		1
Kwok Ka-Ki (Guo Jiaqi)	郭家麒		4
Lala	拉拉		5
Laiwang	來旺		7
laogai ying	勞改營		9
lao guniang	老姑娘		5
Lap-Yan Leung (Liang Liren)	梁立人		8
lazi	拉子		5
Li Dianlang	李殿朗	a.k.a. Margaret Li	Introduction
Li Han-hsiang (Li Hanxiang)	李翰祥		7
Li Ning	李寧		1
Li Ming	黎明	a.k.a. Leon Lai	8
Li Ping'er	李瓶兒		7
Liang Chaowei	梁朝偉	a.k.a. Tony Leung	8
Liaoning	遼寧		9
Liu Dehua	劉德華	a.k.a. Andy Lau	8
luan	亂		1
Lung Kong (Long Gang)	龍剛		7
Luo Zhuoyao	羅卓瑤	a.k.a. Clara Law	7
maide	賣的		1
Mailie Feifei	麥列菲菲	a.k.a. Felice Lieh Mak	8
mamasan	媽媽生		7
Mei Mei or Meimei	美美	film title or person's name	9
Mei Lanfang	梅蘭芳		9
Mei Yanfang	梅艷芳	a.k.a. Anita Mui	9
Meng dao neihe	夢到內河	*Bewildered*	8
Meng Tingwei	孟庭葦		9
mianzi	面子		5

Pinyin or local transliteration (Pinyin)	Chinese	Names and titles in English where applicable	Chapter
Mo Sun-Kwan (Mao Shunjun)	毛舜筠	a.k.a. Teresa Mo	8
Mong Kok (Wang jiao)	旺角		3
Mudanting	牡丹亭	*(The) Peony Pavilion*	8
nantong	男同		5
Ni jiujing you jige hao meimei	你究竟有幾個好妹妹	*How Many Dear Sisters on Earth Do You Have?*	9
Nui Gai (Nü jie)	女街		3
Nüren hua	女人花		9
nütong	女同		5
Pan Jinlian	潘金蓮		7
Pan Jinlian zhi qianshi jinsheng	潘金蓮之前世今生	*The Reincarnation of Golden Lotus*	7
Pao ma di	跑馬地	Happy Valley	3
pek jao (pi jiu)	劈酒		3
Pian cai pian se	騙財騙色	*Love Swindlers*	8
pingtai	平台		1
po (pu)	蒲		3
Qiannü youhun	倩女幽魂	*A Chinese Ghost Story*	8
qingchun fan	青春飯		9
Qing guo qing cheng	傾國傾城	*The Empress Dowager*	7
qu'er/qu'i	酷兒／酷異		Introduction
quan'nei ren	圈內人		1
reqing yanchang hui	熱情演唱會	Passion Tour	8
Renmien taohua	人面桃花	*Beautiful Men*	9
renyao	人妖		4
Shaonü Pan Jinlian	少女潘金蓮	*The Amorous Lotus Pan*	7
shaoye	少爺		1
Shi Nai'an	施耐庵		7
shuangxing	雙性		8
Shui hu zhuan	水滸傳	*The Water Margin*	7
Shuimohua	水墨畫		7
sik jung (tou zhong)	骰盅		3
Sima Ke	司馬可		7
Sinn Lap-man (Shan Liwen)	單立文		7
Song Huilian	宋蕙蓮		7
suzhi	素質		1
Tang Tang or Tangtang	唐唐	film title or person's name	8
Tian Ni	恬妮	a.k.a. Tanny Tien	7
tianxia qishu	天下奇書	Wonder Book(s) of the World	7
tie fanwan	鐵飯碗		9

Pinyin or local transliteration (Pinyin)	Chinese	Names and titles in English where applicable	Chapter
tong xing lian	同性戀		5
tongzhi	同志		Introduction, 1, 5, 6
Tsim Sha Tsui (Jian Sha Zui)	尖沙嘴		3
Tung Lo Wan (Tong Luo Wan)	銅鑼灣	Causeway Bay	3
lun (wan)	擎		Introduction
Wang Zhaojun	王昭君	*Beyond the Great Wall*	7
Wanchai (Wan Zai)	灣仔		3
Wang Po	王婆		7
Wang Wenlan	王文蘭		7
Wang You Gu	忘憂谷	Forget-sadness Valley	3
Wang Zuxian	王祖賢	a.k.a. Joey Wang	7
Wong Kar-wai (Wang Jiawei)	王家衛		8
Wu Dalang	武大郎		7
Wu Song	武松	Chinese film title or protagonist of *Tiger Killer*	7
Wu Wenguang	吳文光		9
Wu Zetian	武則天	*Empress Wu Tse-tien*	7
Xishi	西施	*Hsi Shih: The Beauty of Beauties*	7
Ximen Qing	西門慶		7
xianchang	現場		9
xiao pin bu xiao chang	笑貧不笑娼		9
xianchang gan	現場感		9
Xu Beihong	徐悲鴻		7
yazi	鴨子		1
yanda	嚴打		1
Yanzhi kou	胭脂扣	*Rouge*	8
Yang Guifei	楊貴妃	*Yang Kwei Fei, the Magnificent Concubine*	7
Yau Ma Tei (You Ma Di)	油麻地		3
Yingtai qixue	瀛台泣血	*The Last Tempest*	7
yinfu	淫婦		7
yin shu	淫樹／淫書		7
Yingxiong bense	英雄本色	*A Better Tomorrow*	8
Yü pu tuan	玉蒲團	*The Carnal Prayer Mat*	7
Yuan'nan	怨男	*Grieving Man*	8
Yuen Long (Yuan Lang)	元朗		7
yum cha (yin cha)	飲茶		3
zhan qi lai	站起來		Introduction
zhan chu lai	站出來		Introduction

Pinyin or local transliteration (Pinyin)	*Chinese*	*Names and titles in English where applicable*	*Chapter*
Zhang Hanzi	張涵子		9
Zhang Xueyou	張學友	a.k.a. Jacky Cheung	8
Zhang Yuan	張元		9
Zhizun Bao	至尊寶	a.k.a. *Supremo* (film title and protagonist's name)	7
Zhou Zuoren	周作人		7
Zhu fu ren	竹夫人	*Madame Bamboo*	7
Zhu Mu	朱牧		7
zhuanti pian	專題片		9
Zhuo jian qushi	捉姦趣事	*That's Adultery!*	7
Zung Kai-leon (Zhong Qilin)	鍾啟麟		4

Works Cited

Introduction

Works cited in Chinese

Fang Gang 方剛. *Nanxing xing gongzuozhe nanxing qigai jiangou de zhi xing yanjiu*《男性性工作者男性氣概建構的質性研究》[A Qualitative Research of the Construction of Masculinity of Male Sex Workers].
http://blog.sina.com.cn/s/blog_467a5c9601000ai8.html. Accessed 20 November 2008.
Xianggang xing wenhua xue hui 香港性文化學會 [Hong Kong Sex Culture Society]. *Seqing wu hai! shi fou shenhua?—cong seqing guiguan de zhengyi lun seqing huohai tekan*《色情無害！是否神話？——從色情規管的爭議論色情禍害特刊》 [Pornography Is Harmless! Is That a Myth? Special Issue on the Harm of Pornography Regarding the Debate of Regulating Pornography]. January 2009. http://www.scs.org.hk/publish/081224_ART-pornharm.pdf. Accessed 2 January 2009.
Guan Qiwen 關啟文 [Kwan Kai Man]. *Shifei, quzhi—dui renquan, tongxinglian de lunli fansi*《是非、曲直——對人權、同性戀的倫理反思》[Reflection on Human Rights and Homosexuality ("Truth and Light" series 1)]. Hong Kong: China Alliance Press, 2000.
———. *Liwan kuangchao—xijuan quanqiu de xing jiefang yundong*《力挽狂潮——席捲全球的性解放運動》[*Stem the Tide—The Affection of Sexual Liberation Movement* ("Truth and Light" series 2)]. Hong Kong: China Alliance Press, 2007.
Guan Qiwen, Dai Yaoting et al. 關啟文、戴耀廷等 [Kwan Kai Man, Tai Yiu Ting et al.]. *Ping quan? ba quan?——shen shi tongxinglian yiti*《平權？霸權？——審視同性戀議題》[Equal Rights? Hegemony? Examining the Homosexual Issue]. Hong Kong: Cosmos, 2005.
Guan Qiwen, Hong Ziyun, eds. 關啟文、洪子雲編 [Kwan Kai Man, Andrew Hung eds.]. *Chong xun zhen xing: xing jiefang hongliu zhong jidutu de jinchi yu huiying*《重尋真性：性解放洪流中基督徒的堅持與回應》[In Search of Authentic Sexuality ("Intellectual" Series 1)]. Hong Kong: Fellowship of Evangelical Students, 2003.

Works cited in English

Eng, David, Judith Halberstam, and Estaban José Muñoz. "Introduction: What's Queer about Queer Studies Now?" *Social Text* 2005, 23(3–4, 84–85): 1–17.
Love, Heather. "Compulsory Happiness and Queer Existence." *New Formations* 2007–2008a, 63 (Winter): 52–65.

————. *Feeling Backward: Loss and the Politics of Queer History*. Cambridge, MA: Harvard University Press, 2007b.

Sedgwick, Eve Kosofsky. *Tendencies*. Durham and London: Duke University Press, 1993.

Villarejo, Amy. "Tarrying with the Normative: Queer Theory and Black History." *Social Text* 2005, 23(3–4, 84–85): 69–84.

Warner, Michael. *The Trouble with Normal: Sex, Politics, and the Ethics of Queer Life*. Cambridge, MA: Harvard University Press, 1999.

Yau, Ching. "Bridges and Battles" as part of "Queer Film and Video Festival Forum, Take Two: Critics Speak Out." *GLQ: A Journal of Lesbian and Gay Studies* 2006, 12(4): 599–625.

Chapter 1

Works cited in Chinese

Li, Yinhe 李銀河. *Tongxinglian yawenhua*《同性戀亞文化》[Homosexual Subculture]. Beijing: Jinri Zhongguo chubanshe, 1998.

Samshasha 小明雄. *Zhongguo tongxinglian shilu*《中國同性愛史錄》[History of Homosexuality in China]. Hong Kong: Rosa Winkel Press, 1997 [1984].

Tong, G. 童戈. *Zhongguo de nannan xingxingwei xing yu ziwo rentong zhuangtai diaocha*《中國人的男男性行為性與自我認同狀態調查》[Sexuality and Expression of Self-identities in Chinese MSM Community]. Beijing, China: Beijing Gender Health Education Institute, 2005.

————. *Zhongguo nannan xingjiaoyi zhuangtai diaocha*《中國男男性交易狀態調查》[An Inquiry to Commercial Sex in MSM Community in China]. Beijing, China: Beijing Gender Health Education Institute, 2007.

Works cited in English

Allen, D. M. "Young male prostitutes: A psychosocial study." *Archives of Sexual Behavior* 9.5 (1980): 399–426.

Aggleton, P., ed. *Men Who Sell Sex: International Perspectives on Male Prostitution and AIDS*. London: UCL Press, 1999.

Amnesty International. "China: Internal Migrants: Discrimination and Abuse. The Human Cost of an Economic 'Miracle'." http://www.amnesty.org/en/library/info/ASA17/008/2007. Accessed 30 September 2008.

Blum, S.D., and L.M. Jensen. eds. *China Off Center: Mapping the Margins of the Middle Kingdom*. Honolulu: University of Hawai'i Press, 2002.

Brewis, J., and S. Linstead. "The Worst Thing Is the Screwing (1): Consumption, and the Management of Identity in Sex Work." *Gender, Work and Organization* 7.2 (2000a): 84–97.

————. "The Worst Thing Is the Screwing (2): Context and Career in Sex Work." *Gender, Work and Organization* 7.3 (2000b): 168–180.

Browne, J., and V. Minichiello. "Research Directions in Male Sex Work." *Journal of Homosexuality* 31.4 (1996a): 29–36.

————. "The Social and Work Context of Commercial Sex between Men: A Research Note." *Australian and New Zealand Journal of Sociology* 32.1 (1996b): 86–92.

————. "The Social Meanings behind Male Sex Work: Implications for Sexual Interaction." *The British Journal of Sociology* 46.4 (1995): 598–622.

Calhoun, T.C., and G. Weaver. "Rational Decision-making among Male Street Prostitutes." *Deviant Behavior* 17 (1996): 209–227.

Chapkis, W. *Live Sex Acts: Women Performing Erotic Labor*. New York: Routledge, 1997.

China Ministry of Health, Joint United Nations Program on HIV/AIDS, and World Health Organization. *2005 Update on the HIV/AIDS Epidemic and Response in China*. Beijing, China: National Center for AIDS/STD Prevention and Control, China CDC, 2006.

Choi, K. H., E. Diehl, G. Yaqi, S. Qu, and J. Mandel. "High HIV Risk but Inadequate Prevention Services for Men in China Who Have Sex with Men: An Ethnographic Study." *AIDS and Behavior* 6.3 (2002): 255–266.

Choi, K. H., D. R. Gibson, L. Han, and Y. Guo. "High Levels of Unprotected Sex with Men and Women among Men Who Have Sex with Men: A Potential Bridge of HIV Transmission in Beijing, China." *AIDS Education and Prevention* 16.1 (2004): 19–30.

Cohen, M. S., G. E. Henderson, P. Aiello, and H. Zheng. "Successful Eradication of Sexually Transmitted Disease in the People's Republic of China: Implications for the 21st Century." *Journal of Infectious Diseases* 174 (1996): S223–229.

Coombs, N. R. "Male Prostitution: A Psychosocial View of Behaviour." *American Journal of Orthopsychiatry* 55.5 (1974): 782–789.

Davies, P., and R. Feldman. "Prostitute Men Now." *Rethinking Prostitution: Purchasing Sex in the 1990s*. Eds. G. Scambler and A. Scambler. London: Routledge, 1997. 29–53.

Davis, K. "Prostitution." *Contemporary Social Problems*. Eds. R. K. Merton and R. Nisbit. New York: Harcourt-Brace, 1976.

Dressel, P. L., and D. M. Petersen. "Becoming a Male Stripper: Recruitment, Socialization, and Ideological Development." *Work and Occupations* 9.3 (1982): 387–406.

Escoffier, J. "Gay-for-Pay: Straight Men and the Making of Gay Pornography." *Qualitative Sociology* 26.4 (2003): 531–555.

Farrer, J. *Opening Up: Youth Sex Culture and Market Reform in Shanghai*. Chicago and London: The University of Chicago Press, 2002.

Gil, V. E. "The Cut Sleeves Revisited: A Contemporary Account of Male Homosexuality." *China Off Center: Mapping the Margins of the Middle Kingdom*. Eds. S.D. Blum and L.M. Jensen. Honolulu: University of Hawai'i Press, 2002. 238–248.

Gil, V. E., M. S. Wang, A. F. Anderson, G. M. Lin, and Z. O. Wu. "Prostitutes, Prostitution and STD/HIV Transmission in Mainland China." *Social Science & Medicine* 42 (1996): 141–152.

Glover, E. "The Psychopathology of Prostitution." *Roots of Crime*. Ed. E. Glover. New York: International University Press, 1960. 244–267.

Guang, L. "Rural Taste, Urban Fashion: The Cultural Politics of Rural/Urban Difference in Contemporary China." *positions: east asia cultures critique* 11. 3 (2003): 613–646.

Halberstam, J. *In a Queer Time & Place: Transgendered Bodies, Subcultural Lives*. New York: New York University Press, 2005.

He, N., F. Y. Wong, Z. J. Huang, E. E. Thompson, and C. Fu. "Substance Use and HIV Risks among Male Heterosexual and 'Money Boy' Migrants in Shanghai, China." *AIDS Care* 19. 1 (2007): 109–115.

Hershatter, G. *Dangerous Pleasure: Prostitution and Modernity in Twentieth-Century Shanghai*. Berkeley: University of California Press, 1997.

Hinsch, B. *Passions of the Cut Sleeve: The Male Homosexual Tradition in China*. Oxford: University of California Press, 1990.

Ho, C. J. "Self-empowerment and 'Professionalism': Conversations with Taiwanese Sex Workers." *Inter-Asia Cultural Studies* 1.2 (2000): 283–299.

Hong, Y., and X. Li. "Behavioral Studies of Female Sex Workers in China: A Literature Review and Recommendation for Future Research." *AIDS and Behavior*, 12.4 (2007): 623–636.

Jeffreys, E. "Querying Queer Theory: Debating Male-Male Prostitution in the Chinese Media." *Critical Asian Studies* 39.1 (2007): 151–175.

————. "Introduction: Talking Sex and Sexuality in China." *Sex and Sexuality in China.* Ed. E. Jeffreys London: Routledge, 2006. 1–20.

Joffe, H., and J. E. Dockrell. "Safer Sex: Lessons from the Male Sex Industry." *Journal of Community and Applied Social Psychology* 5 (1995): 333–346.

Jones, R. "Identity, Community, and Social Practice among Men Who Have Sex with Men in China." *Rethinking and Recasting Citizenship: Social Exclusion and Marginality in Chinese Societies.* Eds. M. Tam M., H.B. Ku, T. Kong. Hong Kong: Centre for Social Policy Studies, The Hong Kong Polytechnic University, 2005. 149–166.

Kong, Travis S.K. "The Seduction of the Golden Boy: The Body Politics of Hong Kong Gay Men." *Body and Society* 8.1 (2002): 29–48.

————. "Queer at Your Own Risk: Marginality, Community, and the Body Politics of Hong Kong Gay Men." *Sexualities* 7.1 (2004): 5–30.

————. *The Hidden Voice: The Sexual Politics of Chinese Male Sex Workers.* Hong Kong: Centre for Social Policy Studies, Department of Applied Social Sciences, the Hong Kong Polytechnic University, 2005.

————. "What It Feels Like for a Whore: The Body Politics of Women Performing Erotic Labour in Hong Kong." *Gender, Work and Organization.* 13.5 (2006): 409–434.

————. "Risk Factors Affecting Condom Use among Male Sex Workers Who Serve Men in China: A Qualitative Study." *Sexually Transmitted Infections* 84 (2009a): 444–448.

————. "More Than a Sex Machine: Accomplishing Masculinity among Chinese Male Sex Workers in the Hong Kong Sex Industry," *Deviant Behavior* 30 (2009b): 715–745.

————. *Chinese Male Homosexualities: Memba, Tongzhi, and Golden Boy.* London: Routledge, 2010.

Li, X.M., L.Y. Zhang, X.Y. Fang, Q. Xiong, X.G. Chen, D.H. Lin, A. Mathur, and B. Stanton. "Stigmatization Experienced by Rural-to-urban Migrant Workers in China: Findings from a Qualitative Study." *World Health and Population* 9.4 (2007): 29–43.

Li, Yinhe. "Regulating Male Same-Sex Relationships in the People's Republic of China." *Sex and Sexuality in China.* Ed. E. Jeffreys. London: Routledge, 2006. 82–101.

Liu, J.X., and K. Choi. "Experiences of Social Discrimination among Men Who Have Sex with Men in Shanghai, China." *AIDS and Behavior* 10 (2006): S25–S33.

Liu, L. H. ed. *Tokens of Exchange: The Problem of Transformation in Global Circulation.* Durham and London: Duke University Press, 1999.

Luckenbill, D. F. "Entering Male Prostitution." *Urban Life* 14.2 (1985): 131–153.

————. "Deviant Career Mobility: The Case of Male Prostitutes." *Social Problems* 33.4 (1986): 283–296.

Miles, M.B., and A. M. Huberman, eds. *An Expanded Sourcebook Qualitative Data Analysis.* London: Sage, 1994.

Minichiello, V., R. Marino, and J. Browne "Knowledge, Risk Perceptions and Condom Usage in Male Sex Workers from Three Australian Cities." *AIDS Care* 13.3 (2002): 387–402.

O'Connell Davidson, J. "Prostitution and the Contours of Control." *Sexual Cultures.* Eds. Janet Holland and Jeffrey Weeks. London: Macmillan, 1996. 180–198.

O' Neill, M. *Prostitution and Feminism: Towards a Politics of Feeling.* Cambridge: Polity Press in association with Blackwell Publishers, 2001.

Pan, S.M. "A Sex Revolution in Current China." *Journal of Psychology and Human Sexuality* 6 (1993): 1–14.

Perry, E. J., and M. Selden, eds. *Chinese Society: Change, Conflict and Resistance.* London and New York: Routledge, 2000.

Pheterson, G. *The Prostitution Prism.* Amsterdam: Amsterdam University Press, 1996.

Philips, J. L. "Tourist-oriented Prostitution in Barbados: The Case of Beach Boy and the White Female Tourist." *Sun, Sex, and Gold.* Ed. K. Kempadoo. Oxford: Rowman and Littlefield, 1999. 183–200.

Pruitt, D., and S. LaFont. "For Love and Money: Romance Tourism in Jamaica." *Annals of Tourism Research* 22.2 (1995): 422–440.

Pun, N. "Subsumption or Consumption? The Phantom of Consumer Revolution in 'Globalizing' China." *Cultural Anthropology* 18.4 (2003): 469–492.

———. *Made in China: Women Factory Workers in a Global Workplace.* Durham: Duke University Press, 2005.

Reiss, A. J. "The Social Integration of Queers and Peers." *Social Problems* 9 (1961): 102–120.

Rofel, L. *Desiring China: Experiments in Neoliberalism, Sexuality, and Public Culture.* Durham and London: Duke University Press, 2007.

———. "The Traffic in Money Boys." *positions: east asia cultures Critique,* 2010 (in press).

Ronai, C. R., and R. Cross. "Dancing with Identity: Narrative Resistance Strategies of Male and Female Stripteasers." *Deviant Behavior* 19 (1998): 99–119.

Ruan, F.F. *Sex in China.* New York: Plenum, 1991.

Ryan, G. W., and H. R. Bernard. "Data Management and Analysis Methods." *Handbook of Qualitative Research.* Eds. N. K. Denzin and Y.S. Lincoln. 2nd ed. Thousand Oaks, CA: Sage, 2000. 769–802.

Sanders, T. *Sex Work: A Risky Business.* Devon: Willan, 2005.

Scambler, G., and A. Scambler, eds. *Rethinking Prostitution: Purchasing Sex in the 1990s.* London and New York: Routledge, 1997.

Shaw, I., and I. Butler. "Understanding Young People and Prostitution: A Foundation for Practice?" *British Journal of Social Work* 28.2 (1998): 177–196.

Solinger, D. *Contesting Citizenship in Urban China: Peasant, Migrants, the State, and the Logic of the Market.* Berkeley: University of California Press, 1999.

Strauss, A. L., and J.M. Corbin. *Grounded Theory in Practice.* Thousand Oaks, CA: Sage, 1997.

Tewksbury, R. "Male Strippers: Men Objectifying Men." *Doing "Women's Work": Men in Nontraditional Occupations.* Ed. Christine L. Williams. London: Sage, 1993. 168–181.

Van Gulik, R. H. *Sexual Life in Ancient China: A Preliminary Survey of Chinese Sex and Society from ca. 1500 B.C. till 1644 A.D.* Leiden, Netherlands: E.J. Brill, 1961.

Vanwesenbeeck, I. "Another Decade of Social Scientific Work on Sex Work: A Review of Research 1990–2000." *Annual Review of Sex Research* 12 (2001): 242–289.

Weinberg, M.S., F.M. Shaver, and C.J. Williams. "Gendered Sex Work in San Francisco Tenderloin." *Archives of Sexual Behavior* 28 (1999): 503–521.

Weitzer, R. ed. *Sex for Sale: Prostitution, Pornography, and the Sex Industry.* London and New York: Routledge, 2000.

West, D. J., and B. de Villiers. *Male Prostitution.* London and New York: The Haworth Press, 1993.

Wong, F.Y., Z.J. Huang, N. He, B.D. Smith, Y. Gin, C. Fu, and D. Young. "HIV Risks among Gay- and Non-Gay-Identified Migrant Boys in Shanghai, China." *AIDS Care* 20. 2 (2008): 170–180.

Wong, W.C.W., J. Zhang, S.C. Wu, T.S.K. Kong, and D.C.Y. Ling. "The HIV Related Risks among Men Having Sex with Men in Rural Yunnan, China: A Qualitative Study." *Sexually Transmitted Infections* 82 (2006): 127–130.

Wu, J. "From 'Long Yang' and 'Dui Shi' to Tongzhi: Homosexuality in China." *Journal of Gay & Lesbian Psychotherapy* 7.1/2 (2003): 117–143.

Yan, H.R. "Neoliberal Governmentality and Neo-Humanism: Organizing Suzhi/Value Flow through Labor Recruitment Networks." *Cultural Anthropology* 18. 4 (2003a): 493–523.

————. "Spectralization of the Rural: Reinterpreting the Labor Mobility of Rural Young Women in Post-Mao China." *American Ethnologist* 30.4 (2003b): 578–596.

Zhang, B.C., and Q.S. Chu. "MSM and HIV / AIDS in China." *Cell Research* 15.11-12 (2005): 858–864.

Zhang, B.C., S.W. Wu, X.F. Li, M.Q. Zhu, and L.G. Yang. "Study on High Risk Behaviours among Male Sex Workers Related to STI / HIV." *Chin J STD/AIDS* 10 (2004): 329–331.

Zhang, L. *Strangers in the City: Reconfigurations of Space, Power, and Social Networks within China's Floating Population.* Stanford, CA: Stanford University Press, 2001.

Zhu, Y. "China's Floating Population and Their Settlement in the Cities: Beyond the Hukou Reform." *Habitat International* 31.1 (2007): 65–76.

Chapter 2

"70 Percent of Job-Seekers Underpaid, Overqualified." *Jakarta Post* 17 July 2003.

"Government Urged to Improve Protection of Migrant Workers." *Indonesian Observer* 19 December 2000.

"Indonesia Aiming to Send One Million Workers Overseas Each Year." *Jakarta Post* 25 January 2006.

"Indonesian Migrant Workers Send Home US$2.9 BLN in 2005." *Asia Pulse* 25 January 2006.

"Satu Lagi, Pernikahan Sejenis di Tai Po." *Suara* 23 March 2007.

AMC et al. (Asian Migrant Centre & Asian Domestic Workers Union, Forum of Filipino Reintegration and Savings Groups, Indonesian Migrant Workers Union and Thai Women's Association). *Baseline Research on Gender and Racial Discrimination Towards Filipino, Indonesian and Thai Domestic Helpers in Hong Kong.* Hong Kong: Asian Migrant Centre & Asian Domestic Workers Union, Forum of Filipino Reintegration and Savings Groups, Indonesian Migrant Workers Union and Thai Women's Association, 2001.

Atkinson, Jane Monnig. "How Gender Makes A Difference in Wana Society." *Power and Difference: Gender in Island Southeast Asia.* Eds. Jane Monnig Atkinson and Shelley Errington. Stanford: Stanford University Press, 1990. 59–94.

Belanger, Daniele, and Khuat Thu Hong. "Young Single Women Using Abortion in Hanoi, Viet Nam." *Asia-Pacific Population Journal* 13.22 (1998): 3–26.

Bennett, Linda Rae. *Women, Islam and Modernity: Single Women, Sexuality and Reproductive Health in Contemporary Indonesia.* London, New York: RoutledgeCurzon, 2005.

Blackwood, Evelyn. "Tombois in West Sumatra: Constructing Masculinity and Erotic Desire." *Female Desires: Same-Sex Relations and Transgender Practices Across Cultures.* Eds. Evelyn Blackwood and Saskia E Wieringa. New York: Columbia University Press, 1999. 181–205.

Blackwood, Evelyn, and Saskia E. Wieringa, eds. *Female Desires: Same-Sex Relations and Transgender Practices across Cultures.* New York: Columbia University Press, 1999.

Bourdieu, Pierre. "The Organic Ethnologist of Algerian Migration." *Ethnography,* 1.2 (2000): 173–182.

Butler, Judith. *Gender Trouble: Feminism and the Subversion of Identity.* New York: Routledge, 1990.

————. "Imitation and Gender Insubordination." *Inside/Out: Lesbian Theories, Gay Theories.* Ed. Diana Fuss. New York: Routledge, 1991. 13–31.

Case, Sue-Ellen. "Towards a Butch-Femme Aesthetic." *Discourse 11* (Winter 1988–1989). Reprinted in *The Lesbian and Gay Studies Reader.* Eds. Henry Abelove, Michèle Aina Barale and David M. Halperin. New York: Routledge, 1993. 294–306.

Constable, Nicole. "Sexuality and Discipline among Filipina Domestic Workers in Hong Kong." *American Ethnologies* 24.3 (1997a): 539–558.

———. *Maid to Order in Hong Kong: Stories of Filipina Workers.* New York: Cornell University Press, 1997b.

———. "Dolls, T-Birds, and Ideal Workers: The Negotiation of Filipino Identity in Hong Kong." *Home and Hegemony: Domestic Service and Identity Politics in South and Southeast Asia.* Eds. Kathleen M. Adams and Sara Dickey. Ann Arbor: The University of Michigan Press, 2000. 221–248.

Cook, Blanche Weisen. "Female Support networks and Political Activism." *Chrysalis* 3 (1977): 43–61.

de Lauretis, Teresa. "Sexual Indifference and Lesbian Representation." *The Lesbian and Gay Studies Reader.* Eds. Henry Abelove, Michèle Aina Barale and David M. Halperin. New York: Routledge, 1993. 141–158.

Echols, A. *Daring to Be Bad: Radical Feminism in America 1967–1975.* Minneapolis: University of Minnesota Press, 1989.

Echols, John, and Hassan Shadily. *An Indonesian-English Dictionary.* 3rd Edition. Jakarta: Penerbit, 1989.

Elmhirst, Becky. "Negotiating Gender, Kinships and Livelihood Practices in an Indonesian Transmigration Area." *Women and Households in Indonesia: Cultural Notions and Social Practices.* Eds. Juliette Koning, Marleen Nolten, Janet Rodenburg and Ratna Saptari. Richmond, Surrey: Curzon, 2000. 208–234.

Fenstermaker, Sarah, and Candace West. "'Doing Difference' Revisited: Problems, Prospects, and the Dialogue in Feminist Theory." *Doing Gender, Doing Difference: Inequality, Power & Institutional Change.* Eds. Sarah Fenstermaker and Candace West. New York and London: Routledge, 2002. 205–233.

Fenstermaker, Sarah, Candace West, and Don H. Zimmerman. "Gender Inequality: New Conceptual Terrain." *Doing Gender, Doing Difference: Inequality, Power & Institutional Change.* Eds. Sarah Fenstermaker and Candace West. New York and London: Routledge, 2002. 25–40.

Ferguson, Ann. "Is There A Lesbian Culture?" *Lesbian Philosophies and Cultures.* Ed. Jeffner Allen. New York: State University of New York Press, 1990. 63–88.

Goodloe, Amy. "Lesbian Identity and the Politics of Butch-Femme Roles". http://www.lesbian.org/amy/essays/bf-paper.html. 1996. Accessed 31 October 2006.

Groves, Julian McAllister, and Kimberly A. Chang. "Romancing Resistance and Resisting Romance: Ethnography and the Construction of Power in the Filipina Domestic Worker Community in Hong Kong". *Journal of Contemporary Ethnography* 28.3 (1999): 235–265.

Hawwa, Sithi. "From Cross to Crescent: Religious Conversion of Filipina Domestic Helpers in Hong Kong". *Islam and Christian–Muslim Relations* 11.3 (2000): 347–367.

Hettiarachchy, Tilak, and Stephen L. Schensul. "The Risks of Pregnancy and the Consequences among Young Unmarried Women Working in a Free Trade Zone in Sri Lanka". *Asia-Pacific Journal* (June 2001): 125–140.

Hong Kong Immigration Department. *Statistics May 2006.* Hong Kong: Hong Kong Government.

Hugo, Graeme. "International Labor Migration and the Family: Some Observations from Indonesia." *Asian and Pacific Migration Journal* 4.2-3 (1995): 273–301.

———. "Indonesian Overseas Contract Workers' HIV Knowledge: A Gap in Information". 2000. UNDP. http://www.hiv-development.org/text/publications/IOCWK.pdf. Accessed 28 May 2005.

Johnston, J. *Lesbian Nation*. New York: Simon and Schuster/Touchstone, 1973.

Komnas Perempuan, Commission on Violence Against Women, Solidaritas Perempuan/ Caram Indonesia. "Indonesian Migrant Workers: Systematic Abuse at Home and Abroad." Indonesian Country Report to the UN Special Rapporteur on the Human Rights of Migrants. Kuala Lumpur: Komnas Perempuan, Commission on Violence Against Women, Solidaritas Perempuan/Caram Indonesia, 2002.

Lan, Pei-Chia. *Global Cinderellas: Migrant Domestics and Newly Rich Employers in Taiwan*. Durham and London: Duke University Press, 2006.

Leigh, Barbara. "Learning and Knowing Boundaries: Schooling in New Order Indonesia." *Sojourn* 14.1 (1999): 34–56.

Loveband, Anne. "Positioning the Product: Indonesian Migrant Women Workers in Contemporary Taiwan." *Southeast Asia Research Centre, Working Papers Series* 43. City University, Hong Kong (April 2003).

———. "Positioning the Product: Indonesian Migrant Women Workers in Taiwan." *Journal of Contemporary Asia* 34.3 (2004): 336–348.

Murray, Alison J. "Let Them Take Ecstasy: Class and Jakarta Lesbians." *Female Desires: Same-Sex Relations and Transgender Practices Across Cultures*. Eds. Evelyn Blackwood and Saskia E Wieringa. New York: Columbia University Press, 1999. 139–156.

Oetomo, Dédé. "Gender and Sexual Orientation In Indonesia". *Fantasizing the Feminine in Indonesia*. Ed. Laurie J. Sears. Durham and London: Duke University Press, 1996.

Puri, Mahesh C., and Joanna Busza. "In Forests and Factories: Sexual Behaviour among Young Migrant Workers in Nepal." *Culture, Health and Sexuality* 6.2 (March–April 2004): 145–158.

Radicalesbians. "The Woman-Identified Woman." *Radical Feminism*. Eds. Anne Koedt, Ellen Levine and Anita Rapone. New York: Quadrangle/New York Times Book, 1973. 240–245.

Rich, Adrienne. "Compulsory Heterosexuality and Lesbian Existence." *Signs* 5.4 (Summer 1980): 631–660.

Robinson, Kathryn. "Gender, Islam, and Nationality: Indonesian Domestic Servants in the Middle East." *Home and Hegemony: Domestic Service and Southeast Asia*. Eds. Kathleen M. Adams and Sara Dickey. Ann Arbor: University of Michigan Press, 2000. 249–282.

Roof, Judith. *A Lure of Knowledge: Lesbian Sexuality and Theory*. New York: Columbia University Press, 1991.

Rupp, Leila J. "'Imagine My Surprise': Women's Relationships in Mid-Twentieth Century America." *Hidden From History: Reclaiming the Gay and Lesbian Past*. Eds. Martin Bauml Duberman, Martha Vicinus and George Chauncey, Jr. London, New York, Ontario: Meridian, 1990.

Sassen, Saskia. "Women's Burden: Counter-Geographies of Globalization and the Feminization of Survival." *Journal of International Affairs* (Spring 2000): 503–524.

Sim, Amy. "Organising Discontent: NGOs for Southeast Asian Migrant Workers in Hong Kong." *Asian Journal of Social Sciences* 31.3 (2003): 478–510.

———. Conference paper. "Sapphic Shadows: Sworn Sisterhoods and Cyber Lesbian Communities in Hong Kong." The Second International Symposium on "Chinese Women and Their Network Capital Log-on: Chinese Women and Their Chinese Networks". University of Hong Kong, Hong Kong, 20–21 October 2004a.

———. Conference paper. "Sexuality in Migration: The Case of Indonesian Domestic Workers in Hong Kong." 8th Asian Studies Conference. Institute of Asian Cultural Studies and International Christian University, Tokyo, June 19–20 2004b.

Suryakusuma, Julia I. *Sex, Power and Nation: An Anthology of Writings 1979–2003*. Jakarta: Metafor, 2004.

United Nations Commission on Human Rights. "Forced Labour and Exploitation of Indonesian Migrant Workers." *Sub-Commission on the Promotion and Protection of Human Rights,* Working Group on Contemporary Forms of Slavery, 28th Session. Geneva 16–20 June 2003.

Wee, Vivienne, and Amy Sim. "Transnational labour networks in female labour migration." *International Migration in Southeast Asia.* Eds. Aris Ananta and Evi N. Arifin. Singapore: Institute of Southeast Asian Studies, 2004. 166–198.

———. "Hong Kong as a Destination for Migrant Domestic Workers." *Asian Women as Transmigrant Domestic Workers.* Eds. Shirlena Huang et al. Singapore: Marshall Cavendish Academic, 2005. 175–209.

Wee Vivienne, Amy Sim, and Celine Lim. Conference paper. "Class, Gender and Agency: The Employment and Abuse of Migrant Domestic Workers in East and Southeast Asia." Workshop of Migration, Ethnicity and Workforce Segmentation in the Asia Pacific. Southeast Asia Research Centre, City University and the Centre for Asia Pacific Social Transformations, University of Wollongong, Wollongong, 11–12 August 2003.

Wieringa, Saskia. Conference paper. "Jakarta's Butches: Transgendered Women or Third Gender?" *Beyond Boundaries: Sexuality Across Culture.* Amsterdam. 1997.

———. "Desiring Bodies or Defiant Cultures: Butch-Femme Lesbians in Jakarta and Lima." *Female Desires: Same-Sex Relations and Transgender Practices across Cultures.* Eds. Evelyn Blackwood and Saskia E Wieringa. New York: Columbia University Press. 1999. 206–229.

Williams, Catharina Purwani Budi. "Maiden Voyages: Eastern Indonesian Women on the Move." Doctoral thesis. Australian National University, 2003.

Chapter 3

Works cited in Chinese

Chen, Cui-Er, et al. 陳翠兒、陳麗喬、蔡宏興、吳啟聰、陳建國. *Bi cheng: wo men de kong jian*《The 逼 City: 我們的空間》[The Congested City: Our Spaces]. Hong Kong: Home Affairs Bureau, 2006.

Feng, Bang-Yan 馮邦彥. *Xianggang dichanye bainian*《香港地產業百年》[A Century of Hong Kong Real Estate Development]. Hong Kong: Joint Publishing, 2001.

Zhang, Qiao Ting 張喬婷. *Xufu yu dikang: shi wei xiaoyuan nü jingying lazi de qingyu yayi*《馴服與抵抗：十位校園女菁英拉子的情慾壓抑》[Campus Memory, Identity and the Emerging of Lesbian Subjectivities in Taiwan]. Taipei: Tangshan chubanshe, 2000.

Works cited in English

Bell, David, and Gill Valentine, eds. *Mapping Desire: Geographies of Sexualities.* London: Routledge, 1995.

Bouthillette, Anne-Marie. "Queer and Gendered Housing: A Tale of Two Neighbourhoods in Vancouver." *Queers in Space: Communities, Public Spaces, Sites of Resistance.* Eds. Gordon Brent Ingram, Anne-Marie Bouthillette and Yolanda Retter. Seattle, WA: Bay Press, 1997. 213–232.

Castells, Manuel. *The City and the Grassroots: A Crosscultural Theory of Urban Social Movements.* Berkeley, CA: University of California Press, 1983.

Chao, Antonia. "Global Metaphors and Local Strategies in the Construction of Taiwan's Lesbian Identities." *Culture, Health & Sexuality,* 2.4 (2000): 377–390.

————. "'How Come I Can't Stand Guarantee for My Own Life?': Taiwan Citizenship and the Cultural Logic of Queer Identity." *Inter-Asia Cultural Studies*, 3.3 (2002): 369–381.

Chauncey, George. *Gay New York: Gender, Urban Culture, and the Making of the Gay Male World, 1890–1940*. New York: Basic Books, 1994.

Chua, Beng-Huat. *Consumption in Asia: Lifestyles and Identities*. London and New York: Routledge, 2000.

Corteen, Karen. "Lesbian Safety Talk: Problematizing Definitions and Experiences of Violence, Sexuality and Space." *Sexualities*, 5.3 (2002): 259–280.

De Certeau, Michel. *The Practice of Everyday Life*. Berkeley, Los Angeles and London: University of California Press, 1984.

Désert, Jean-Ulrick. "Queer Space." *Queers in Space: Communities, Public Spaces, Sites of Resistance*. Eds. Gordon Brent Ingram, Anne-Marie Bouthillette and Yolanda Retter. Seattle, WA: Bay Press, 1997. 17–26.

Duncan, Nancy. "Renegotiating Gender and Sexuality in Public and Private Spaces." *Body Space: Destabilizing Geographies of Gender and Sexuality*. Ed. Nancy Duncan. London: Routledge, 1996. 127–145.

Eves, Alison. "Queer Theory, Butch/Femme Identities and Lesbian Space." *Sexualities*, 7.4 (2004): 480–496.

Faderman, Lillian. *Odd Girls and Twilight Lovers: A History of Lesbian Life in Twentieth-Century America*. New York: Penguin Books, 1992.

Foucault, Michel. "Of Other Spaces." *Diacritics*, 16.1 (1986): 22–27.

Fraser, Nancy. "Rethinking the Public Sphere: A Contribution to the Critique of Actually Existing Democracy." *Habermas and the Public Sphere*. Ed. Craig Calhoun. Cambridge, MA: The MIT Press, 1992. 109–142.

Hankin, Kelly. *The Girls in the Back Room: Looking at the Lesbian Bar*. Minneapolis: University of Minnesota Press, 2002.

Harvey, David. "Social Justice, Postmodernism and the City." *International Journal of Urban and Regional Research*, 16.4 (1992): 588–601.

Herng-Dar, Bih. *The Power of Space*. Taipei: PsyGarden Publishing Company, 2001.

Highmore, Ben. *Everyday Life and Cultural Theory: An Introduction*. London and New York: Routledge, 2002. 1–17.

Ingram, Gordon, Anne-Marie Bouthillette, and Yolanda Retter, eds. *Queers in Space: Communities, Public Spaces, Sites of Resistance*. Seattle: Gay Press, 1997.

Jeffreys, Sheila. "Butch and Femme: Now and Then." *Not a Passing Phase: Reclaiming Lesbians in History 1840–1985*. Eds. Lesbian History Group. London: Women's Press, 1989. 158–187.

Kennedy, Elizabeth Lapovsky, and Madelaine Davis. *Boots of Leather and Slippers of Gold: The History of a Lesbian Community*. New York: Routledge, 1993.

Kenney, Moira Rachel. *Mapping Gay L.A.: The Intersection of Place and Politics*. Philadelphia: Temple University Press, 2001.

Lai, Yuen-Ki. "Lesbian Masculinities: Identity and Body Construction among Tomboys in Hong Kong." MPhil Thesis. Hong Kong: The Chinese University of Hong Kong, 2003. 41–42.

Lee, Ji-eun. "Beyond Pain and Protection: Politics of Identity and *Iban* Girls in Korea." *Journal of Lesbian Studies*, 10.3/4(2006): 49–68.

Lefebvre, Henri. *The Production of Space*. 1974. Oxford: Basil Blackwell, 1991. 1–68.

Lorde, Audre. *Zami; Sister Outsider; Undersong*. New York: Quality Paperback Book Club, 1993.

Ma, Kit-Wai Eric. "The Hierarchy of Drinks: Alcohol and Social Class in Hong Kong." *Consuming Hong Kong*. Hong Kong: Hong Kong University Press, 2001.

Massey, Doreen. *For Space*. London: Sage Publications Ltd., 2005.

Nestle, Joan. *A Persistent Desire: The Femme-Butch Reader*. Boston: Alyson Publications, 1992.

Pellegrini, Ann. "Consuming Lifestyle: Commodity Capitalism and Transformations in Gay Identity." *Queer Globalizations: Citizenship and the Afterlife of Colonialism*. Eds. Arnaldo Cruz-Malavé and Martin F. Manalansan IV. New York: New York University Press, 2002. 134–148.

Pile, Steve, and Keith Michael, eds. *Geographies of Resistance*. London and New York: Routledge, 1997. 1–32.

Rothenberg, Tamar. "'And She Told Two Friends': Lesbians Creating Urban Social Space." *Mapping Desire: Geographies of Sexualities*. Eds. David Bell and Gill Valentine. London: Routledge, 1995. 165–181.

Thorpe, Rochella. "'A House Where Queers Go': African-American Lesbian Nightlife in Detroit 1940–1975." *Inventing Lesbian Cultures in America*. Ed. Ellen Lewin. Boston: Beacon Press, 1996. 40–61.

Tonkiss, Fran. *Space, the City and Social Theory*. Cambridge: Polity Press, 2005. 59–147.

Valentine, Gill. "Out and About: Geographies of Lesbian Landscapes." *International Journal of Urban and Regional Research* 19 (1995): 96–111.

———. "Introduction: From Nowhere to Everywhere: Lesbian Geographies." *From Nowhere to Everywhere: Lesbian Geographies*. Ed. Gill Valentine. Binghamton, New York: Harrington Park Press, 2000. 1–9.

Wolfe, Maxine. "Invisible Women in Invisible Places: The Production of Social Space in Lesbian Bars." Eds. Gordon Brent Ingram, Anne-Marie Bouthillette and Yolanda Retter. *Queers in Space: Claiming the Urban Landscape*. Seattle: Bay Press, 1997. 301–323.

Chapter 4

Works cited in Chinese

"Huan xingquxiang shitiaozheng huanxingqijian zaifanan yifu han chuang nüce xiajing yayi" 〈患性取向失調症緩刑期間再犯案易服漢闖女廁嚇驚牙醫〉 [Sexual Orientation Disorder Man Re-offended by Barging into a Female Toilet and Frightened a Dentist during His Suspension of Sentence], *Pingguo Ri Bao* 《蘋果日報》 [Apple Daily], 19 August 2007.

"Yifupi huanxing you chuang nüce" 〈易服癖緩刑又闖女廁〉 [Transvestite Barged into the Female Toilet during His Suspension of Sentence], *Dongfang Ri Bao* 《東方日報》 [Oriental Daily], 19 August 2007.

"Mali tu che dujia bianxing fudao zhensuo" 〈瑪麗突撤獨家變性輔導診所〉 [Queen Mary Suddenly Removed Its Exclusive Sex-change Counseling Clinic], *Ming Bao* 《明報》 [Ming Pao Daily News], 8 March 2005. http://www.mpinews.com/content.cfm?newsid=200503 080854gb20854t. Accessed 10 December 2005.

Works cited in English

American Psychiatric Association. *Diagnostic and Statistical Manual of Mental Disorders: DSM-III*. 3rd ed. Washington, DC: American Psychiatric Association, 1980.

———. *Diagnostic and Statistical Manual of Mental Disorders: DSM-IV*. 4th ed. Washington, DC: American Psychiatric Association, 1994.

————. *Diagnostic Criteria from DSM-IV-TR.* Washington, DC: Amercian Psychiatric Association, 2000.

Beauvoir, Simone de. *The Second Sex.* New York: Alfred A. Knopf Inc., 1993.

Benjamin, Harry. "Introduction." *Transsexualism and Sex Reassignment.* Eds. Richard Green and John Money. Baltimore: Johns Hopkins Press, 1969. 1–10.

Butler, Judith. *Gender Trouble: Feminism and the Subversion of Identity.* New York: Routledge, 1990.

Garber, Marjorie B. *Vested Interests: Cross-Dressing & Cultural Anxiety.* New York: Routledge, 1992.

Hamburger, C., G. K. Stump, and E. Dahl-Iversen. "Transvestism, Hormonal, Psychiatric and Surgical Treatment." *The Journal of the American Medical Association* 152 (1953): 391–396.

Harry Benjamin International Gender Dysphoria Association. "The Standards of Care for Gender Identity Disorders." *The International Journal of Transgenderism.* 6th ed. 5 vols. 2001. Retrieved on 11 December 2005. http://www.symposion.com/ijt/soc_2001/index.htm.

Hirschfeld, Magnus. "Die Intersexuelle Konstitution" [the Intersexual State]. *Jahrbuch fuer sexuelle Zwischenstufen* 23 (1923): 3–27.

Hooker, Evelyn. "The Adjustment of the Male Overt Homosexual." *Journal of Projective Techniques* 21 (1957): 18–31.

Kenagy, Gretchen P. "Transgender Health: Findings from Two Needs Assessment Studies in Philadelphia." *Health & Social Work* 30.1 (2005): 19–26.

Kessler, Suzanne J., and Wendy McKenna. *Gender: An Ethnomethodological Approach.* Chicago: University of Chicago Press, 1985.

King, Mark, S. J. Winter, and Beverley Webster. "Etiological and Biological Essentialist Beliefs: Attitudes Towards Transgenderism and Transgender Civil Rights in Hong Kong." Unpublished, 2007.

Ko, J.S.N. *A Descriptive Study of Sexual Dysfunction and Gender Identity Clinic in the University of Hong Kong Psychiatric Unit, 1991–2001.* Department of Psychiatry, The University of Hong Kong, Queen Mary Hospital, 2003.

Lev, Arlene Istar. *Transgender Emergence: Therapeutic Guidelines for Working with Gender-Variant People and Their Families.* New York: The Haworth Clinical Practice Press, 2004. 400.

Lorber, Judith. *Paradoxes of Gender.* New Haven: Yale University Press, 1994.

Ma, Joyce L. C. "Social Work Practice with Transsexuals in Hong Kong Who Apply for Sex Reassignment Surgery." *Social Work in Health Care* 29.2 (1999): 85–103.

Meyer, Ilan H. "Prejudice, Social Stress, and Mental Health in Lesbian, Gay, and Bisexual Populations: Conceptual Issues and Research Evidence." *Psychological Bulletin* 129.5 (2003): 674–697.

Money, J. *Gendermaps: Social Constructionism, Feminism, and Sexosophical History.* New York: Continuum, 1995.

Namaste, Viviane K. *Invisible Lives: The Erasure of Transsexual and Transgendered People.* Chicago; London: University of Chicago Press, 2000. 2.

Ng, M.L., et al. "Transsexualism: Service and Problems in Hong Kong." *Hong Kong Practitioner* 11.12 (1989): 591–602.

Pauly, I. B. "Current Status of Change of Sex Operation." *Journal of Nervous and Mental Disease* 147 (1968): 460–471.

Raymond, Janice G. *The Transsexual Empire: The Making of the She-Male.* Athene Series. New York: Teachers College Press, 1994.

Wilson, Katherine K. "The Disparate Classification of Gender and Sexual Orientation in American Psychiatry." 1997. http://www.priory.com/psych/disparat.htm. Accessed 27 October 2007.

"Suicide of Transsexual Triggers Activists' Plea for Better Support." *South China Morning Post,* 22 September 2004.

"Suicide Leap." *South China Morning Post,* 24 September 2004.

"Gender Bender Stole Brother's ID Card to Get Job at Wing On." *The Standard,* 4 August 2007. http://www.thestandard.com.hk/news_detail.asp?pp_cat=11&art_id=50551&sid=147866 84&con_type=1. Accessed 27 October 2007.

Chapter 5

Works cited in Chinese

China Statistics Press. *2004 Zhongguo Renkou* 2004《中國人口》[2004 China Population]. Beijing: China Statistics Press, 2005.

Fang, Gang 方剛. *Zhongguo Duoxinghuoban Gean Kaocha*《中國多性夥伴個案考察》[Case Studies of Multiple Sexual Partnership in China]. Beijing: Zhongguo Shehui Chubanshe, 2005.

Li, Yinhe 李銀河. *Zhongguo Nüxing de Gangqing yu Xing*《中國女性的感情與性》[Love and Sexuality of the Chinese Women]. Beijing: Zhongguo Youyi Chuban Gongshi, 2002a.

———. *Zhongguo'ren de Xing'ai yu Hunying*《中國人的性愛與婚姻》[Love, Sexuality, and Marriage of the Chinese People]. Beijing: Zhongguo Youyi Chuban Gongshi, 2002b.

———. *Tongxinglian Ya Wenhua*《同性戀亞文化》[Subculture of Homosexuality]. Beijing: Zhongguo Youyi Chuban Gongshi, 2002c.

Lu, Xueyi 陸學藝, ed., *Dangdai Zhongguo Shehui Liudong*《當代中國社會流動》[Social Mobility in Contemporary China]. Beijing: Social Sciences Documentation Publishing House, 2004.

Zheng, Meili 鄭美里. *Nü'er Quan: Taiwan Nü Tongzhi de Xingbie, Jiating yu Quannei Shenghuo*《女兒圈：臺灣女同志的性別、家庭與圈內生活》[The Female Circle: Gender, Family and Community Life of Lesbians in Taiwan]. Taipei: Nüshu Wenhua, 1997.

Zhou, Hua Shan 周華山. *Xingbie Yueje Zai Zhongguo*《性別越界在中國》[Gender Transgression in China]. Hong Kong: Xianggang Tongzhi Yanjiu She, 2000.

Works cited in English

Census and Statistics Department, Hong Kong Special Administrative Region, 2005. "Population Aged 15 and over by Marital Statues, 1991, 1996, 2001." http://www.censtatd.gov.hk. Accessed 1 December 2008.

China Statistics Press. *China Statistical Yearbook.* Beijing: China Statistics Press, 2000.

Evans, Harriet. *Women and Sexuality in China: Female Sexuality and Gender Since 1949.* New York: The Continuum Publishing Company, 1997.

National Statistics, Republic of China. "Monthly Bulletin of Statistics." December 2005a. http://eng.stat.gov.tw. Accessed 1 December 2008.

———. "Population of Age 15 Years or Over by Sex and Marital Status." 2005b. http://eng.stat.gov.tw. Accessed 1 December 2008.

Chapter 7

Works cited in Chinese

Chen Qingwei 陳清偉. *Xianggang dianying gongye jiegou ji shichang fenxi*《香港電影工業結構及市場分析》[The Structure and Marketing Analysis of Hong Kong Film Industry]. Hong Kong: Hong Kong Film Biweekly, 2000.

Chen, W. Edwin 陳煒智. "Renwu Texie: Li Hanxiang" 〈人物特寫：李翰祥〉[Profile: Li Han-hsiang], *Taiwan Dianying Biji*《台灣電影筆記》[Taiwan Cinema Note], Chinese Taipei Film Archive. http://movie.cca.gov.tw/People/Content.asp?ID=234. 1 December 2007. Accessed 7 March 2008.

Dou Yingtai 竇應泰. *Dadaoyan Li Hanxiang*《大導演李翰祥》 [Master Director Li Han-hsiang]. Harbin: Harbin Press, 1997.

Hong Kong Film Critics' Association 香港影評人協會, *Xianggang Seqing Dianying Fazhan (Yanjiu Baogao)*《香港色情電影發展（研究報告）》[The Development of Hong Kong Pornographic Film (A Study Report)], 2000.

Lan Ling Xiao Xiao Sheng 蘭陵笑笑生, *Jin Ping Mei*《金瓶梅》[The Plum in the Golden Vase]. Jilin: Changchun University Press, 1994 [circa 1610].

Li Han-hsiang 李翰祥. *Sanshinian Xishuo Congtou*《三十年細說從頭》[Passing Flickers]. Hong Kong: Cosmos Books, 1983.

———. *Jin Ping Mei Sanbuqu*《金瓶梅三部曲》[The Golden Lotus Trilogy]. Hong Kong: Racing Stallion Press, 1985.

———. *Yingcheng Neiwai*《影城內外》[Inside and Beyond the Cinema City]. Hong Kong: Cosmos Books, 1997a.

———. *Yinhe Qianqiu*《銀河千秋》[A Thousand-Year Milky Way]. Hong Kong: Cosmos Books, 1997b. 34–35.

———. *Yinhe Shangxia*《銀河上下》[Above and Below the Milky Way]. Hong Kong: Cosmos Books, 1997c.

Shi Nai'an 施耐庵. *Shuihu Zhuan*《水滸傳》[The Water Margin]. Hong Kong: Chung Hwa Book Company, 1970 [circa 1570].

Wei Chongxin 魏崇新. *Shuobujin De Pan Jinlian*《説不盡的潘金蓮》[The Inexhaustible Lotus Pan]. Taipei: Yeqiang Press, 1997.

Yu Yeying ed. 宇業熒編. *Yongyuan De Li Hanxiang Jinian Zhuanji*《永遠的李翰祥紀念專輯》[Forever Li Han-hsiang Commemorative Collection]. Taipei: Jinxiu Press, 1997.

Zeng Qingyu and Xu Jianping 曾慶雨、許建平. *Gaofeng Suyun: Jin Ping Mei De Nürenmen*《高風俗韵——金瓶梅的女人們》[The Noble and the Earthly: The Women in Jin Ping Mei]. Kunming: Yunnan University Press, 2000.

Zhou Zuoren 周作人. "Xiaoshuo De Huiyi" 〈小説的回憶〉[Memory of Novel] *Zhi Tang Yiyou Wenbian*《知堂乙酉文編》[An Anthology from Zhitang in the Year Yiyou]. Hong Kong: Sanyu Publishing Company, 1961.

Works cited in English

Ding Naifei. *Obscene Things: Sexual Politics in Jin Ping Mei*. Durham: Duke University Press, 2002.

Dowrkin, Andrew. *Pornography: Men Possessing Women*. New York: Perigee, 1981.

Dyer, Richard. "Don't Look Now: Richard Dyer Examines the Instabilities of the Male Pin-up." *Screen* 23.4 (1982): 61–73. Reprinted in *The Sexual Subject: A Screen Reader in Sexuality*. New York: Routledge, 1992. 265–276.

Griffin, Susan. *Rape: The Power of Consciousness*. New York: Harper and Row, 1979.

———. *Pornography and Silence: Culture's Revenge against Nature*. New York: Harper and Row, 1981.

Hunt, Lynn. "Introduction: Obscenity and the Origins of Modernity 1500–1800." *The Invention of Pornography: Obscenity and the Origins of Modernity, 1500–1800*. New York: Zone Books, 1993. 9–45.

Kam, Louie. *Theorising Chinese Masculinity: Society and Gender in China*. Cambridge, UK: Cambridge University Press, 2002.

Kendrick, Walter. *The Secret Museum: Pornography in Modern Culture*. New York: Penguin, 1987.

Kipnis, Laura. *Bound and Gagged: Pornography and the Politics of Fantasy in America*. Durham: Duke University Press, 1999.

Marcus, Maria. *A Taste for Pain: On Masochism and Female Sexuality*. New York: St. Martin's Press, 1981.

McMahon, Keith. *Misers, Shrews, and Polygamists: Sexuality and Male-Female Relations in Eighteenth-Century Chinese Fiction*. Durham, NC: Duke University Press, 1995.

Merck, Mandy. "From Minneapolis to Westminister." *Sex Exposed: Sexuality and the Pornography Debate*. Eds. Lynne Segal and Mary McIntosh. London: Virago, 1992.

Nikunen, Kaarina, and Paasonen, Susanna. "Porn Star as Brand: Pornification and the Intermedia Career of Rakel Liekki." *Velvet Light Trap* 59 (Spring 2007): 30–42.

Roy, David. "Chang Chu-po's Commentary on the *Chin P'ing Mei*." *Chinese Narrative: Critical and Theoretical Essays*. Ed. Andrew H. Plaks. Princeton: Princeton University Press, 1977.

Sek, Kei. "The Journey of Desires." *A Study of Hong Kong Cinema in the Seventies (The Eighth Hong Kong International Film Festival Publication)*. Hong Kong: Hong Kong Urban Council, 1984. 82–89.

Soble, Alan. *Marxism, Feminism, and the Future of Sexuality*. New Haven and London: Yale University Press, 1986.

Sommer, Matthew H. *Sex, Law and Society in Late Imperial China*. Stanford: Stanford University Press, 2000.

Song, Geng. *The Fragile Scholar: Power and Masculinity in Chinese Culture*. Hong Kong: Hong Kong University Press, 2004.

Sontag, Susan. "The Pornographic Imagination." *Styles of Radical Will*. New York: Dell, 1969.

Steinem, Gloria. "Erotica and Pornography: A Clear and Present Difference." *Ms.*, November 1978.

Teo, Stephen. "Li Hanxiang's Aesthetics of the Cynical." *A Study of Hong Kong Cinema in the Seventies (The Eighth Hong Kong International Film Festival Publication)*. Hong Kong: Hong Kong Urban Council, 1984. 94–98.

———. *Hong Kong Cinema: The Extra Dimensions*. London: BFI, 1997.

Vitiello, Giovanni. "The Fantastic Journey of an Ugly Boy: Homosexuality and Salvation in Late Ming Pornography." *Positions* 4: 2 (1996): 291–320.

———. "Exemplary Sodomites: Chivalry and Love in Late Ming Culture." *Nannuu* 2: 2 (2000): 1–51.

Willemen, Paul. "Letter to John." *The Sexual Subject: A Screen Reader in Sexuality*. London: Routledge, 1992. 171–83.

Williams, Linda. *Hard Core: Power, Pleasure and the "Frenzy of the Visible"*. Berkeley and Los Angeles: University of California Press, 1989.

Wu, Yenna. "The Inversion of Marital Hierarchy: Shrewish Wives and Henpecked Husbands in Seventeenth-Century Chinese Literature." *Harvard Journal of Asiatic Studies* 48: 2 (1988): 371–372.

Yau, Ching. *Filming Margins: Tang Shu Shuen, a Forgotten Hong Kong Woman Director.* Hong Kong: Hong Kong University Press, 2004.

Yau, Ching. "A Sensuous Misunderstanding: Women and Sexualities in Li Han Hsiang's *Fengyue* Films." *Li Han-hsiang, The Storyteller.* Ed. Wong Ain-ling. Hong Kong: Hong Kong Film Archive, 2007. 112–38.

Filmography

Diau Charn (dir: Li Han-hsiang, 1958)
The Kingdom and the Beauty (dir: Li Han-hsiang, 1959)
Yang Kwei Fei, the Magnificent Concubine (dir: Li Han-hsiang, 1962)
Empress Wu Tse-tien (dir: Li Han-hsiang, 1963)
Beyond the Great Wall (dir: Li Han-hsiang, 1964)
Hsi Shih: The Beauty of Beauties (dir: Li Han-hsiang, 1966)
The Winter (dir: Li Han-hsiang, 1967)
The Warlord (dir: Li Han-hsiang, 1972)
Legends of Lust (dir: Li Han-hsiang, 1972)
Illicit Desire (dir: Li Han-hsiang, 1973)
Facets of Love (a.k.a. *Northern Ladies of China*) (dir: Li Han-hsiang, 1973)
Golden Lotus (dir: Li Han-hsiang, 1974)
The Empress Dowager (dir: Li Han-hsiang, 1975)
That's Adultery! (dir: Li Han-hsiang, 1975)
The Last Tempest (dir: Li Han-hsiang, 1976)
Love Swindlers (dir: Li Han-hsiang, 1976)
Supremo (a.k.a. *Badge 369*) (dir.: Zhu Mu; scr.: Sima Ke a.k.a. Li Han-hsiang, 1974)
Tiger Killer (dir: Li Han-hsiang, 1982)
The Burning of the Imperial Palace (dir: Li Han-hsiang, 1983)
Reign Behind a Curtain (dir: Li Han-hsiang, 1983)
Take Care, Your Majesty! (dir: Li Han-hsiang, 1983)
The Reincarnation of Golden Lotus (dir: Clara Law, 1989)
The Golden Lotus: Love and Desire (dir: Li Han-hsiang, 1991)
The Amorous Lotus Pan (dir: Li Han-hsiang, 1994)
Madame Bamboo (dir: Li Han-hsiang, 1994)

Chapter 8

Works cited in Chinese

Cheung, William Su-ping 張叔平. "Zhang Guorong de fang yu jin" 〈張國榮的放與盡〉 [Leslie Cheung's Indulgence and Uttermost]. *The One and Only: Leslie Cheung.* Ed. Leslie Cheung CyberWorld. Hong Kong: City Entertainment, 2004. 44–45.

Chu, Wing-lung 朱永龍. "Zhang Guorong: Meiyou Dongzuodi Wudao" 〈張國榮：沒有動作的舞蹈〉 [Leslie Cheung: The Dance Without Steps]. *The One and Only: Leslie Cheung.* Ed. Leslie Cheung CyberWorld. Hong Kong: City Entertainment, 2004. 34–35.

Lee, Po-neng. "The Weakness of Leslie Cheung as a Male-Cross-dresser". Hong Kong: *Apple Daily*, 2 August 2000. C3.

Lin, Yan-ni 林燕妮 (a.k.a. Eunice Lam). "Milian Dang Daoyan: Fangwen Zhang Guorong"〈迷戀當導演：訪問張國榮〉[Want to be a Director: An Interview with Leslie Cheung].《明報週刊》*Ming Pao Weekly*, March (2002): 54–57.

Law, Wei-ming 羅維明. "Leslie, Dance, Dance, Dance". *Yongyuan Huainian Cheung Kwokwing*《永遠懷念張國榮》[In Memory of Leslie Cheung]. Ed. Chan Bak-seng. Hong Kong: City Entertainment, 2003. 17–19.

Leslie Cheung CyberWorld, ed. *Zhang Guorong huiyi zhuan*《張國榮回憶傳》[The One and Only: Leslie Cheung]. Hong Kong: City Entertainment, 2004.

Luo Feng 洛楓 (a.k.a. Natalia Chan). *Shijimo Chengshi: Xianggang Liuxing Wenhua*《世紀末城市：香港的流行文化》[Decadent City: Hong Kong Popular Culture]. Hong Kong: Oxford University Press, 1995.

———. *Shengshi bianyuan: Xianggang Dianying di Xingbie, Teji yu Jiuqi Zhengzhi*《盛世邊緣：香港電影的性別、特技與九七政治》[City on the Edge of Time: Gender, Technology, and the 1997 Politics in Hong Kong Cinema]. Hong Kong: Oxford University Press, 2002.

———. *Jinse di Hudie: Zhanguorong di Yishu Xingxiang.*《禁色的蝴蝶：張國榮的藝術形象》[Butterfly of Forbidden Colours: The Artistic Image of Leslie Cheung]. Hong Kong: Joint Publishing Co. Ltd. 2003.

Ng, Cheng-Bang, et al., ed. 伍城邦等編, *Tongzhi yu Chuanmei*《同志與傳媒》[Tongzhi and the Mass Media]. Hong Kong: Chi Heng Foundation, 2000.

Works cited in English

Arnold, Rebecca. *Fashion, Desire and Anxiety: Image and Morality in the 20th Century*. New Jersey: Rutgers University Press, 2001. 111.

Bruzzi, Stella. "The Erotic Strategies of Androgyny." *Undressing Cinema: Clothing and Identity in the Movie*. New York: Routledge, 1997.

Butler, Judith. *Gender Trouble: Feminism and the Subversion of Identity*. New York: Routledge, 1990.

———. "Imitation and Gender Insubordination". *The Lesbian and Gay Studies Reader*. Eds. Henry Abelove, Michele Aina Barale and David M. Halperin. New York: Routledge, 1993. 307–320.

Chenoune, Farid. *Jean Paul Gaultier*. New York: Universe Publishing, 1998.

Chow, Rey. "Nostalgia of the New Wave: Structure in Wong Kar-wai's *Happy Together*." *Camera Obscura: Feminism, Culture, and Media Studies* 42 (1999): 30–48.

Chung, Winnie. "Inner Secret." *South China Morning Post*. 10 April 2002.

Cixous, Helene. "The Laugh of the Medusa." *Feminism: An Anthology of Literary Theory and Criticism*. Eds. Robyn R. Warhol and Diane Price Herndl. New Jersey: Rutgers University Press, 1996. 334–349.

Corliss, Richard. "Forever Leslie." *Time*. 7 May 2001. 44–46.

Garber, Marjorie. *Vested Interests: Cross-Dressing and Cultural Anxiety*. New York: Routledge, 1997.

Kristeva, Julia. "Manic Eros, Sublime Eros: On Male Sexuality." *Tales of Love*. New York: Columbia University Press, 1987. 59–82.

Leung, Helen Hok-Sze. "In Queer Memory: Leslie Cheung (1956–2003)." *Undercurrents: Queer Culture and Postcolonial Hong Kong*. Toronto: University of British Columbia Press, 2008. 85–105.

Smith, Barbara. "Homophobia: Why Bring It Up?" *The Lesbian and Gay Studies Reader.* Eds. Henry Abelove, Michèle Aina Barale and David M. Halperin. New York: Routledge, 1993. 99–102.

Sontag, Susan. "Notes on Camp." *A Susan Sontag Reader.* New York: Vintage Books, 1983. 103–119.

Stewart, Clare. "About Face: Wong Kar-Wai's Leslie Trilogy." *Leslie Cheung.* Eds. Clare Stewart and Philippa Hawker. Australia: ACMI, 2003. 63–75.

Weil, Kari. "Androgyny, Feminism, and the Critical Difference." *Androgyny and the Denial of Difference.* Charlottesville: University Press of Virginia, 1992. 145–169.

Woolf, Virginia. *A Room of One's Own and Three Guineas.* London: Penguin Books, 1993.

Yue, Audrey. "What's So Queer about *Happy Together*? a.k.a. Queer (N)Asian: Interface, Community, Belonging." *Inter-Asia Cultural Studies* 1.2 (2000): 251–264.

———. "The Wind Blows on: Forever Leslie ... King of Pop, Queen of Hearts." *Leslie Cheung.* Eds. Clare Stewart and Philippa Hawker. Australia: ACMI, 2003. 39–54.

Discography

Cheung, Leslie. *Forever Leslie.* Universal Music Ltd., 2001.

———. *In Memory of Leslie.* Rock Records (HK), 2003.

———. *Leslie Cheung Live in Concert 97.* Rock Records (HK), 2003.

———. *Passion Tour.* Universal Music Ltd., 2001.

Piazzolla, Astor. *The Rough Dancer and the Cyclical Night (Tango Apasionado).* Nonesuch Records, 2000.

Wong, Kar-wai. *Happy Together* (The Soundtrack). Block 2 Picture Inc. 1997.

Filmography

Farewell My Concubine (dir: Chen Kaige, 1993)
Happy Together (dir: Wong Kar-wai, 1997)

Chapter 9

Works cited in Chinese

Liu Bin 劉兵. "Di san jie jilupian jiaoliuzhou yingpian: Mei Mei" 〈第三屆紀錄片交流周影片：美美〉[A Film in the Third "Week for Documentary Film Communication": *Mei Mei*]. September 2006. http://www.fanhall.com/show.aspx?id=11688&cid=40.

Lu Xinyu 呂新雨. *Jilu Zhongguo: Dandai Zhongguo xin jilupian yundong* 《記錄中國：當代中國新紀錄運動》[Documenting China: Contemporary Chinese New Documentary Movement]. Shanghai: Sanlian Shudian, 2003.

Wu, Wenguang 吳文光. "He jilu fangshi youguande shu" 〈和紀錄方式有關的書〉[A Book That Has Something to Do with the Way of Documenting]. *Xianchang* 《現場》[Document]. Ed. Wu Wenguang. Tianjin: Tianjin Shehui Kexueyuan Chubanshe, 2000. 174–175.

Works cited in English

Appadurai, Arjun. "Disjuncture and Difference in the Global Cultural Economy". *Public Culture* 2.2 (Spring 1990): 1–24.

Bell, David, and Jon Binnie. "Turn It Into Love." *The Sexual Citizen: Queer Politics and Beyond*. Cambridge: Polity Press, 2000. 123–140.

Berry, Chris. "Getting Real: Chinese Documentary, Chinese Postsocialism." *The Urban Generation*. Ed. Zhang Zhen. Durham: Duke University Press, 2007. 115–134.

———. "Watching Time Go By: Narrative Distention, Realism, and Postsocialism in Jia Zhangke's *Xiao Wu*." *South Atlantic Quarterly*. Forthcoming.

Butler, Judith. *Gender Trouble: Feminism and the Subversion of Identity*. New York: Routledge, 1990.

———. "Imitation and Gender Insubordination." *Inside/Out: Lesbian Theories, Gay Theories*. Ed. Diana Fuss. New York: Routledge, 1991. 13–31.

———. "Gender Is Burning: Questions of Appropriation and Subversion." *Bodies That Matter: On the Discursive Limits of "Sex"*. New York: Routledge, 1993. 121–140.

Catalogue of the 2006 New Festival (The 18th New York Lesbian, Gay, Bisexual and Transgender Film Festival). 74.

Dirlik, Arif, and Zhang Xudong, "Introduction: Postmodernism and China." *Boundary* 2 24: 3 (Fall 1997): 1–18.

Dyer, Richard. *Pastiche: Knowing Imitation*. New York: Routledge, 2007.

Flynn, Norman, Ian Holliday and Linda Wong, "Introduction." *The Market in Chinese Social Policy*. Eds. Linda Wong and Norman Flynn. New York: Palgrave, 2001. 1–11.

Giddens, Anthony. *The Consequences of Modernity*. Stanford: Stanford University Press, 1990. 21–29.

———. *The Transformation of Intimacy: Sexuality, Love and Eroticism in Modern Societies*. Stanford: Stanford University Press, 1992.

Jamieson, Lynn. *Intimacy: Personal Relationships in Modern Societies*. Cambridge: Polity Press, 1998.

———. "Intimacy Transformed? A Critical Look at The 'Pure Relationship'." *Sociology* 33.3 (August 1999): 477–494.

Kaplan, Caren. *Questions of Travel: Postmodern Discourses of Displacement*. Durham: Duke University Press, 1996. 110.

Lee, Grace O. M. "Labour Policy Reform." *The Market in Chinese Social Policy*. Eds. Linda Wong and Norman Flynn. New York: Palgrave, 2001. 12–37.

Nichols, Bill. "Documentary Modes of Representation." *Representing Reality: Issues and Concept in Documentary*. Bloomington: Indiana University Press, 1991. 32–75.

———. "What Types of Documentary Are There?" *Introduction to Documentary*. Bloomington: Indiana University Press, 2001. 99–138.

Ong, Aihwa. "Chinese Modernities: Narratives of Nation and of Capitalism." *Undergrounded Empirers: The Cultural Politics of Modern Chinese Transnationalism* Eds. Aihua Ong and Donald M. Nonini. New York: Routledge, 1997. 171–202.

Rofel, Lisa. *Other Modernities: Gendered Yearnings in China After Socialism*. Berkeley: University of California Press, 1999.

Sang, Tze-lan D. "The Brave New World of Post-Mao China: An Overview." *The Emerging Lesbian: Female Same-Sex Desire in Modern China*. Chicago: The University of Chicago Press, 2003. 163–174.

Sedgwick, Eve K. "Queer Performativity: Henry James's The Art of the Novel." *GLQ* 1.1 (1993): 1–16.

———. "Affect and Queer Performativity." *Working Papers in Gender/Sexuality Studies* Nos. 3 & 4 (Sept. 1998): 90–108.

Spivak, Gayatri C. "Subaltern Studies: Deconstructing Historiography." *In Other Worlds: Essays in Cultural Politics.* New York: Routledge, 1987. 197–221.

———. "The Problem of Cultural Self-Representation." *The Post-Colonial Critic: Interviews, Strategies, Dialogues.* Ed. Sarah Harasym. New York: Routledge, 1990. 50–58.

Stam, Robert. *Reflexivity in Film and Literature: From Don Quixote to Jean-Luc Godard.* New York: Columbia University Press, 1992.

Stam, Robert, Robert Burgoyne and Sandy Flitterman-Lewis. *New Vocabularies in Film Semiotics: Structuralism, Post-structuralism and Beyond.* New York: Routledge, 1992.

Straayer, Chris. "Transgender Mirrors: Queering Sexual Difference." *Between the Sheets, In the Streets: Queer, Lesbian, Gay Documentary.* Eds. Chris Holmlund and Cynthia Fuchs. Minneapolis: University of Minnesota Press, 1997. 207–223.

Trinh, Minh-ha. "The Totalizing Quest of Meaning." *When the Moon Waxes Red: Representation, Gender and Cultural Politics.* New York: Routledge, 1991. 29–50.

Yang, Mayfair Mei-hui. "Mass Media and Transnational Subjectivity in Shanghai: Notes on (Re)Cosmo-politanism in a Chinese Metropolis." *Undergrounded Empires: The Cultural Politics of Modern Chinese Transnationalism.* Eds. Aihua Ong and Donald M. Nonini. New York: Routledge, 1997. 287–319.

Zhang, Hanzi. "Tang Tang." The official catalogue of the 29th Hong Kong International Film Festival. 2005. 40.

Zhang, Zhen. "Mediating Time: The 'Rice Bowl of Youth' in Fin de Siecle Urban China." *Public Culture* 12.1 (Winter 2000): 93–113.

———. "Building on the Ruins: The Exploration of New Urban Cinema of the 1990s." *Reinterpretation: A Decade of Chinese Experimental Art (1990–2000).* Eds. Wu Hung, Wang Huangsheng and Feng Boyi. Guangzhou: Guangdong Museum of Art, 2002. 113–20.

———. "Introduction: Bearing Witness: Chinese Urban Cinema in the Era of 'Transformation' (Zhuanxing)." *The Urban Generation: Chinese Cinema and Society at the Turn of the Twenty-first Century.* Ed. Zhang Zhen. Durham: Duke University Press, 2007. 1–45.

Index

Amorous Lotus Pan, The 114, 120, 126–128, 192; see also *Golden Lotus, The*
androgyny 134, 136–7, 138, 140–141; *see also* cross-gender identity, *cixiongtongti*
Asahi Shimbun, the 147

BDSM 125; *see also* S/M
Beijing 6, 20, 22, 23, 29, 31, 34, 103, 107, 110, 135, 154; Beijing-based 152, 164, 165, 166, 167, 169, 175, 183n6, 186n3; Beijing Film Academy 186n3; Beijing Gender Health Education Institute 196; see also *jingju*
beiyangde 21, 189
bisexuality 133–136; see also *shuangxing* and intersexuality 136–137
butch-femme 38, 40–41, 58, 200, 201, 203; butches 47; femmes 38, 48; *see also* lesbi; lesbian; *Po*; T; TBs; *tomboi*
Butler, Judith 40, 41, 83, 140, 142, 143, 161, 162, 174, 185 n10, 199, 200, 206, 211, 213

Call Girls, The 117
camp 138–142, 212; campy 135
censor 147; censored 185; censorship 116; uncensored 117; *see also* three-tier rating system
Chao, Antonia 57, 59, 203
Chatroom 55
Chen Dieyi 135–136
chengshi hua 166, 189
Chenoune, Farid 144, 185
Cheung Kwok-wing, Leslie 4, 11–13, 133–149, 185–186, 189, 210
Cheung, William 139
chi daguo fan 169, 189

Chinese New Documentary Movement 12, 151, 212
Christian Right 177 n3; *see also* religious fundamentalisms
chutai 21, 189
Circus 55
cixiongtongti 137, 190; *see also* androgyny
Cixous, Helene 136, 184n4, 211
closet, the 33, 35, 103; *see also* coming out
coming out 9, 44, 71, 103, 141, 144, 186; see also *zhan chu lai*
Constable, Nicole 37, 44, 180, 201
Coombs, N. R. 24, 197
cross-dressing 137–138, 152, 167, 170, 175
cross-gender identity 134, 141–142; *see also* androgyny, *cixiongtongti*

daling qingnian 92, 190
dandyism 140–141
danggongzai 23
danwei 89,168, 178–189n2, 190; *danwei* system 90–91, 93
Deng Xiaoping 17
documentary 12, 151–175, 212–214; reflexive documentary 160; see also *jishi* and Chinese New Documentary Movement
drag 105, 142–143, 152; cross-dressing performance 174; gender performance 142–143; performing gender 151–152; gender performativity 161–162; and intimacy 163; *see also* transvestite
Duan Xiaolou 135–136

è nü 183n8, 190
Evans, Harriet 92

Facets of Love 117, 189
fanchuan 152, 162, 166, 190
Fang Gang 91
Farewell My Concubine 5, 134–136, 141, 184, 189, 212
fengyue pian (*fengyue* genre) 10–11, 113–131, 182–184, 190, 210
Foucault, Michel 53, 204
freedom panic 177; *see also* moral panic; homosexual panic

Gaultier, Jean Paul 133, 141, 144–147, 185n11, 185n13, 211
Gender Identity Disorder (GID) 76–85, 206; Standards of Care for Gender Identity Disorders 77
Gender Identity Team (GIT) 77–83
Gender Reassignment Surgery 77
Giddens, Anthony 163, 172
Golden Lotus, The 114, 122, 124–125, 127, 191; and *Golden Lotus: Love and Desire, The* 122, 125, 128, 191; *Golden Lotus Trilogy, The* 34, 124, 184, 208; *The Reincarnation of Golden Lotus* 126, 128, 192; *see also Jin Ping Mei*; Pan Jinlian; Wu Dalang; Wu Song
gongwei 113; 190
Grieving Man 142, 193
guocui 166

H2O 55, 57
hangdang 166
hao jiemei 160, 190
Happy Together 5, 134, 135, 139–140, 184, 185, 190, 211, 212
Happy Valley 55, 192
Harvey, David 53, 204
Highmore, Ben 56–57, 204
homophobia 3, 61, 146, 174, 212; International Day Against Homophobia 56
homosexual panic 146; *see also* freedom panic; moral panic
Hong Kong Sex Culture Society 177, 195, *see also* Kwan Kai Man
huangmei diao 113, 114, 120, 121, 191
hukou 31, 179, 190, 200
Hugo, Graeme 43, 180, 201

Illicit Desire 117, 124, 210
International HIV/AIDS Alliance, the 103
intersexuality 136–137; intersexed 8; *see also* bisexuality; *shuangxing*; transgender

jingju 12, 166–167, 191; Beijing plays 12; Peking opera 135; *see also chengshi hua; guocui; hangdang*
Jin Ping Mei 121–125, 128, 183n 9, 183n10, 184n13, 191, 208; *see also Golden Lotus, The*
jishi 157, 191

kantil 38, 179
Kennedy, Elizabeth Lapovsky and Madelaine D. Davis 59, 204
Kwan Kai Man 177n4, 195; *see also* Hong Kong Sex Culture Society; Society for Truth and Light

labour 6, 7, 12, 17, 35, 44–46, 169–171, 175, 180; "labour camp" (*laogai ying*) 187; labour market 168–169; labour migration 38–40; 42–50, 203; labour productivity 168; labour reform 168–170; 213; Indonesian Labour Department 45; erotic labour 198; forced labour 203; physical and emotional labour 27; private realm and unwaged labour 53; public sphere and waged labour 53–54; transient labour 35; and leisure 57; *see also* "rice bowl of youth"
lala and *lalas* 4, 9, 87–102, 182n1, 191
lao guniang 92, 191
Law, Clara 126, 128, 191, 210; *see also Reincarnation of Golden Lotus, The*
Lefebvre, Henri 57, 204
Legends of Lust 129–130, 190, 210
lesbi 38
lesbian 4, 7, 38–41, 44, 46, 50, 51–55, 87–102, 196, 199, 200, 201, 202, 203, 204, 205, 211, 212, 213, 214; "lesbian continuum" 46; lesbian relationship 47; lesbian relationships 37, 50; lesbian spaces 8, 51–71; lesbian subjectivities 57, 203; *see also* butch-femme; *tombois*; *sentul*; *kantil*; *lesbi*; *lala*; *lalas*
Li Han-hsiang 113–149, 182–184, 191, 208–210

Li Ning 18, 191
Li Yinhe 91, 196, 198, 207
luan 32, 191

Madame Bamboo 129, 194
mamasans 129; *see also* prostitution; sex work
marriage 5, 7, 9, 11, 43, 63, 87, 89–102,
    103–110, 207; co-operative marriage
    87–88, 99–102; fake marriage 4, 105–109;
    same-sex marriage 63, 103; strategies of
    marriage 97–102
mass media 147–149, 173–175, 186, 211, 214
Mei Mei 12, 151–152, 164, 168–172, 186, 191,
    212
mianzi 96, 191
Mo, Teresa 184n5, 192
money boys 4, 7, 10, 17–35, 179n3, 199
Mong Kok   55, 59, 60, 64, 68–71, 192; "MK
    look" 70
moral panic 177, *see also* homosexual panic;
    freedom panic

neo-heterosexuality 7, 40–41
Ni jiujing you jige hao meimei 174, 192
Nishijima Kazuhiro 147
nü'er quan 207; see also *quan'nei ren*
nui gai 68, 192
Nüren hua 174, 192

Ogura Eiji 147

Pan Jinlian 114, 120–128, 179, 192, 208; see
    also *Golden Lotus, The; Water Margin, The;*
    Wu Dalang; Wu Song
Passion Tour 133, 144, 146, 147, 149, 185n15,
    192, 212
pingtai 31, 192
Po 59; *see also* butch-femme; lesbian; T
pornography 1, 11, 115–116, 119, 127,
    129–130, 195, 199, 208, 209; porn film
    industry 117; pornographic affect, the
    121; pornographic books 125, 127–128;
    pornographic gaze 11; pornographic
    imagination 127; period dramas 5,
    10, 113; and erotica 115, 183, 209; and
    philosophy 127; and pornification 122;
    and women 120; 127; anti-porn 125; gay
    pornography 197
prostitution 18–35; *see also* labour; money
    boys; sex work

qingchun fan 170, 192, 214; "rice bowl of
    youth" 214
quan'nei ren 21; *quannei* 207; see also *nü'er*
    quan
queer 1–5, 6–7, 9, 10, 11, 12, 13, 35, 51, 56, 58,
    59, 63, 66, 68, 70, 113, 134, 138, 139, 140,
    143, 145, 146, 147, 151, 153, 161–2, 166,
    169, 175, 178n6, 178n9, 184n6, 184n7,
    185n14, 187n10, 195, 196, 197, 198, 203,
    204, 205, 211, 212, 213, 214; *Queer Eye*
    for the Straight Guy 2; queer family 102;
    queer-friendly 61, 62–63; queer icon 5,
    11; queering 5, 9, 133; queerness 3, 12,
    56, 136, 148, 178; queer performativity
    162–3; queerphobic 12, 214; queer
    private sphere 102; queers 199, 205;
    queer studies 2, 5, 195; queer subjectivity
    and subjectivities 139, 151, 154, 158, 163,
    167; and normativity 3–4

Red 55, 57
reflexivity 153, 158–160, 163; *see also*
    documentary
Reincarnation of Golden Lotus, The 126, 128; *see*
    also Law, Clara
religious fundamentalisms 1; *see also*
    Christian Right
renyao 75, 152, 192
Robinson, Kathryn 42–43, 202
Rofel, Lisa 169–170, 173
Roof, Judith 40, 202
Room of One's Own, A 134, 212
Rouge 5, 134–135, 193

S/M 110; *see also* BDSM
sentul 38, 179
sex work 6, 24–25, 27, 31, 42, 179n4, 199;
    female sex workers 28, 197; male sex
    workers 4, 7, 19–20, 21–23, 33–35, 178n7,
    178n1, 179n3, 179n5, 195, 196, 198,
    200; sex workers 1, 26, 28, 30, 33, 129;
    transvestite sex workers 33; and social
    stigma 32; *see also* labour; prostitution;
    money boys
Shanghai 4, 6, 9, 20, 22, 34, 87–102, 118,
    164, 167, 172, 182, 183, 197, 198, 199,
    212, 214; Shanghai Drama School 183;
    Shanghainese 118
shuangxing 137, 192; *see also* bisexuality and
    intersexuality

Sixth-Generation cinema 158
Society for Truth and Light 177n4; *see also* Kwan Kai Man; Hong Kong Sex Culture Society
Sontag, Susan 140, 142, 209, 212; *see also* camp
Spivak, Gayatri 161, 214; *see also* strategic essentialism
Straayer, Chris 161, 214
Straight Boy Complexes 3
strategic essentialism 161; 163; *see also* Spivak, Gayatri
suzhi 31, 32, 33, 192, 199

T 57, 59; T-bars 57; T-Birds 201; see also *Po; tomboi*
Tang Tang 12, 151–163, 168, 171–172, 174, 175, 186, 192, 214
TBs 55, 60, 63, 178n8; TB vests 67, 181n8; *see also* T; *tomboi*
Tianxia Qishu 122, 192
TEAM 79
That's Adultery 114, 130, 194, 210
tie fanwan 168, 192
Tiger Killer 114, 125–126, 193, 210; see also *Golden Lotus, The*; Pan Jinlian; Wu Dalang, Wu Song; Ximen Qing
three-tier film rating system 116–117
tomboi 49; *tombois* 38–39, 47–48, 178, 200; dress code 44; *see also* T; TBs
tongzhi 21, 23, 62, 87, 103, 177n2, 178n6, 182n1, 193, 198, 199, 207; *tongzhi* activist movements 1; *tongzhi* studies 2, 8, 11, 87; and the Mass Media 186n16, 211
transgender 5, 8, 12, 56, 81, 161, 200, 202, 206, 213, 214; transgendered 81, 83, 179, 181, 197, 203, 206; transgendering 151; transgenderism 4, 12, 76, 83, 147, 206; transgenders 75, 84; New York Lesbian, Gay, Bisexual and Transgender Film Festival 186; *see also* intersexuality; transexual; transvestism
transitional sexuality 7
transsexual 75–85, 143, 181n1, 181n2, 181n11, 206, 207; transsexuals 5, 178n8, 206; transsexualism 206; transsexuality 8, 9; and transvestite sex workers 33; *see also* transgender
transvestite 33, 135, 148, 181n5, 181n6, 205; transvestites 142; transvestism 9, 138, 140, 151, 206; *see also* drag; transgender; transsexual
Trinh Minh-ha 159, 214
Tung Lo Wan 8, 51, 54–57, 59, 60, 64, 65, 67, 68, 180n4, 193; and Mong Kok 68–70

Vitiello, Giovanni 127, 209

Wang Wenlan 118; 193
Wang You Gu 57, 193
Wannabes 48
Water Margin, The 122–123, 126, 128, 192, 208; *see also* Pan Jinlian; Wu Dalang; Wu Song
Wei Chongxin 123, 208
Winter, The 121, 190, 210
women's liberation 54, 173; *funü jiefang* 190
Wong Kar-wai 134, 140, 184, 185, 193, 211, 212; see also *Happy Together*
Woolf, Virginia 134–135, 138, 212; *see also* androgyny
Wu Dalang 121, 123, 126, 183, 193
Wu Song 114, 120–129, 183n10, 193; Wu Sung 120; see also *Golden Lotus, The; Tiger Killer; Water Margin, The*; Wu Dalang
Wu Wenguang 151, 156, 193, 212

xianchang 151, 152–158, 175, 193, 212; *xianchang gan* 157–158, 193
xiao pin bu xiao chang 171, 193; *see also* prostitution; sex work
Ximen Qing 120, 121, 123–126, 128–129, 183, 193; see also *Golden Lotus, The*; Pan Jinlian; *Tiger Killer; Water Margin, The*; Wu Dalang; Wu Song

Yang, Mayfair Mei-hui 173, 214
yinfu 116, 118, 123, 183n8, 193; *yinfus* 10
yinshu 116, 118, 129, 193

zhan chu lai 9, 193; *see also zhan qi lai*; closet, the; coming out
zhan qi lai 9, 193
Zhang Hanzi 12, 151, 153, 158, 186n1, 186n3, 194
Zhang Zhen 156–158, 170, 186n1, 213, 214
zhuanti pian 151, 194
Zhou Huashan 88, 91, 207
Zhou Zuoren 123, 194, 208